SpringerBriefs in P

SpringerBriefs present concise summaries of cutting-edge research and practical applications across a wide spectrum of fields. Featuring compact volumes of 50 to 125 pages, the series covers a range of content from professional to academic. Typical topics might include:

- A timely report of state-of-the-art analytical techniques
- A bridge between new research results as published in journal articles and a contextual literature review
- A snapshot of a hot or emerging topic
- An in-depth case study or clinical example
- A presentation of core concepts that readers must understand to make independent contributions

SpringerBriefs in Psychology showcase emerging theory, empirical research, and practical application in a wide variety of topics in psychology and related fields. Briefs are characterized by fast, global electronic dissemination, standard publishing contracts, standardized manuscript preparation and formatting guidelines, and expedited production schedules.

More information about this series at http://www.springer.com/series/10143

Tabea Scheel · Christine Gockel

Humor at Work in Teams, Leadership, Negotiations, Learning and Health

Springer

Tabea Scheel
Department of Work and Organizational Psychology
FernUniversitaet in Hagen
Hagen
Germany

Christine Gockel
SRH University of Applied Sciences
Berlin
Germany

ISSN 2192-8363 ISSN 2192-8371 (electronic)
SpringerBriefs in Psychology
ISBN 978-3-319-65689-2 ISBN 978-3-319-65691-5 (eBook)
DOI 10.1007/978-3-319-65691-5

Library of Congress Control Number: 2017950031

Printed on acid-free paper

This Springer imprint is published by Springer Nature
The registered company is Springer International Publishing AG
The registered company address is: Gewerbestrasse 11, 6330 Cham, Switzerland

The original version of the book was revised: Chapter author names have been included in respective chapters. The erratum to the book is available at https://doi.org/10.1007/978-3-319-65691-5_9

Acknowledgements

We would like to thank the following individuals for their support in completing this book: our editor Stefan Einarson at Springer for his encouragement and patience; the anonymous reviewers for providing us with invaluable feedback; Jakob Weers for formatting the chapters of this book; and several of our students for literature searches, especially Christian Schär and Jakob Weers.

Contents

Chapter 1
Introduction

Tabea Scheel and Christine Gockel

Abstract This chapter contains (1) introductory explanations on the relevance of studying humor in work and organizational psychology and what to expect from the book as a whole, as well as (2) an organizer for the reader, including short paragraphs on every topic. The core chapters cover the role of humor for teams, leadership, negotiation, learning, and health in the work context. Each chapter will conclude with a summary of the main findings, an outline of research gaps for future studies, and a paragraph about the implications for practice in work and organizational psychology (e.g., consequences for employees and organizations). References for further reading will be provided in the texts and at the end of the main chapters of this SpringerBrief. In the appendix, a collection of humor measures useful in work contexts is provided.

Keywords Workplace humor · State-of-the art · Humor theories · Teams · Leadership · Negotiations · Learning · Health · Diversity · Virtuality

1.1 Why Humor in Work and Organizational Psychology

Humor is inescapable, and humor may have far reaching consequences—these are two intriguing reasons for the relevance of studying humor in relation to work and in organizations.

Humor is inherent in human beings and their interactions. Polimeni and Reiss (2006) relate the evolutionary origin of humor to adaptivity with regard to, for instance, the origins of language, hominid group size, and primate teasing. Likewise, Ramachandran (1998) combines neurology and the evolution of humor, laughter and smiling in the "false alarm theory": following initial threat perceptions, laughter signals that there is no such (interpersonal) threat.

The original version of this chapter was revised: See the "Chapter Note" section at the end of this chapter for details. The erratum to this chapter is available at https://doi.org/10.1007/978-3-319-65691-5_9

T. Scheel and C. Gockel, *Humor at Work in Teams, Leadership, Negotiations, Learning and Health*, SpringerBriefs in Psychology,
DOI 10.1007/978-3-319-65691-5_1

Much has been written on the semantics of jokes, on humor and health or romantic relationships, but less about humor at work—though humor is potentially related to all aspects of work. Part of the reasons for the lack of empirical research on workplace humor may be the immanent non-seriousness and related fear of jeopardizing one's reputation with such a "fun topic". However, humor is not just fun: "Humor is an inherently unstable phenomenon that can be used for a variety of purposes, from worker resistance to management discipline" (Butler, 2016, p. 421). Thus, ambiguity is fundamental for humor.

Types of humor in the workplace can be puns, slapstick, jokes, anecdotes, and teasing, mainly used for bonding in order to reach unity and common purpose (Huang & Kuo, 2011). With joking practices, workers undermine management control and subvert power structures, but humor also functions as a safety valve for employee dissatisfaction. Jokes serve as a reflection on how things could be otherwise, showing a counter-reality to the one offered by the dominant corporate culture, thus temporarily interrupting the serious world of work (Butler, 2016). From organizational side, humor is a resource for motivating organizational members and for fostering creativity and productivity (Butler, 2016).

Likewise, Barsoux (1996) viewed spontaneous humor as an important organizational resource with multiple benefits like closing the communication gap between leader and follower, helping to reduce barriers between people, and making organizations more participative and responsive. This way, trust and a plurality of visions may foster learning and renewal. Using and managing humor in the workplace is also said to provide such benefits as stress relief, team unification, employee motivation, idea generation, and diffusion of frustration through venting (Lyttle, 2007).

Despite these positives, humor in this context has its downsides as well. For example, humor can distract us from the job at hand, hurt our credibility, or cause offense in increasingly diverse work settings. For instance, Gruber, Mauss and Tamir (2011) describe the Dark side of happiness, negative humor styles include self-defeating and aggressive types (e.g., Martin, Puhlik-Doris, Larsen, Gray, & Weir, 2003), and group research has a strong research history on disparagement humor (e.g., Ford, Richardson, & Petit, 2015). Accordingly, humor can be divided into adaptive and maladaptive types with a multitude of functions each (e.g., Romero & Cruthirds, 2006). Among others, managers are responsible for fostering beneficial and reducing dangerous effects of humor.

That said, several reviews about workplace humor cover the organization management perspective (Huang & Kuo, 2011), like managerial communication (Wood, Beckmann, & Rossiter, 2011) and managing humor in the workplace (Lyttle, 2007). Also, humor in workplace relationships is reviewed by Cooper (2008), humor styles and their implications for work contexts such as leadership are summarized by Romero and Cruthirds (2006), and humor and emotion for workplace climate are described by Robert and Wilbanks (2012). Butler (2016) provides an organizational perspective on humor. Though all these reviews are very useful, most proposed humor functions lack sound empirical support—making them prime starting points for future research attempts.

Mirroring the practical relevance of humor, the business press frequently takes up the topic (e.g., Romero & Cruthirds, 2006), with catchy titles like "Are you weird enough?" (Castelli, 1990) or "Transforming a conservative company—One laugh at a time" (Hudson, 2001). Joking practices were rather prohibited in most workplaces for much of the twentieth century—today, we observe "cultures of fun" in contemporary organizations, most famous of them being Google (Google Company Culture, 2016). Both, the prohibition as well as an artificially induced atmosphere of playfulness can backfire. There is nothing less likely to raise a smile than being forced to enjoy yourself—especially when determined by your employer.

Humor accompanies the whole life cycle of organizations. At one extreme, start ups with their loose, innovative appeal and informal culture may vent their ways via becoming established formal organizations by using humor for developing their culture. In Coworking Spaces, coworkers with their flexible work in diverse businesses and employment types may use humor for fulfilling their much-sought social needs (e.g., social support, Gerdenitsch, Scheel, Andorfer, & Korunka, 2016). At the other end, the global spread of—originally Mexican (http://fuckupnights.com/)—Fuck-up nights presents the aftermath of organizational development: Entrepreneurs speak publically about their biggest failures and mistakes, sharing their insolvencies, misfortunes and a laugh with their audience.

Even in science, the notion of the seriousness of scientific knowledge production changed to the recent popularity of positive psychology. That said, our work is not based in the tradition of the positive psychology—its neglect of the negative side makes it a less useful approach for grasping the multidimensional and ambiguous nature of humor. When scientists allow themselves to be funny, the reactions are heterogeneous—in 2011, an article titled "25 Years of Portative Behavior as a Problem of Modern Psychology—Status Quo" ("25 Jahre portatives Verhalten als Problem der modernen Psychologie—Status quo") was published in the German journal Psychologische Rundschau, authored by Budischewski and Nock (2011). Taken up a satirical article about the so-called door-related behavior (Salzgraf, 1985, which is a pseudonym of a German professor), the authors introduce a comprehensive model relating the intensity, frequency, and speed of knocking to the dichotomous outcome "opened" or "not opened" door. Personality factors like impulsivity and dominance are modeled as mediators, resulting in portative or even contra-portative behavior. Budischewski and Nock (2011) also link the "new area of psychological research—PoPsy" to several established areas of psychology (e.g., psychiatry with the "locked-in" syndrome). After publication, it created an outrage in the scientific community, which forced the editors to explain and reply (Schmitz, 2011). It was never quite clear whether some scholars did not *get* the joke, or seriously perceived a violation of norms. Recently, Pennycook, Cheyne, Barr, Koehler, and Fugelsang (2015) published a paper "On the reception and detection of pseudo-profound bullshit", taking the same line of satirical perspective on the scientific profession and its ways. In some cases, the very topic of the research lends itself to being made fun of, such as the book of Ringenbach (1971; cf. Steel 2007) cited by Knaus (1979; cf. Steel 2007) about the history of procrastination—only that this book was never actually written. It turned out to be a joke between author and publisher (see Steel, 2007). The paper by Upper (1974) is legendary: titled "The Unsuccessful Self-treatment of a Case of 'Writer's Block'" it is basically a blank page—with the fictional (*really?*) reply of a reviewer praising the paper for concision and recommending print without revision. Also, the sometimes humiliating and frustrating digestion of reviewer comments inspired papers with mocking replies to some virtual reviewer (e.g., Glass, 2000).

When writing this issue of the SpringerBrief series, we kept asking ourselves whether there is any aspect in and of work that could not be related to the presence or absence of humor. We concluded that—if humans are involved—humor seems to be inevitable. Finally, something we—as humor researchers—are quite used to being asked for is our favorite joke. To provide you with an answer before the question can even distract you, we agreed on this famous quote from Einstein: "We all know that light travels faster than sound. That's why certain people appear bright until you hear them speak" (see also Butler, 2016, p. 422).

Our aim was to prepare the ground for more methodologically sound and meaningful future humor research, and thus for evidence-based humor practice. We hope you find this book informative and useful in this regard.

1.2 What to Expect from the Book

We provide a state of the art about humor at work, that is, an extensive review of existing results from work and organizational psychology as well as additional results from other fields of humor research, if adaptable (e.g., social and cognitive psychology, sociology, linguistics). Thus, we include the latest of the relevant humor research. Our focus is on workplace humor. However, as most research is not conducted in work contexts, the chapters of this SpringerBrief refer to general results, too—sometimes extensively. However, in order to lay the ground for future research, including transferring results to the work context, this is done on purpose.

Approaches in humor research are diverse (Martin, 1998). They not only originate from different disciplines (e.g., linguistics, sociology, psychology), but include different methods ranging from participant observations to diary studies with factor analytical or multidimensional approaches. Also, the focus and levels vary (e.g., liberation, mental health, emotion-based temperament, reversal theory, comedians) as well as the conceptualization of humor (e.g., humor as a characteristic of a person or a message).

Our review depends heavily on the quality and quantity of the original work and the shortcomings of the empirical and theoretical work it is based on. The methods (e.g., quantitative/diary, qualitative/interview) and generalizability with regard to the nature of the setting and the sample are (mostly) reported in order to evaluate the contributions of the findings. We also comment on current theories and point out where further theory refinement is necessary.

Each chapter concludes with a summary of the main findings, an outline of research gaps for future studies, and the implications for practice in work and organizational psychology (e.g., consequences for employees and organizations, like well-being or turnover intentions). References for further reading will be provided in the text and at the end of the main chapters (Chaps. 3–7).

As both the authors were responsible for specific chapters, different approaches will be apparent: Christine wrote Chaps. 3, 4, 5, and Sect. 8.2. Her writing follows a US/American style with a narrower focus on the topic and a view on big-picture issues. Tabea wrote Chaps. 2, 6, 7, and Sect. 8.1. Her writing follows a German style with a broad focus on the topic and attention to detail. Both styles are strongly affected by our academic training on two different continents.

As a consequence of concerning ourselves with the state of the art of humor research, we strongly encourage research of virtually all topics presented here—small and large—with a sophisticated mixed-method approach, across time and levels where appropriate, and with regard to different cultures/across cultures. Not least this latter ambition implies that even the rare high-quality research conducted in the field of humor at work deserves sound replication.

1.3 What the Chapters Will Provide

In Chap. 2 (Tabea Scheel), the foundations for humor research are laid in that the concept(s) (and definitions) of humor and the most prominent theories are introduced. While the three main approaches of humor are superiority, incongruence and arousal theories, other useful theories for humor research are supplemented. Finally, the diverse functions of humor are introduced and the different approaches to the assessment of humor are briefly described.

The Chaps. 3–7 are the core chapters with regard to specific topics of humor at work. Chapter 3 (Christine Gockel) starts with a focus on humor in teams. Positive forms of humor have been found to increase cohesion and identification in teams. A close look at the evolution of laughter and humor might help to explain these bonding effects of humor in groups. We summarize under which conditions humor should increase or undermine cohesion, how humor is related to group productivity, and why it is beneficial to foster a humor-friendly climate in teams.

Chapter 4 (Christine Gockel & Laura Vetter) focuses on humor in leadership. We first present various functions of humor use by leaders and place a special emphasis on the relationship between leader and subordinate. We explain why humorous leaders are perceived to be more effective and vice versa. But we also point out that the association between humor and perceived effectiveness is not so simple. Recent research shows which task and subordinate characteristics influence the effect of leader humor on outcomes. The chapter closes with findings of how female and male leaders differ in their use of humor.

In Chap. 5 (Christine Gockel), we highlight the role of humor in negotiations. First, we describe the general functions and explain the verbal signs for humor in this special context. We then explain the outcomes of humor in negotiations, such as financial concessions, and clarify some mediators of these effects. We present divergent findings of how power is related to the production of humor in negotiations and close by explaining the potential effects of humor in online negotiations.

Chapter 6 (Tabea Scheel) focuses on humor in learning. As most of the research is done in academic settings rather than in work contexts, this chapter relies heavily on general empirical findings. We introduce two theoretical approaches, that is, the Instructional Humor Processing Theory as well as the perceived humor hypothesis. The cognitive, social and psychological functions and consequences of humor in learning and instruction are presented. For example, research about memory, immediacy, and motivation are discussed. The sparse knowledge about the mode of humor presentation (i.e., textbooks, tests) and about humor in online instruction are an additional aspect.

Chapter 7 (Tabea Scheel) summarizes research on humor and mental as well as physical health, in work as well as general contexts. Findings for the relationship between humor and well-being, anxiety, depression, and burnout are presented. Additionally to mental health aspects, related concepts, which are especially important in work contexts, are introduced with their relation to humor—for instance, work engagement and withdrawal. The stress-buffering hypothesis and social facilitation are discussed as mechanisms for the health-beneficial effects of humor. Empirical findings for the relation between laughter as well as trait humor and physiological processes are presented. Future research has to replicate studies in the work context. Also, it is worthwhile to investigate the mediating role of humor between newer concepts like job crafting and passion for work and mental health.

In Chap. 8 (Tabea Scheel & Christine Gockel), two new avenues for future research topics with regard to humor are introduced, that is, diversity and virtuality. Moderators for the effects of humor like age, gender, and culture become more salient due to globalization as well as the socio-demographic development in industrialized countries. Work becoming ever more virtual challenges former routines of cooperation and makes it more difficult to send and receive cues for humorous messages. We show how people have adapted their humorous communication to the scarcity of nonverbal cues, for example by using emoticons.

Finally, in the Appendix A.1 (Tabea Scheel), a list of scales is provided which might be useful for future research about humor in work contexts. This compilation encompasses scales with a focus on coping, personality, humor types, as well as scales especially for communication and for work contexts.

References

Barsoux, J.-L. (1996). Why organisations need humour. *European Management Journal, 14*(5), 500–508.

Budischewski, K., & Nock, L. (2011). 25 Jahre portatives Verhalten als Problem der modernen Psychologie—Status quo. [25 years of portative behavior as problem of modern psychology—status quo.]. *Psychologische Rundschau, 62*(3), 144–146. doi:10.1026/0033-3042/a000057.

Butler, N. (2016). Humour and organization. In R. Mir, H. Willmott, & M. Greenwood (Eds.), *The Routledge companion to philosophy in organziation studies* (pp. 421–429). London: Routledge.

Castelli, J. (1990). Are you weird enough? *HR Magazine*, 38–41.

Cooper, C. (2008). Elucidating the bonds of workplace humor: A relational process model. *Human Relations, 61*(8), 1087–1115. doi:10.1177/0018726708094861.

Ford, T. E., Richardson, K., & Petit, W. E. (2015). Disparagement humor and prejudice: contemporary theory and research. *HUMOR, 28*(2), 171–186. doi:10.1515/humor-2015-0017.

Gerdenitsch, C., Scheel, T., Andorfer, J., & Korunka, C. (2016). Coworking spaces—Providing a source of social support for independent professionals. *Frontiers of Psychology*. doi:10.3389/fpsyg.2016.00581.

Glass, R. L. (2000). A letter from the frustrated author of a journal paper. *Journal of Systems and Software*, 54(1).

Google. (2016). *Google Company Culture*. Retrieved from https://www.google.com/about/company/facts/culture/

Gruber, J., Mauss, I. B., & Tamir, M. (2011). A dark side of happiness? How, when, and why happiness is not always good. *Perspectives on Psychological Science, 6*(3), 222–233. doi:10.1177/1745691611406927.

Huang, K.-P., & Kuo, W. -C. (2011). Does humor matter? From organization management perspective. *Journal of Social Sciences, 7*(2), 141–145.

Hudson, K. M. (2001). Transforming a conservative company—One laugh at a time. *Harvard Business Review, 79*(7), 45–53.

Lyttle, J. (2007). The judicious use and management of humor in the workplace. *Business Horizons, 50*(3), 239–245. doi:10.1016/j.bushor.2006.11.001.

Martin, R. A. (1998). Approaches to the sense of humor: A historical review. In W. Ruch (Ed.), *The sense of humor: Explorations of a personality characteristic* (pp. 15–60). Berlin/New York: De Gruyter.

Martin, R. A., Puhlik-Doris, P., Larsen, G., Gray, J., & Weir, K. (2003). Individual differences in uses of humor and their relation to psychological well-being: Development of the Humor Styles Questionnaire. *Journal of Research in Personality, 37*(1), 48–75.

Pennycook, G., Cheyne, J. A., Barr, N., Koehler, D. J., & Fugelsang, J. A. (2015). On the reception and detection of pseudo-profound bullshit. *Judgement and Decision Making, 10*(6), 549–563.

Polimeni, J., & Reiss, J. P. (2006). The first joke: Exploring the evolutionary origins of humor. *Evolutionary Psychology, 4,* 347–366.

Ramachandran, V. S. (1998). The neurology and evolution of humor, laughter, and smiling: The false alarm theory. *Medical Hypotheses, 51*(4), 351–354.

Robert, C., & Wilbanks, J. E. (2012). The wheel model of humor: Humor events and affect in organizations. *Human Relations, 65*(9), 1071–1099. doi:10.1177/0018726711433133.

Romero, E. J., & Cruthirds, K. W. (2006). The use of humor in the workplace. *Academy of Management Perspectives, 5,* 58–69.

Salzgraf, F. R. (1985). Das portative Verhalten als Problem der modernen Psychologie. [Portative behavior as a problem of modern psychology.] *Psychologische Rundschau, 36,* 102–103.

Schmitz, B. (2011). Nachrichten (Editorial). *Psychologische Rundschau, 62*(4), 256.

Steel, P. (2007). The nature of procrastination: A meta-analytic and theoretical review of quintessential self-regulatory failure. *Psychological Bulletin, 133*(1), 65–94. doi:10.1037/0033-2909.133.1.65.

Upper, D. (1974). The unsuccessful self-treatment of a case of "writer's block". *Journal of Applied Behavior Analysis, 7*(3), 497.

Wood, R. E., Beckmann, N., & Rossiter, J. R. (2011). Management humor: Asset or liability? *Organizational Psychology Review, 1*(4), 316–338. doi:10.1177/2041386611418393.

Chapter 2
Definitions, Theories, and Measurement of Humor

Tabea Scheel

Abstract This chapter provides an overview of conceptualizations of humor, the most prominent theories, and theories that may be a useful foundation for research on humor at work. Definitions of humor are manifold, ranging from a communicative activity with positive emotional reactions in perceivers to an individual trait (e.g., sense of humor, cheerfulness). Humor is seen as multidimensional and includes the abilities to produce, recognize, and appreciate humor and to use humor as a coping strategy. The three most prominent humor theories are the superiority, incongruity, and arousal-relief theories. We discuss the intra- and interpersonal function of humor in general, the function of humor at work, and humor measurement. Measures of (usually self-assessed) humor range from more trait-focused and internal perspectives to humor styles and humor in work contexts. A collection of humor scales and tests is presented in Appendix A.1.

Keywords Humor definitions · Incongruence theory · Arousal-relief theory · Superiority theory · Humor functions · Humor styles

2.1 Introduction

The complexity of humor and humor theories is comparable to the experience of blind men touching an elephant. This originally Indian (but nowadays widespread) story describes how blind men touch an elephant to get an idea of what it looks like. As each one feels a different part of the elephant, they experience complete disagreement when comparing their descriptions (https://en.wikipedia.org/wiki/Blind_men_and_an_elephant). Likewise, humor is a very complex phenomenon, and although each theory or definition may be correct, it may also acknowledge only part of the phenomenon.

The original version of this chapter was revised: See the "Chapter Note" section at the end of this chapter for details. The erratum to this chapter is available at https://doi.org/10.1007/978-3-319-65691-5_9

T. Scheel and C. Gockel, *Humor at Work in Teams, Leadership, Negotiations, Learning and Health*, SpringerBriefs in Psychology,
DOI 10.1007/978-3-319-65691-5_2

There are many different approaches, including social and neurological ones, which can be used to grasp the concept of humor or to explain its origins. One can also explain humor from an evolutionary or cognitive perspective (Hurley, Dennett, & Adams, 2011), or collect jokes to diagnose the humor of a whole generation—as Winick (1976) did in the US.

Nearly everyone laughs when a person slips—when it is clear that she or he is not seriously hurt. Slapstick works at work, too. Maybe you have a colleague who often dropped his (full) cup, so that later the mere expectation produces witty comments and laughter in your team. Maybe you share a joke about your supervisors' mood, or your colleague makes everyone giggle by wearing bright colorful shoes to an otherwise expensive, elegant suit. Or some comments of your boss may embarrass yourself while all your colleagues laugh. This list of diverse situations may be continued endlessly and demonstrates the variety of humor. As evolution got us hooked on humor, we long to eat titbits of that "endogenous mind candy" (Hurley et al., 2011).

This chapter explains why such diverse phenomena as described above are labeled humor. More theory about the evolution of humor and laughter can be found in the chapter about humor in teams (Chap. 3). In the following, we provide an overview of definitions, theories, and concepts of humor as well as the ambiguous functions of humor (at work) and its measurement.

2.2 Definitions of Humor

The term "humor" has undergone several changes of meaning and has evolved from a physiological to a mental quality. One of the earliest meanings of humor (humores) was bodily fluids (lat. *ūmor:* liquid, moistness). According to Hippocrates (400 BC), the regulation of blood, phlegm, and yellow and black bile was central for health (in Schubert & Leschhorn, 2006). During the Middle Ages, humor was understood as a quirky or odd character trait and was brought to the stage by Ben Jonson as objects of the *Comedy of humours* (1600, 1927). The shift toward an active term was initiated by Morris (1744), including the ability to perceive and depict the comic. Paul (1804/1990) was one of the first to develop a full theory of humor, with humor becoming a matter of aesthetics. Establishing a genuine psychological perspective, Freud (1905/1960, 1927/1961) labeled humor as the "most frugal of the types of the comic" and as the supreme defense mechanism in (re)gaining pleasure as he introduced the relevance of humor and jokes into psychotherapy.

Definitions of humor are manifold, depending on whether humor is seen as a communicative activity (e.g., Martineau, 1972) with positive emotional reactions in perceivers (e.g., Romero & Cruthirds, 2006) or as an individual trait-like sense of humor (Martin, 1998) or cheerfulness in personality psychology research (Ruch, Köhler, & van Thriel, 1996). Humor is nowadays seen as having multidimensional characteristics. Martin (2007) summarized humor as (1) the ability to understand jokes and other humorous stimuli, (2) an expression of humor and cheerfulness,

(3) the ability to make humorous comments or have humorous perceptions, (4) the appreciation of diverse types of jokes, cartoons, and other humorous material, (5) the active seeking of sources that elicit laughter (e.g., comedies), (6) the memorizing of jokes and funny anecdotes in life, as well as (7) the tendency to use humor as a coping mechanism. Thus, Martin (2007) describes humor as a characteristic of a person rather than of a statement. Likewise, humor includes the abilities to produce, recognize, and appreciate humor and to use humor as a coping strategy (Thorson & Powell, 1993)—a description that demonstrates circular reasoning. In line with the multitude of humor perspectives, the characteristics of humor vary, including surprise, incongruity, comprehension, and funniness (Aillaud & Piolat, 2012). According to Martin (2007), humor may be viewed as a habitual pattern, an ability, a temperament, an aesthetic response, an attitude, a world view, a coping strategy, or a defense mechanism. Furthermore, Martin (2007) distinguished four components of the humor process, that is, a social context, a cognitive-perceptual process, an emotional response, and the vocal-behavioral expression of laughter.

According to Long and Graesser (1988), humor is "anything done or said, purposely or inadvertently, that is found to be comical or amusing" (p. 4). Martineau (1972) defined humor as any communication that is perceived as humorous (reflecting circular reasoning), whereas Crawford (1994) highlighted the positive cognitive or affective reactions of listeners when witnessing someone else's verbal or nonverbal humorous behavior. Similarly, Romero and Cruthirds (2006) defined humor as amusing communications that create a positive cognitive and emotional reaction in a person or a group. All these definitions are problematic in that they refer to the reactions of the audience. They would thus not include attempts at humor.

Also, humor is seen as an international form of social communication (Robert & Yan, 2007) and as a verbal or nonverbal message that evokes amusement and positive feelings by the receiver (Hurren, 2006). Booth-Butterfield and Booth-Butterfield (1991) emphasized the intentional use of both verbal and nonverbal communication behaviors that elicit positive responses such as laughter and joy. Though intention is not a crucial element of definitions of humor (e.g., unintentional humor; Martin, 2007; definition by Long & Graesser, 1988), it is an appropriate characterization of much of the instructional (and also organizational) humor examined so far. All these approaches view humor as a communicative activity, which ideally leads to laughter, but none of these definitions really refer to what kinds of statements are humorous as compared with nonhumorous (apart from the reaction of the audience).

Meyer (2000) defined humor as a cognitive state of mirth. Focusing on humor appreciation, Weisfeld (1993) defined humor appreciation as "a distinct, pleasurable affect that often is accompanied by laughter" (p. 142). Laughter is the most obvious behavioral expression of humor (or rather: is caused by humor) and includes a distinctive behavioral pattern that also has psychophysiological correlates (Ruch & Ekman, 2001). Ruch and Ekman (2001) defined *laughter* as a vocal expressive-communicative signal and provided an overview of laughter in terms of respiration, vocalization, facial action, body movement, mechanisms, and element definition.

In line with Weisfeld (1993), laughter caused by humor is associated with a pleasant emotional state connected with cheerfulness and exhilaration.

There is no fully satisfactory comprehensive definition of humor. However, scholars agree that humor involves the communication of multiple, incongruous meanings that are amusing in some manner (Banas, Dunbar, Rodriguez, & Liu, 2011; Martin, 2007). In line with this idea, Gervais and Wilson (2005) summarized the fundamental nature of humor as "nonserious social incongruity" (p. 399). In the Encyclopedia of Quality of Life and Well-being Research (Michalos, 2014), Svebak defined humor as a "social phenomenon that is reflected in playful interaction and mirthful communication" (2014, p. 3048). Overall, an appropriate and comprehensive definition will probably have to be based on a theory of humor.

Few attempts have been made to define humor in work contexts. Cooper (2005) defined organizational humor as "any event shared by an agent (e.g., an employee) with another individual (i.e., a target) that is intended to be amusing to the target and that the target perceives as an intentional act" (pp. 766–767). Dikkers, Doosje, and de Lange (2012) presented a model of organizational humor based on interacting communication levels. They built on Cooper's (2005) as well as Romero and Cruthirds' (2006) definitions and defined organizational humor as "*non-serious incongruity shared in work settings aimed at the intentional amusement of individuals, groups or organizations*" (Dikkers et al., 2012, p. 76, Italics in Orignial). Incongruity is a cognitive-perceptual process in which conflicting ideas or events are combined. The attempt to provide a definition for organizational humor is worthwhile. However, it is limited in the sense that it is narrow in scope (only amusement intention).

As humor has internal and communicational facets, our **working definition** encompasses humor as a communicative process that includes incongruence and evokes a variety of emotions, either in the "producer" of humor, in the "receiver" of humor, or in both. Thus, our definition of humor at work as "nonserious social incongruity" follows Gervais and Wilson (2005, p. 399).

2.3 Theories of Humor

Three main theories about the origin of humor are repeatedly drawn on, that is, incongruity theory, superiority theory, and relief/release/arousal theories (e.g., Banas et al., 2011; Buijzen & Valkenburg, 2004; Ferguson & Ford, 2008; Martin, 1998; McCreaddie & Wiggins, 2008; Meyer, 2000). Thus, humor emerges in human thought through perceptions of incongruity, superiority, and relief (Meyer, 2000). Ferguson and Ford (2008) applied the three theories to disparagement humor to explain why it is amusing. In his comprehensive book on the psychology of humor, Martin (2007) provided an extensive overview of several theories.

According to Ferguson and Ford (2008), the theories differ in many ways but particularly in the relative emphasis they place on the structure of the contents of humor versus the centrality of the social context in eliciting amusement: incongruity and cognitive theories emphasize irony and surprise in the contents of humor (representative: Attardo, 1993; Berger, 1987; Raskin, 1985; Suls, 1972), whereas the psychoanalytic (a type of relief theory) and the superiority theories emphasize antagonistic social relationships between humorists and targeted individuals, groups, or objects in a given context (representative: Berger, 1987; Freud, 1960, 1905). These latter theories focus more on context, thus more directly and fully addressing disparaging humor.

Most research has been conducted on the enjoyment of certain types of humor, mainly disparagement humor. Whereas there is some evidence for superiority and incongruity in humor, the psychoanalytic idea of a catharsis or tension relief has not yet been clearly demonstrated (Ferguson & Ford, 2008). In the following, we provide an overview of the three approaches, including a brief discussion of empirical evidence.

2.3.1 *Incongruity Theory*

According to Kant (1724–1804), incongruity is "Humour where the punchline or resolution is inconsistent or incongruous with the set-up" (cf. McCreaddie & Wiggins, 2008, p. 585). Traced back to Aristotle, incongruity is the most widely accepted philosophical theory of humor to date (Morreall, 1989)—"amusement is the enjoyment of something which clashes with our mental patterns and expectations" (p. 1). People understand humorous communication if they are (cognitively) able to resolve the incongruity (Banas et al., 2011). Surprise is a key element (Meyer, 2000), and absurdity, nonsense, and surprise are *typical themes* (Buijzen & Valkenburg, 2004). For example, a customer might perceive a humorous incongruence if a (usually serious) bank employee wears a clown nose (maybe at carnival time).

Forabosco (1992) views incongruity as the "divergence from a cognitive model of reference" and "resolution" as well as "cognitive mastery" as essential components of the humor process. Thus, incongruity theory emphasizes *cognition*, requiring the mental capacity to note, understand, and categorize incongruous changes and thus to comprehend a situation and its implications before humor (the cognitive state of mirth) can be experienced. Thus, humor comprehension, but not humor appreciation, is at the core of incongruity theories. In a review of the past 50 years of humor research, Westwood and Johnston (2013) extended theory in relating incongruity and the ambiguities of humor as a basis for subversive potential, advocating for a view of organizational humor as subversion and resistance.

Evidence for Incongruity Theory According to the review by Martin (1998), empirical *evidence for incongruity* and individual differences in sense of humor are based on creative thought processes that are involved in the production and comprehension of humor. That is, the creation and resolution of incongruence is inherent in humor and in creativity. He concluded that evidence for a close relationship between the ability to create humor and creative abilities, in general, is considerable. Accordingly, humor production is positively related to divergent thinking (creativity) and humor comprehension to convergent thinking (intelligence; Martin, 1998). In a comprehensive review of studies about humor and incongruity, Martin (2007) concluded that incongruity theories "do not adequately account for all aspects of humor" (p. 74). In particular, the emotional and social aspects of humor remain largely unexplained.

2.3.2 Superiority Theory

Among the oldest theories, dating back to Plato and Aristotle, superiority results "from the disparagement of another person or of one's own past blunders or foolishness" (Martin, 1998, p. 29). McCreaddie and Wiggins (2008) traced the Superiority Theory (or tendentious or disparagement theory) back to another famous advocate: Hobbes (1588–1679) "considered an aggressive form of humour which takes pleasure in others' failings or discomfort. A 'sudden glory of some eminency in ourselves, compared with infirmity of others'" (cf. McCreaddie & Wiggins, 2008, p. 585) characterizes aggressive humor, including humor used against the self, for example, self-deprecating/-defeating/-disparaging humor. Based on aggressiveness or playful competition (Banas et al., 2011), a *typical theme* is ridicule and making fun of those who are less fortunate or who deviate from a given norm (Buijzen & Valkenburg, 2004). For example, a superior could demonstrate his/her achieved status by saying something funny at the expense of a subordinate in a meeting; most probably, the people attending the meeting, including the target, will laugh.

According to Buijzen and Valkenburg (2004) and Meyer (2000), humor has a primarily *emotional* function when laughter and mirth result from seeing oneself as superior, right, or triumphant. The superiority or disparagement theory emphasizes the ways in which negative or hostile *attitudes* are expressed through humor (Martin, 1998). Being laughed at threatens our identity, making it an unpleasant experience for the targets of such superiority humor (Meyer, 2000).

Evidence for Superiority Theory Martin (1998) summed up the superiority or disparagement approach as focusing on the ways in which negative or hostile attitudes are expressed through humor and explained "that people laugh more at jokes that disparage people toward whom they have negative attitudes and laugh less at jokes that disparage those with whom they identify" (p. 33). Furthermore, the distinction between the disparagement of a specific social group (i.e., intergroup disparagement) and the disparagement of a person (i.e., intragroup disparagement) serve different functions: the morale and cohesion of the ingroup versus conformity in and control over ingroup behavior (Janes & Olson, 2015). For instance, students who observed other students being ridiculed (in cartoons) conformed more and performed better on a quiz (Bryant, Brown, & Parks, 1981).

Some evidence for superiority has been collected by running experiments that included racial jokes or jokes about specific ethnic or cultural groups—depending on whether the joke teller was part of the group, the jokes were more or less funny; thus, membership in reference groups is important. Humor that disparages social outgroups is funnier than humor that disparages social ingroups (Ferguson & Ford, 2008). Ferguson and Ford (2008) summarized that (informal) attitudinal affiliation with a social group—regardless of whether one actually belongs to it—influences the extent to which humor that disparages that group will be considered amusing; and according to affective disposition (attitude), humor appreciation depends on membership in a social group or attitudes toward the disparaged group (Zillmann & Cantor, 1976/1996; cf. Ferguson & Ford, 2008).

As disparagement humor is at the heart of superiority theory, research on its effects has provided evidence for superiority theory. In a special issue of *Humor: International Journal of Humor Studies* (2015) on disparagement humor and intragroup and intergroup differences and effects, Ford (2015) brought together several empirical studies.

2.3.3 Arousal Theories /Relief

According to Freud (1856–1938), relief or release theory implies "Humour released by 'excess' nervous energy which actually masks other motives and/or desires" (cf. McCreaddie & Wiggins, 2008, p. 585). The relief theory focuses on the *physiological* release of tension (Buijzen & Valkenburg, 2004; Meyer, 2000) by laughing. Berlyne (1972) described two ways in which the associated positive hedonic value can arise: either arousal is raised moderately ("arousal boost"), or a sequence of conditions generates an uncomfortable state of heightened arousal that is subsequently reversed ("arousal jag"). For example, in a meeting with a tense atmosphere, a manager could say something funny and thus take the audience by surprise, resulting in an arousing outburst of laughter and a subsequently looser atmosphere. e.g.

An advancement of arousal theory describes pleasure from increasing arousal to an optimal level (Martin, 2007). The shifting from a paratelic (i.e., a playful frame of mind such as humor) to a telic state (i.e., goal-directed, serious) is described in *reversal* theory (Apter, 2013). Arousal theories combine cognitive appraisal with an optimal level of physiological arousal (Banas et al., 2011); thus, cognition and emotion interact (Martin, 2007). The coping functions of humor are based on the tension–relief element of arousal theory (Banas et al., 2011). *Typical themes* are sexual or aggressive (Buijzen & Valkenburg, 2004).

Evidence for Arousal-Relief Theory The arousal-relief theory has mainly been explored in the psychoanalytic tradition (Ferguson & Ford, 2008) by testing the catharsis hypothesis. A number of studies have examined Freud's hypothesis that the enjoyment of hostile jokes is related to repressed aggressive drives (Martin, 1998). Many of the studies on psychoanalytic theory and individual differences in sense of humor reviewed by Martin (1998) were based on samples of psychiatric patients or students and most focused on the appreciation of humor (of prepared cartoons or jokes). Contrary to psychoanalytic theory, most of these studies found that aggressive humor is enjoyed more by persons who express hostility and aggression rather than by those who suppress or repress it, and the majority of the evidence suggests that people laugh the most at humor that is related to impulses that they themselves express overtly—rather than repress (Martin, 1998). Martin (1998) and Ferguson and Ford (2008) similarly concluded that exposure to hostile humor is related to *more* expressions of aggression, though some studies found an association between hostile humor appreciation and reductions in aggression and tension (e.g., Singer, 1968). Psychoanalytic assumptions were tested with negative (i.e., aggressive or hostile) humor because positive humor is not assumed to refer to repressed feelings or thoughts.

2.3.4 Additional Theoretical Approaches

In addition, other theoretical approaches might be useful for explaining the functions and consequences of humor. While not claiming to be exhaustive, we mention the following theories because they appear useful for explaining the role of humor at work.

Social identity theory (Tajfel, 1978) is applied to the explanation of disparagement humor, that is, why it elicits amusement and what elicits this kind of humor (Ferguson & Ford, 2008). Social identity theory is aligned with superiority theory. Judging one's own groups as superior to other groups enhances positive social identity and can be achieved with disparaging humor against the outgroup (e.g., Janes & Olsen, 2015), thus accounting for the use of disparagement humor as a social lubricant (see Chap. 3 on teams).

Three more affective approaches are emotional contagion, the Broaden-and-Build-Theory of Positive Emotions and the feelings-as-information-theory (see Chap. 3 on teams). *Emotional contagion* (Hatfield, Rapson, & Le, 1994) might explain how humor actually functions as a social lubricant. Primitive emotional contagion was defined as "the tendency to automatically mimic and synchronize facial expressions, vocalizations, postures, and movements with those of another person and, consequently, to converge emotionally" (Hatfield et al., 1994, p. 5). The *Broaden-and-Build-Theory of Positive Emotions* by Fredrickson (1998, 2001) proposes that positive emotions broaden people's momentary thought-action repertoires and thus build enduring resources—physical, intellectual, social, and psychological. In addition to improved functioning due to positive emotions, Fredrickson (2001) assumed a general transformation of thought and action for the better. Likewise, Schwarz (1990) included negative and positive affect in his *feelings-as-information-theory* and stated that affective states provide an informational basis about the (negative or positive) state of a person's environment.

Banas et al. (2011) introduced the *Instructional Humor Processing Theory* (*IHPT*), which is a combination of incongruity-resolution theory, disposition theory, and the elaboration likelihood model (ELM) of persuasion (Wanzer, Frymier, & Irwin, 2010). The IHPT is useful for explaining why certain types of humor used by instructors might result in increased student learning whereas others might not (Wanzer et al., 2010) (see Sect. 6.3 on learning).

In conclusion, there is not yet an overarching theory of humor or even humor at work. Rather, different theories explain distinct aspects of humor. Likewise, there are several different functions served by humor beyond amusement. We will examine these functions after introducing specific concepts of humor in the next section.

2.4 Specific Concepts of Humor

There are several specific concepts that are related to humor, and we will introduce those that are relevant for the work context. The two most frequently researched constructs are sense of humor and humor style. We do not discuss gelotology, the study of laughter, and its effects on the body. However, gelotophobia, the fear of being laughed at, may have implications at work such as self-selecting specific jobs that provide fewer opportunities to be laughed at (Ruch, Hofmann, Platt, & Proyer, 2014). For the recent state of the art on gelotophobia, see Ruch et al. (2014).

Sense of Humor is defined as "habitual individual differences in all sorts of behaviors, experiences, affects, attitudes, and abilities relating to amusement, laughter, jocularity, and so on" (Martin, 1998, p. 17). In his historical review of individual differences in sense of humor, Martin (1998) referred to Eysenck's (1972) three meanings of humor when ascribing sense of humor to a person: laughing at the same things (conformist meaning), laughing often (quantitative meaning), and telling funny stories or amusing other people (productive meaning). The three are not necessarily related within individuals. In a more recent definition, Svebak (2014) stated that sense of humor is "a characteristic of the individual and reflects readiness for understanding as well as producing humorous cognitive processes and to display related effects of smiling and laughter" (p. 3048). According to Craik, Lampert, and Nelson (1996), overall sense of humor subsumes a delimited and specific set of humor-related behaviors, specifically "socially constructive and competent forms of humorous conduct within interpersonal contexts" (p. 273); for instance, maintaining group morale through humor or displaying a quick wit.

Humor Styles describe the ways in which people use humor (Martin, Puhlik-Doris, Larsen, Gray, & Weir, 2003) and are thus narrower than a sense of humor: *Self-enhancing* humor involves a tendency to be amused by the incongruities of life (e.g., adversity) and helps people attain distance from problems in stressful situations, *affiliative* humor describes a person's tendency to facilitate relationships by telling jokes and engaging in funny banter. Both styles provide an adaptive function, thus being called positive humor. *Aggressive* humor refers to irony, sarcasm, teasing, and mockery as well as to sexist and racist humor and is associated with manipulating or belittling others (e.g., Janes & Olsen, 2000). People who tell funny anecdotes or do funny things at their own expense in order to gain the appreciation of others use *self-defeating* humor (Martin et al., 2003). These latter two (negative) humor styles are maladaptive, because humor at one's own or another's expense jeopardizes social relationships and self-worth. There are also two approaches to categorizations: self-directed (self-enhancing/-defeating) versus other-directed (affiliative/aggressive, e.g., Cann, Stilwell, & Taku, 2010) and enhancing the self (self-enhancing/aggressive) or relationships with others (affiliative/self-defeating; Martin et al., 2003).

Humor Styles at Work Building on the two adaptive and two maladaptive humor styles (Martin et al., 2003), Romero and Cruthirds (2006) tied specific ways to use humor in organizations to their respective functions. As we judge this systematization to be especially useful and as it is one of the most prominent in recent research in work contexts, we will introduce it in more detail. In general, the styles are intended to function as enhancers of the self or relationships with others. Affiliative and self-enhancing humor are categorized as "positive" styles; aggressive and self-defeating humor are categorized as "negative" styles. Lang and Lee (2010) reported three functions of humor in the workplace that have similarities with affiliative (liberating humor), self-enhancing (stress-relieving humor), and aggressive or mild aggressive humor styles (controlling humor). According to Mak, Liu and Deneen (2012), humor functions as a regulating (mild aggressive, affiliative) and coping mechanism (self-enhancing) in workplace socialization. Although all four styles might serve interpersonal functions, the self-enhancing style in particular is said to serve an intrapersonal function. Using the literature, Martin et al. (2003) developed these four factors (Humor Style Questionnaire, HSQ) and subsequently empirically confirmed their validity by showing that they are distinctly related to certain consequences (e.g., health). Scheel, Gerdenitsch and Korunka (2016) introduced an adapted shorter work-related Humor Style Questionnaire (swHSQ; see Appendix). The following discussion of the four styles and their functions are mainly based on the review by Romero and Cruthirds (2006).

Affiliative humor serves the (lubricating; Martineau, 1972) function of enhancing liking and nonthreatening perceptions between persons; utilizing this style should lessen interpersonal tension and aid in building relationships. Thus, it facilitates interpersonal interactions and creates a positive environment; the intention is to bring people together (Romero & Cruthirds, 2006). By eliciting positive feelings through the successful sharing of humor, affiliative humor may foster group cohesion. Also, socialization is facilitated as interactions are less tense. Communication (e.g., in public speaking) may profit from affiliative humor by creating similarities between the speaker and the audience and through shared humor. Sharing humor is not compatible with being offended and thus involves honest and free communication. Affiliative humor within a group may reduce stress by easing tension from stressful events. Promoting openness to new ideas by making people less critical facilitates risk taking and thus creative thinking.

A humorous environment can stimulate creative problem-solving. By the same mechanisms of creating a positive environment for knowledge sharing and interpersonal relationships, organizational culture profits from affiliative humor. Organizational values and behavioral norms are communicated without negative affect for the audience or new personnel. Affiliative humor may reduce the social distance between leaders and subordinates by identifying similarities (e.g., intelligence, values) and because it causes subordinates to perceive the leader as a group member.

Self-enhancing humor is a coping mechanism for dealing with stress and is centered on the person. This style can be found on an individual or a group level. The intention is enhancement of a person's image relative to others in the group or organization (Romero & Cruthirds, 2006). Self-enhancing humor at the group level fosters favorable perceptions of the group and thus enhances group cohesion. Self-enhancing humor in communication helps speakers to connect with an audience. This type of humor is especially beneficial for stress reduction, for instance, by reframing stressful situations and achieving distance from problems. Self-enhancing humor fosters creative thinking by making light of errors or failures, which inevitably occur with novel ideas. By promoting the ability to cope with problems, self-enhancing humor fosters team-oriented as well as organizationally desired behavior. For leadership, self-enhancing humor may be beneficial for acquiring power from superiors by increasing appeal.

Holmes and Marra (2006) analyzed workplace discourses and likewise found that the positive types of humor were beneficial for strengthening collegiality, softening instruction or a criticism, releasing tension, or defusing anger.

Self-defeating humor is meant to enhance relationships with others by amusing them and gaining their acceptance. At moderate levels, it may reduce status and render people more approachable (Romero & Cruthirds, 2006). For instance, the use of moderate self-defeating humor in a speaker's communication may release tension and also temporarily reduce the speaker's status. When credibility is at stake, self-defeating humor is especially unfavorable when leaders aim to secure power over subordinates. However, to reduce their social distance from subordinates, leaders can use this type of humor to help them seem more approachable and appealing.

Aggressive humor is used to victimize, belittle, and disparage others (Romero & Cruthirds, 2006). Consistent with superiority theory, people with aggressive humor try to enhance their own status and feel better at the expense of others. Aggressive humor (e.g., making jokes about outgroup members) bonds the group, thereby enhancing cohesion. It is also a means for securing power in leadership by defining the leader's status and elucidating power relations. Aggressive humor, targeted toward employees with lower status, demonstrates the initiator's power over others in order to, for instance, gain behavioral compliance. Aggressive humor may be detrimental to relationships and organizational culture when it is used to ridicule and manipulate maliciously. The costs of this negative humor can be particularly high when some people are offended, and lawsuits may even result.

2.5 Functions of Humor

In Janes and Olson's (2015) words: "Humor is ubiquitous in daily life and extraordinarily complex in its consequences" (p. 286). There are several reviews about the general functions of humor (e.g., Banas et al., 2011; Martin, 1998, 2007). Assumptions about how the general or specific functions of humor are related to humor theories are limited. For instance, interpersonal functions such as enhancing one's own liking and status might refer to superiority theories. Also, stress reduction via humor and laughter may be explained by arousal-relief theories.

It is very challenging to disentangle the functions and intended consequences of humor. For instance, the function of protecting the self with an aggressive joke at the expense of a potentially threatening person might lead to protection (e.g., the person is no longer perceived as threatening) or might worsen the situation (e.g., the person reacts with an aggressive joke in return). Olsson, Backe, Sörensen, and Kock (2002) asked 20 people from Sweden what humor means to them and categorized the essence of humor as possibilities/obstacles (e.g., happiness, unforeseen events/situations, real humor/art form, jokes, plays on words/puns, situation comedy) and weapons/protection (e.g., political satire). The contents of both categories demonstrate once more that the functions and consequences of humor, the types of humorous stimuli, and the level of abstraction are intertwined.

The proposed functions of humor are often inductively derived theoretical assumptions or generalizations of empirical investigations of details. Thus, empirical research on nearly every function is recommended. That said, we will now summarize the proposed intrapersonal and interpersonal functions of humor and humor at work.

2.5.1 Intrapersonal Functions

Humor may serve to enhance relationships with others (e.g., affiliative, self-defeating) or the self (e.g., self-enhancing; Martin et al., 2003). Humor may also help individuals cope with stress: Humor can help people see the amusing side of problems and can help them distance themselves from stressors (Banas et al., 2011). Humor is said to enable a change in perspective and to buffer the effects of stress by serving as a coping strategy (see also Chap. 7 on Health). In the same way, humor helps to regulate emotions. The intrapersonal function of disparagement humor, according to Freud (1905, 1960), is the venting of aggressive feelings in a socially acceptable way. Based on his experiences in Nazi concentration camps, Obrdlik (1942) saw the main function of gallows humor as morale strengthening—enhancing for the ingroup, disparaging for the outgroup. As this example demonstrates, the boundaries between intra- and interpersonal functions of humor are blurry. Though these functions apply to humor in general, they naturally apply to work settings, too. However, the relevance and consequences might differ between nonwork and work contexts.

2.5.2 *Interpersonal Functions*

The (*interpersonal*) functions of humor have been viewed as an apparent paradox. Martineau (1972) described the social functions of humor as abrasive or lubricating; laughter, as a result of humor, may create both closeness and distance between individuals (Olsson et al., 2002). Beyond providing amusement, humor can facilitate liking and can bring people together, but it may be also used to disparage others and socially isolate them (Banas et al., 2011). Thus, several authors have indicated that humor can increase/decrease closeness and power and can, therefore, influence the two main dimensions in person perception: liking and status. Among the positive functions is an increase in group cohesion, but it might also serve negative functions such as derision and social isolation. In the same line of thinking, Alexander (1986) distinguished between affiliative humor with its focus on creating or maintaining group cohesiveness, and ostracizing humor, which singles out a victim. Whereas most functions of aggressive humor elicit negative consequences, some may be potentially positive. For instance, relying on the face-saving ambiguity of humor may enable groups to resolve conflict without engaging in destructive behavior (Kahn, 1989).

The lubricating and abrasive functions of humor continue in communication. According to Meyer (2000), humor serves four basic functions in communication: Two tend to *unite* communicators (mutual identification, clarification of positions and values), and two tend to *divide* communicators from each other (enforcement of norms, differentiation of acceptable vs. unacceptable behaviors or people). These functions of humor in communication as, alternately, unifier or divider, allow humor to be used to delineate social boundaries.

2.5.3 *Specific Functions at Work*

The interpersonal functions—or rather the consequences—of humor at work encompass attention and immediacy (see Chap. 6 on Learning), cohesion (see Chap. 3 on Teams), and emotional contagion (see Sect. 2.3.4 on additional theories), status and power (see Chap. 4 on Leadership), face-saving (see Chap. 5 on Negotiation), and norm enforcement (see Chaps. 3 and 4 on Teams and Leadership).

A core function of humor in workplace talk is to provide entertainment or amusement (Holmes & Marra, 2006). However, humor in the workplace involves more than telling jokes (Vinton, 1989). In his review, Duncan (1982) discussed management humor as an influence on group characteristics (cohesiveness, communications, power, status) and a link between group dynamic variables and performance. Morreall (1991) listed three benefits of humor in the workplace: to promote health, enhance mental flexibility, and smooth social relations.

2.6 Measuring Humor

According to the variety of definitions and conceptualizations and to state/trait perspectives, measures of (usually self-assessed) humor range from more trait-focused (e.g., State-Trait-Cheerfulness-Inventory, STCI; Ruch et al., 1996) and internal perspectives (e.g., Sense of Humor Questionnaire, SHQ-6; Svebak, 1974, 2010) to the more behavior-related humor styles (Humor Styles Questionnaire, HSQ; Martin et al., 2003) or humor assessment in work contexts (Questionnaire of Occupational Humorous Coping, QOHC; Doosje, De Goede, van Doornen, & Goldstein, 2010; Humor Climate Questionnaire, HCQ; Cann, Watson, & Bridgewater, 2014). For an extensive overview of established but also lesser known scales, please see Appendix A.1.

Several compilations of measures exist: In a special issue on the measurement of humor, Ruch (1996) provided an overview of several measurement approaches. Also, Martin (1998) reviewed approaches to the study of sense of humor and described several measures in his integrative book about humor in psychology (Martin, 2007). In a book on sense of humor, Ruch (2007) provided an extensive appendix with a list of humor measurement tools sorted by the method that was applied (e.g., questionnaire, cartoon test, etc.). Ruch's (2007) list is very useful for researchers interested in general tools for state and trait measures of humor. In a more specific attempt, Beermann and Ruch (2009) discussed the relation between virtue and vice with regard to 12 different humor tools. On the basis of their review of positive humor at work, Mesmer-Magnus, Glew, and Viswesvaran (2012) provided a comprehensive list of the humor scales used in the 49 studies they analyzed (including conceptualization and sample items). There is a considerable amount of overlap between the instruments we introduce in Appendix A.1 and these lists, but we focus on scales that seem useful in field research and in a work context.

Appendix A.1 provides a selective overview of (mostly self-report) measures that might be relevant for the assessment of workplace humor or were even designed for such a purpose. Among the various measures, the HSQ (i.e., affiliative, self-enhancing, self-defeating, aggressive styles) is currently one of the most frequently used as it recognizes the adaptive and maladaptive functions of humor. It seems worthwhile to rely on the HSQ for the assessment of humor at work as it seems to provide a solid basis and has often been used in the work context (Mesmer-Magnus et al., 2012). In this regard, the application of the HSQ to the workplace by developing the short and work-oriented version (swHSQ; Scheel et al., 2016) seems promising. Also, the Humor Climate Questionnaire (HCQ; Cann et al., 2014), which is based in part on the HSQ, measures employees' perceptions of the role of humor in the workplace with four factors. Whereas the HSQ has a clear focus on a person's own use of humor, the HCQ shifts between perceptions of coworkers' and supervisors' use of humor and a person's own use of humor as a group member. In addition, the positive factor of the HCQ combines the two distinct factors of the HSQ (affiliative, self-enhancing), and the negative factor represents aggressive humor while not adopting the self-defeating style of the HSQ. The outgroup humor factor operationalizes only management as the outgroup, whereas the fourth factor (i.e., supervisor support) is reverse coded and actually represents supervisors' nonapproval of humor in the workplace. However, the measurement of humor provides other potential pitfalls. As "sense of humor" is a highly valued characteristic, people might be biased in their ratings. Also, for instance, prior exposure to a named (known!) comedian primes an expectancy of forthcoming humor, and this expectancy influences humor ratings (Johnson & Mistry, 2013). As mentioned, more scales are presented in the Appendix (A.1).

Early research used methods from ethnography such as participant observers (e.g., Roy, 1959; Seckman & Couch, 1989; Vinton, 1989). For instance, Sykes (1966) acted as a participant observer in a glass production company and "analyzed/classified" joking relationships between old/young women and old/young men. Horowitz et al. (2004) conducted focus groups with 11- to 14-year-old US middle school children guided by semistructured interviews to identify sources of teasing and bullying.

As experimental approaches are less applicable to the work context, the respective instruments are not presented in the Appendix but briefly introduced here. A range of experiments have included humor production (e.g., Terror Management Theory; Long & Greenwood, 2013). One of the first attempts at research on humor focused on humor appreciation and assessed the appreciation of jokes and cartoons (e.g., Eysenck, 1942). Cartoons have often been applied in experimental settings to assess humor appreciation and creation. For instance, the 3WD consists of a set of 70 jokes and cartoons (Ruch, 1995, unpublished; cf. Hempelmann & Ruch, 2005). The humor questionnaire (in Hebrew, Ziv, 1981; cf. Ehrenberg, 1995) is a 16-item self-report scale that captures pleasure from humor and is accompanied by a test of humor creation (10 cartoons without captions). This cartoon-caption test covers the use of humor for emphasis, the originality of funny ideas, and the ability to make someone laugh. It also includes a sociometric humor measure. Likewise, the Humor Appreciation Scale (HAS; Overholser, 1992) includes 14 captioned cartoons to be rated for funniness, and the Humor Creativity Ratings (HCR; Overholser, 1992) contain eight cartoons (drawings on stressful situations) without captions. Participants are asked to provide a humorous caption for each cartoon. The Cartoon Measure of Perspective-Taking Humor (CMPTH; Lefcourt et al., 1995) is a composite of the Cartoon Measure of Funniness (CMF) and the Comprehension of Perspective-Taking Humor (CMPT). Six cartoons are rated for funniness (CMF), respondents are asked to explain the humor in each cartoon (CMPT), and the level of abstraction of their explanations is rated. The composite score combines the enjoyment and comprehension of perspective-taking humor. Finally, the Escala de Apreciación del Humor (EAHU in Spanish, Carretero-Dios, Pérez, & Buela-Casal, 2010; "Humor Appreciation Scale") is a 32-item scale involving the contents of humor (incongruity-resolution, nonsense) and the structure of humor (sexual, black, disparaging men, and disparaging women); the items are rated on funniness and aversiveness.

Among the promising newer approaches are diary studies. As early as 1926, Kambouropoulou tested the sense of humor of 70 female students with daily diary entries for a period of 1 week. She discovered that they used different types of humor, that is, passive and directed personal as well as impersonal humor involving incongruity in ideas or nonsense. Also, a higher frequency of laughter during a week was related to higher abilities (academic success, psychological tests). Kuiper and Martin (1998) recorded the actual frequency of laughter for a 3-day period and stressful life events every evening. For men with a higher frequency of laughter, stressful life events were positively related to positive affect. One recent study by Guenter, Schreurs, Van Emmerik, Gijsbers, and Van Iterson (2013) implemented a 2-week-long diary study and found that adaptive humor was related to engagement, and emotional exhaustion was related to maladaptive humor (see also Chap. 7 on health).

Thus, self-report measures may suffer from the participants being primed with the knowledge that they are participating in "a humor study." These scales may be adapted for other-ratings, of course. Although observations of interactions would be especially fruitful for research, such observations do not address all—especially intrapersonal—aspects of humor and may also be very extensive. Mixed-method approaches seem most recommendable.

2.7 Conclusion

Humor is a multidimensional phenomenon and has ambiguous functions within and between persons—in general as well as in work contexts. Our working definition describes humor at work as "nonserious social incongruity" (Gervais & Wilson, 2005). This definition is essentially an invitation for researchers to proceed elaborating on concepts and definitions of humor at work.

Three different theoretical approaches for the explanation of humor are mainly used, that is, incongruity, superiority, and arousal. In the following chapters, they will appear again in the context of work. Specifically, in the following Chaps. 3–7 we provide overviews with regard to teams, leadership, negotiations, learning, and health at work. We discuss humor research in these areas and give implications for future research and practice. Now, we invite you to dig deeper into the ambiguous but fascinating nature of humor at work.

References

Aillaud, M., & Piolat, A. (2012). Influence of gender on judgment of dark and nondark humor. *Individual Differences Research, 10*(4), 211–222.

Alexander, R. D. (1986). Ostracism and indirect reciprocity: The reproductive significance of humor. *Ethology and Sociobiology, 7*(3), 253–270. doi:10.1016/0162-3095(86)90052-X.

Apter, M. J. (2013). Developing reversal theory: Some suggestions for future research. *Journal of Motivation, Emotion, and Personality, 1*(1), 1–8. doi: 10.12689/jmep.2013.101.

Attardo, S. (1993). Violation of conversational maxims and cooperation: The case of jokes. *Journal of Pragmatics, 19*(6), 537–558. doi:10.1016/0378-2166(93)90111-2.

Banas, J. A., Dunbar, N., Rodriguez, D., & Liu, S.-J. (2011). A review of humor in educational settings: Four decades of research. *Communication Education, 60*(1), 115–144. doi:10.1080/03634523.2010.496867.

Beermann, U., & Ruch, W. (2009). How virtuous is humor? What we can learn from current instruments. *The Journal of Positive Psychology, 4*(6), 528–539. doi:10.1080/17439760903262859.

Berger, A. A. (1987). Humor: An introduction. *American Behavioral Scientist, 30*(3), 6–15. doi:10.1177/000276487030003002.

Berlyne, D. E. (1972). Humor and its kin. In J. H. Goldstein & P. E. McGhee (Eds.), *The psychology of humor* (pp. 43–60). New York: Academic Press.

Booth-Butterfield, S., & Booth-Butterfield, M. (1991). Individual differences in the communication of humorous messages. *Southern Journal of Communication, 56*(3), 205–218. doi:10.1080/10417949109372831.

Bryant, J., Brown, D., & Parks, S. L. (1981). Ridicule as an educational corrective. *Journal of Educational Psychology, 73*(5), 722–727. doi:10.1037/0022-0663.73.5.722.

Buijzen, M., & Valkenburg, P. M. (2004). Development a typology of humor in audivisual media. *Media Psychology, 6*, 147–167. doi:10.1207/s1532785xmep0602_2.

Cann, A., Stilwell, K., & Taku, K. (2010). Humor styles, positive personality and health. *Europe´s Journal of Psychology, 6*(3), 213–235. doi:10.5964/ejop.v6i3.214.

Cann, A., Watson, A. J., & Bridgewater, E. A. (2014). Assessing humor at work: The humor climate questionnaire. *Humor—International Journal of Humor Research, 27*(2), 307–323. doi:10.1515/humor-2014-0019.

Carretero-Dios, H., Pérez, C., & Buela-Casal, G. (2010). Assessing the appreciation of the content and structure of humor: Construction of a new scale. *Humor—International Journal of Humor Research, 23*(3), 307–325. doi:10.1515/humr.2010.014.

Cooper, C. D. (2005). Just joking around? Employee humor expression as an ingratiatory behavior. *Academy of Management Review, 30*(4), 765–776. doi:10.5465/AMR.2005.18378877.

Craik, K. H., Lampert, M. D., & Nelson, A. J. (1996). Sense of humor and styles of everyday humorous conduct. *Humor—International Journal of Humor Research, 9*(3–4), 273–302. doi:10.1515/humr.1996.9.3-4.273.

Crawford, C. B. (1994). Theory and implications regarding the utilization of strategic humor by leaders. *Journal of Leadership & Organizational Studies, 1*(4), 53–68. doi:10.1177/107179199400100406.

Dikkers, J. S. E., Doosje, S., & de Lange, A. H. (2012). Humor as a human resource tool in organizations. In J. Houdmont, S. Leka, & R. S. Sinclair (Eds.), *Contemporary occupational health psychology: Global perspectives on research and practice* (pp. 74–91). Chichester: Wiley-Blackwell.

Doosje, S., De Goede, M., van Doornen, L., & Goldstein, J. (2010). Measurement of occupational humorous coping. *Humor—International Journal of Humor Research, 23*(3), 275–305. doi:10.1515/humr.2010.013.

Duncan, W. J. (1982). Humor in management: Prospects for administrative practice and research. *The Academy of Management Review, 7*(1), 136. doi:10.2307/257259.

Ehrenberg, T. (1995). Female differences in creation of humor relating to work. *Humor—International Journal of Humor Research, 8*(4), 349–362. doi:10.1515/humr.1995.8.4.349.
Eysenck, H. J. (1942). The appreciation of humour: An experimental and theoretical study. *British Journal of Psychology, 32*(4), 295–309. doi:10.1111/j.2044-295.1942.tb01027.x.
Eysenck, H. J. (1972). Foreword. In J. H. Goldstein & P. E. McGhee (Eds.), *The psychology of humor: Theoretical perspectives and empirical issues* (pp. xii–xvii). New York: Academic Press.
Ferguson, M. A., & Ford, T. E. (2008). Disparagement humor: A theoretical and empirical review of psychoanalytic, superiority, and social identity theories. *Humor—International Journal of Humor Research, 21*(3), 283–312. doi:10.1515/HUMOR.2008.014.
Forabosco, G. (1992). Cognitive aspects of the humor process: The concept of incongruity. *Humor—International Journal of Humor Research, 5*(1–2), 45–68. doi:10.1515/humr.1992.5.1-2.45.
Ford, T. E. (2015). The social consequences of disparagement humor: Introduction and overview. *Humor—International Journal of Humor Research, 28*(2), 163–169. doi:10.1515/humor-2015-0016.
Fredrickson, B. L. (1998). What good are positive emotions? *Review of General Psychology, 2*(3), 300–319. doi:10.1037/1089-2680.2.3.300.
Fredrickson, B. L. (2001). The role of positive emotions in positive psychology. The broaden-and-build theory of positive emotions. *American Psychologist, 56*(3), 218–226. doi:10.1037/0003-066X.56.3.218.
Freud, S. (1905). *Der Witz und seine Beziehung zum Unbewussten*. Leipzig/Wien: Franz Deuticke.
Freud, S. (1960). *Jokes and their relation to the unconscious*. New York: W. W. Norton & Company.
Freud, S. (1927/1961). *The future of an illusion*. London: Norton.
Gervais, M., & Wilson, D. S. (2005). The evolution and functions of laughter and humor: A synthetic approach. *The Quarterly Review of Biology, 80*(4), 395–430. doi:10.1086/498281.
Guenter, H., Schreurs, B., Van Emmerik, H., Gijsbers, W., & Van Iterson, A. (2013). How adaptive and maladaptive humor influence well-beeing at work: A diary study. *Humor—International Journal of Humor Research, 26*(4), 573–594. doi:10.1515/humor-2013-0032.
Hatfield, E., Rapson, R. L., & Le, Y. L. (1994). Primitive emotional contagion: Recent research. In J. Decenty & W. Ickes (Eds.), *The social neuroscience of empathy*. Boston, MA: MIT Press.
Hempelmann, C. F., & Ruch, W. (2005). 3 WD meets GTVH: Breaking the ground for interdisciplinary humor research. *Humor—International Journal of Humor Research, 18*(4), 353–387. doi:10.1515/humr.2005.18.4.353.
Holmes, J., & Marra, M. (2006). Humor and leadership style. *Humor—International Journal of Humor Research, 19*(2), 119-138. doi: 10.1515/HUMOR.2006.006.
Horowitz, J. A., Vessey, J. A., Carlson, K. L., Bradley, J. F., Montoya, C., McCullough, B., et al. (2004). Teasing and bullying experiences of middle school students. *Journal of the American Psychiatric Nurses Association, 10*(4), 165–172. doi:10.1177/1078390304267862.
Hurley, M. M., Dennett, D. C., & Adams, R. B. (2011). *Inside jokes: Using humor to reverse-engineer the mind*. Cambridge, Massachusetts: MIT Press.
Hurren, B. L. (2006). The effects of principals' humor on teachers' job satisfaction. *Educational Studies, 32*(4), 373–385. doi:10.1080/03055690600850321.
Janes, L. M., & Olson, J. M. (2000). Jeer pressure: The behavioral effects of observing ridicule of others. *Personality and Social Psychology Bulletin, 26*(4), 474–485. doi:10.1177/0146167200266006.
Janes, L., & Olson, J. (2015). Humor as an abrasive or a lubricant in social situations: Martineau revisited. *Humor—International Journal of Humor Research, 28*(2), 271–288. doi:10.1515/humor-2015-0021.
Jonson, B. (1600). *Every man out of his humour*. London: William Holme.
Jonson, B. (1927). Every man out of his humour. In C. H. Herford & P. Simpson (Eds.), *Ben Jonson* (Vol. III, pp. 405–601). Oxford: Clarendon Press.

Johnson, A. J., & Mistry, K. (2013). The effect of joke-origin-induced expectancy on cognitive humor. *Humor—International Journal of Humor Research, 26*(2), 321–341. doi:10.1515/humor-2013-0011.

Kahn, W. A. (1989). Toward a sense of organizational humor: Implications for organizational diagnosis and change. *The Journal of Applied Behavioral Science, 25*(1), 45–63. doi:10.1177/0021886389251004.

Kambouropoulou, P. (1926). Individual differences in the sense of humor. *The American Journal of Psychology, 37*(2), 268–278. doi:10.2307/1413696.

Kuiper, N. A., & Martin, R. A. (1998). Laughter and stress in daily life: Relation to positive and negative affect. *Motivation and Emotion, 22*(2), 133–153. doi:10.1023/A:1021392305352.

Lang, J. C., & Lee, C. H. (2010). Workplace humor and organizational creativity. *The International Journal of Human Resource Management, 21*(1), 46–60. doi:10.1080/09585190903466855.

Lefcourt, H. M., Davidson, K., Shepherd, R., Phillips, M., Prkachin, K., & Mills, D. (1995). Perspective-taking humor: Accounting for stress moderation. *Journal of Social and Clinical Psychology, 14*(4), 373–391. doi:10.1521/jscp.1995.14.4.373.

Long, D. L., & Graesser, A. C. (1988). Wit and humor in discourse processing. *Discourse Processes, 11*(1), 35–60. doi:10.1080/01638538809544690.

Long, C. R., & Greenwood, D. N. (2013). Joking in the face of death: A terror management approach to humor production. *Humor—International Journal of Humor Research, 26*(4), 493–509. doi:10.1515/humor-2013-0012.

Mak, B. C. N., Liu, Y., & Deneen, C. C. (2012). Humor in the workplace: A regulating and coping mechanism in socialization. *Discourse & Communication, 6*(2), 163–179. doi:10.1177/1750481312437445.

Martin, R. A. (1998). Approaches to the sense of humor: A historical review. In W. Ruch (Ed.), *The sense of humor: Explorations of a personality characteristic* (pp. 15–60). Berlin/New York: De Gruyter.

Martin, R. A. (2007). *The psychology of humor: An integrative approach*. Burlington, MA: Academic Press.

Martin, R. A., Puhlik-Doris, P., Larsen, G., Gray, J., & Weir, K. (2003). Individual differences in uses of humor and their relation to psychological well-being: Development of the Humor Styles Questionnaire. *Journal of Research in Personality, 37*(1), 48–75. doi:10.1016/S0092-6566(02)00534-2.

Martineau, W. H. (1972). A model of the social functions of humor. In J. Goldstein &, P. McGhee (Eds.), *The Psychology of Humor* (pp. 101–125). New York: Academic Press.

McCreaddie, M., & Wiggins, S. (2008). The purpose and function of humour in health, health care and nursing: a narrative review. *Journal of Advanced Nursing, 61*(6), 584–595. doi:10.1111/j.1365-2648.2007.04548.x.

Mesmer-Magnus, J., Glew, D. J., & Viswesvaran, C. (2012). A meta-analysis of positive humor in the workplace. *Journal of Managerial Psychology, 27*(2), 155–190. doi:10.1108/02683941211199554.

Meyer, J. C. (2000). Humor as a double-edged sword: Four functions of humor in communication. *Communication Theory, 10*(3), 310–331. doi:10.1111/j.1468-2885.2000.tb00194.x.

Michalos, A. C. (Ed.). (2014). *Encyclopedia of quality of life and well-being research*. Dordrecht: Springer, Netherlands.

Morreall, J. (1991). Humor and work. *Humor—International Journal of Humor Research, 4*(3–4), 359–374. doi:10.1515/humr.1991.4.3-4.359.

Morreall, J. (1989). Enjoying incongruity. *Humor—International Journal of Humor Research, 2* (1), 1–18. doi:10.1515/humr.1989.2.1.1.

Morris, C. (1744). *An essay towards fixing the true standards of wit, humour, raillery, satire, and ridicule*. London: Printed for J. Roberts.

Obrdlik, A. J. (1942). "Gallows humor"-A sociological phenomenon. *American Journal of Sociology, 47*(5), 709–716. doi:10.1086/219002.

Olsson, H., Backe, H., Sörensen, S., & Kock, M. (2002). The essence of humour and its effects and functions: A qualitative study. *Journal of Nursing Management, 10*(1), 21–26. doi:10.1046/j.0966-0429.2001.00272.x.

Overholser, J. C. (1992). Sense of humor when coping with life stress. *Personality and Individual Differences, 13*(7), 799–804. doi:10.1016/0191-8869(92)90053-R.

Paul, J. (1804/1990). *Vorschule der Ästhetik: Nebst einigen Vorlesungen in Leipzig über die Parteien der Zeit.* Hamburg: Friedrich Perthes/Meiner.

Raskin, V. (1985). *Semantic mechanisms of humor.* Dordrecht/Boston/Lancaster: D. Reidel Publishing Company.

Robert, C., & Yan, W. (2007). The case for developing new research on humor and culture in organizations: Toward a higher grade of manure. *Research in Personnel and Human Resources Management, 26,* 205–267. doi:10.1016/S0742-7301(07)26005-0.

Romero, E. J., & Cruthirds, K. W. (2006). The use of humor in the workplace. *The Academy of Management Perspectives, 20*(2), 58–69. doi:10.5465/AMP.2006.20591005.

Roy, D. (1959). "Banana time": Job satisfaction and informal interaction. *Human Organization, 18* (4), 158–168. doi: 10.17730/humo.18.4.07j88hr1p4074605.

Ruch, W. (1996). Measurement approaches to the sense of humor. Introduction and overview. In W. Ruch (Ed.), Measurement of the Sense of Humor (special issue). *Humor—International Journal of Humor Research, 9*(3–4), 239–250.

Ruch, W. (2005). Humor-Test 3 WD. Unpublished manuscript, University of Duesseldorf, Germany.

Ruch, W. (2007). Appendix: Humor measurement tools. In W. Ruch (Ed.), *The sense of humor: Explorations of a personality characteristic* (pp. 405–412). Berlin: De Gruyter.

Ruch, W., & Ekman, P. (2001). The expressive pattern of laughter. In A. W. Kaszniak (Ed.), *Emotion, qualia, and consciousness* (pp. 426–443). Tokyo: World Scientific Publishers.

Ruch, W., Köhler, G., & van Thriel, C. (1996). Assessing the "humorous temperament": Construction of the facet and standard trait forms of the State-Trait-Cheerfulness-Inventory–STCI. *Humor—International Journal of Humor Research, 9*(3–4), 303–339. doi: 10.1515/humr.1996.9.3-4.303.

Ruch, W., Hofmann, J., Platt, T., & Proyer, R. (2014). The state-of-the art in gelotophobia research: A review and some theoretical extensions. *Humor—International Journal of Humor Research, 27*(1), 23–45. doi: 10.1515/humor-2013-0046.

Scheel, T. E., Gerdenitsch, C., & Korunka, C. (2016). Humor at work—Validation of the Short and Work-related Humor Styles Questionnaire (swHSQ). *Humor—International Journal of Humor Research, 29*(3), 439–465. doi: 10.1515/humor-2015-0118.

Schubert, C., & Leschhorn, W. (2006). *Hippokrates. Ausgewählte Schriften.* Düsseldorf/Zürich: Artemis & Winkler.

Schwarz, N. (1990). Feeling as information: Infomational and motivational functions of affective states. In E. T. Higgins & R. M. Sorrentino (Eds.), *Handbook of motivation and cognition: Foundations of social behavior* (Vol. 2). New York, London: Guilford.

Seckman, M. A., & Couch, C. J. (1989). Jocularity, sarcasm, and relationships: An empirical study. *Journal of Contemporary Ethnography, 18*(3), 327–344. doi:10.1177/089124189018003004.

Singer, D. L. (1968). Aggression arousal, hostile humor, catharsis. *Journal of Personality and Social Psychology Monograph Supplement, 8*(1), 1–14. doi:10.1037/h0021361.

Suls, J. (1972). A two-stage model for the appreciation of jokes and cartoons: An information-processing analysis. In J. H. Goldstein & P. E. McGhee (Eds.), *The Psychology of Humor. Theoretical Perspectives and Empirical Issues* (pp. 81–100). New York: Academic Press.

Svebak, S. (1974). Revised questionnaire on the sense of humor. *Scandinavian Journal of Psychology, 15*(1), 328–331. doi:10.1111/j.1467-9450.1974.tb00597.x.

Svebak, S. (2010). The sense of humor questionnaire: Conceptualization and review of 40 years of findings in empirical research. *Europe's Journal of Psychology, 6*(3), 288–310. doi:10.5964/ejop.v6i3.218.

Svebak, S. (2014). Humor. In A. C. Michalos (Ed.), *Encyclopedia of quality of life and well-being research* (pp. 3048–3050). Dordrecht: Springer Netherlands. doi: 10.1007/978-94-007-0753-5_1353.

Sykes, A. J. (1966). Joking relationships in an industrial setting. *American Anthropologist, 68*(1), 188–193. doi:10.1525/aa.1966.68.1.02a00250.

Tajfel, H. (1978). The psychological structure of intergroup relations. In H. Tajfel (Ed.), *Differentiation between social groups: Studies in the social psychology of intergroup relations*. London: Academic Press.

Thorson, J. A., & Powell, F. C. (1993). Development and validation of a multidimensional sense of humor scale. *Journal of Clinical Psychology, 49*(1), 13–23. doi:10.1002/1097-4679(199301)49:13.0.CO;2-S.

Vinton, K. L. (1989). Humor in the workplace it is more than telling jokes. *Small Group Behavior, 20*(2), 151–166. doi:10.1177/104649648902000202.

Wanzer, M. B., Frymier, A. B., & Irwin, J. (2010). An explanation of the relationship between instructor humor and student learning: Instructional humor processing theory. *Communication Education, 59*(1), 1–18. doi:10.1080/03634520903367238.

Weisfeld, G. E. (1993). The adaptive value of humor and laughter. *Ethology and Sociobiology, 14*(2), 141–169. doi:10.1016/0162-3095(93)90012-7.

Westwood, R. I., & Johnston, A. (2013). Humor in organization: From function to resistance. *Humor—International Journal of Humor Research, 26*(2), 219–247. doi: 10.1515/humor-2013-0024.

Winick, C. (1976). The social contexts of humor. *Journal of Communication, 26*(3), 124–128. doi:10.1111/j.1460-2466.1976.tb01915.x.

Zillmann, D., & Cantor, J. R. (1976/1996). A disposition theory of humour and mirth. In A. J. Chapman & H. C. Foot (Eds.), *Humor and laughter: Theory, research, and application.* London: Wiley.

Chapter 3
Humor in Teams: Interpersonal Functions of Humor

Christine Gockel

Abstract Teams and groups are central in our lives. We work in teams and are confronted with teams in our private lives. In this chapter, we will describe the duality of humor in teams—that is, its capacity to unite and to divide. Four processes explain why humor impacts social outcomes in teams—affect-reinforcement, perceived similarity, self-disclosure, and hierarchical salience. A closer look at how laughter and humor developed in our hominid ancestors can deepen our understanding of interpersonal humor effects—laughter is an acoustic signal that the environment is safe and helps positive affect to spread among group members. Current research based on evolutionary theory investigates the spread of positive affect in work teams, the size of natural laughter groups and fake laughter. A micro-level look at specific humorous comments reflects the duality of humor as well. We close with a note of caution, future research ideas, and implications.

Keywords Humor · Team · Work group · Cohesion · Effectiveness · Evolution · Duchenne laughter · Affect · Linguistic analysis · Functionalist perspective

3.1 Introduction

Teams are central in our lives—both inside and outside of organizations. We work in teams because today's complex tasks require the interplay of several competent people who strive toward the same goal. We are confronted with teams in our lives outside work as well, for example when an airline crew flies us to another city, when a surgical team operates on us, or when we drop off our kid at school to learn with a group of other kids from a team of teachers. Thus, teams are everywhere. They are defined as two or more individuals who interact, possess a common goal, and are interdependent (Kozlowski & Ilgen, 2006). In this chapter, we will focus on humor in teams and groups. We use the two terms, team and group, interchangeably.

The original version of this chapter was revised: See the "Chapter Note" section at the end of this chapter for details. The erratum to this chapter is available at https://doi.org/10.1007/978-3-319-65691-5_9

T. Scheel and C. Gockel, *Humor at Work in Teams, Leadership, Negotiations, Learning and Health*, SpringerBriefs in Psychology,
DOI 10.1007/978-3-319-65691-5_3

Research on humor in teams has focused mostly on humor as a social phenomenon that is a certain kind of communication between team members, instead of humor as an individual characteristic. We will therefore describe the duality of positive and less positive effects of humor in teams, and will also explain which processes specifically impact team relationships. We will chronicle how and why laughter and humor evolved in our hominid ancestors. This background knowledge helps to understand the beneficial effects of humor on positive affect and cohesion in teams. A micro-level look at humorous statements reflects the duality of humor as well. We will close with a note of caution, ideas for future research and implications.

3.2 A Positive Look on Humor in Teams

Humor in teams has generally been described positively. Romero and Cruthirds (2006), for example, list the effects of humor as "reducing stress and enhancing leadership, increasing group cohesiveness, improving communication, fostering creativity, and building organizational culture" (p. 58). They describe humor as a multifunctional management tool which can be selectively used by managers in order to achieve desired outcomes. Others (e.g., Morreall, 1991) describe general functions of humor, which are all positive: humor is supposed to bring people together, create cohesion, help groups change their perspective on problems and help groups work together smoothly.

Empirical research supports a positive view on humor in teams—at first sight. A recent meta-analysis (of self-report cross-sectional studies) included three studies with group cohesion as an outcome (out of 49 studies overall; Mesmer-Magnus, Glew & Viswesvaran, 2012). When a group is cohesive, members report a sense of belonging to the group, they feel included in the group and report that the group is a part of who they are (Bollen & Hoyle, 1990; Forsyth, 2006). Furthermore, cohesive groups "stick together," have high levels of solidarity and are unified (Forsyth, 2006). Results of the meta-analysis indicate a small positive effect of employee humor on work group cohesion. The correlation coefficient corrected for unreliability was 0.20. A second positive effect of (perceived) leader humor on group cohesion was found as well. The correlation coefficient corrected for unreliability was 0.42 in this case. One reason for the positive relation of humor with cohesion is certainly that previous research has been relatively narrow in scope. This, and focusing mostly on friendly and positive humor as compared to detrimental and negative humor, as the authors point out (Mesmer-Magnus et al., 2012).

Aside from quantitative research summarized in the meta-analysis above, qualitative research illustrates the positive effects of humor in groups as well. Lynch (2010) conducted an ethnographic study over the course of one year in a hotel kitchen and examined the use of spontaneous humor among chefs who were all equal in status. As a method, he chose participant observation, took notes on humorous episodes and followed up with three rounds of interviews to ensure the authenticity of his descriptions. He interprets that humor helps in making sense, forming identity, reproducing organizing practices and processes, and in shielding the group from management. His findings therefore support the results of quantitative studies mentioned above. Interestingly, his study also showed that the seemingly cruel nature of some humorous comments increased bonding. It seems as though "if humor is a binding ingredient in social relations, it can also be used to add spice to provide a little bite" (Lynch, 2010, p. 130).

Some researchers even suggest that humor increases group effectiveness. Romero and Pescosolido (2008) provide a framework and explain how the successful use of humor impacts three facets of group effectiveness. First, humor should increase group productivity because it improves communication, develops a strong performance orientation, increases the acceptance of group goals, and helps to manage group emotions. Second, humor should positively impact learning because it strengthens psychological safety within the team. And third, it should impact team viability (which is the degree to which team members want to work together in the future; Hackman, 1986) because it increases positive affect, group cohesion and reduces employee turnover. To date, direct and indirect effects of humor on any facet of group effectiveness remain to be tested.

3.3 A Look at the Dark Side of Humor in Teams

Humor certainly has positive effects on teams, yet it also has a dark side. The duality of humor means that it can unite (as mentioned above) and divide. Meyer (2000) outlines four functions of humor that fit this division. With regard to unity, he explains that humor helps to build group cohesion, to clarify issues and to enforce social norms. With regard to division, he explains that humor can help to contrast one's view with an opponent's or to differentiate one's group from another group. In a similar vein, Wilkinson, Rees, and Knight (2007) found in an examination of eight focus groups that humor served one of three functions: to cope with embarrassing information, to show solidarity or lack of solidarity with others or to exert power and control.

This view on the duality of humor is corroborated by Robinson and Smith-Lovin (2001), who used event history techniques to analyze recorded lab group discussions. Based on their results, the authors developed a theory of humor and status in groups. This theory predicts, among other things, who will produce humor, who will be successful in producing humor, or how producing humor changes the speaker's subsequent interactions within the group. Most importantly for this purpose though is that the theory also provides explanations of how and under which circumstances humor can increase or undermine cohesion in a group. Robinson and Smith-Lovin (2001) hypothesize that humor can strengthen affective ties within the group—that is, increase cohesion—when the humorous comment refers either to the group as a whole or to outsiders. They hypothesize further that humor can undermine cohesion when the comment refers to one's self or to another group member.

Lab

Lyttle's research (2007) reflects the duality of humor in teams as well. He details the positive effects of humor on physical, psychological, cognitive, and social levels; he expresses the dangers of using humor as well. In addition to dividing a group, humor can also cause offense, erode a person's authority, and distract one from work.

In two laboratory experiments, we examined the duality of humor more closely (Gockel & Kerr, 2015). We focused on put-down humor, which always has a specific target and is used to make fun of someone or something. Our assumption was that put-down humor would increase cohesion only when it was targeted at outgroup members and followed by laughter. The results of these two experiments showed that put-down humor of outgroup members, as compared to no humor, did not increase team members' own feelings of cohesion. However, it changed team members' perception of cohesion among their fellow team members: They were regarded to be more cohesive among each other—excluding the participant. In summary, our studies indicate that potentially aggressive forms of humor can change the perception of other team members while not changing an individual's feeling toward the team.

There is currently one questionnaire that can measure the two faces of humor in teams, the "Short Scale for Evaluating Affiliative and Aggressive Humor in Groups" (Curseu & Fodor, 2016; see Appendix A.1). It distinguishes between two types of humor that are used in groups. Affiliative humor is used to amuse others and facilitate interactions (Martin, Puhlik-Doris, Larsen, Gray, & Weir, 2003). In contrast, aggressive humor is used to criticize, manipulate and offend others (Martin et al., 2003).

3.4 A Look at Relevant Processes

Researchers who study humor in teams often examine how strongly humor can unite or divide a group. However, it is not as clear as to why and how humor impacts these social outcomes in groups. Cooper (2008) describes four important processes to explain why humor impacts these outcomes in relationships at work. The four processes can be applied well to the study of humor in teams.

Before we describe these processes in detail, we would like to point out that they fit the two basic dimensions of person perception, namely warmth and competence (Fiske, Cuddy, & Glick, 2007). Social psychological research has shown that when people spontaneously form impressions of others, two dimensions can explain how they characterize others. The first dimension is warmth: it captures all traits related to perceived intent, namely trustworthiness, friendliness, and helpfulness. The second dimension is competence: it captures traits related to perceived ability, namely skill, efficacy, and intelligence (Fiske et al., 2007). Out of the four processes described by Cooper (2008), the first three seem to be related to the warmth dimension of person perception and impact the degree of trustworthiness and friendliness with which someone is regarded. The last dimension however, seems to be related to the competence dimension and impacts the degree of competency with which someone is regarded. All four processes are detailed below.

The first process is *affect-reinforcement* (Cooper, 2008). Humor, especially affiliative humor, can lead to positive affect. This in turn makes people appear to be more sympathetic (Wanzer, Booth-Butterfield, & Booth-Butterfield, 1996). A lab experiment with a creative set-up illustrates this effect. Fraley and Aron (2004) had same-sex strangers participate in a series of interactions that created a humorous experience (e.g., by asking participants to act out a television commercial of their choice in a language made up by them) or did not create a humorous experience (e.g., by asking participants to act out a television commercial in English). Participants, who shared a humorous experience and therefore reinforced each other's positive affect, felt closer to one another after the interaction than participants who had interacted without any humor.

The second process is *perceived similarity.* According to the similarity-attraction-paradigm (Byrne, 1971), people are attracted to others who are similar. This should also be true for similarity in finding hilarity in certain events and not in others. Seeing someone else laugh about a humorous comment shows that one has interpreted the comment correctly; in other words, the other person's behavior validates one's own view (Cooper, 2008). Furthermore, if all group members start laughing loudly after a humorous comment, they display the same behavior, which may make them conclude that they share the same feelings and thoughts on the issue at hand. This realization could make them feel closer to each other and increase cohesion in the group. Eventually, shared experiences facilitate group interactions and help to build a group culture (Fine & De Soucey, 2005). Schachter's classic research on affiliation (1959) supports the claim that perceived similarity can lead to an increase in cohesion. In his well-known studies, Schachter (1959) showed that anxious people preferred to be in the company of others who were similarly anxious. One plausible and well-supported reason for this was the individual's desire to receive comfort and support from another person. Schachter hypothesized that the presence of the other person, who is in the same situation, can have a direct anxiety-reducing effect and reported experimental evidence supporting this hypothesis (e.g., Wrightsman, 1959).

The third process is *self-disclosure.* Previous research has shown that the more people self-disclose, the more others like them (Collins & Miller, 1994). Humor is a way of self-disclosure because people show what they find funny and what they find serious. Though a disclaimer must be added here. There is an important sequence regarding the kind of information that people self-disclose when they get to know others. It is certainly not advisable to share one's funny divorce stories on a first date.

The fourth process is *hierarchical salience.* Humor can make power and status differences salient. For example, a leader can use humor to point out a mistake to an employee or to control employee behavior (Holmes, 2000). Alternatively, a leader can use humor to overcome status differences (Vinton, 1989). In both cases, differences in the hierarchy become salient for both leader and employee. This fact is particularly well illustrated in a naturalistic study in a small organization with 13 employees (Vinton, 1989). The author showed that teasing served two purposes.

First, it helped in completing the necessary work. Teasing allowed higher status employees to order their subordinates in a pleasant way to finish a task. Second, teasing lessened status differentials between employees by putting everyone on the same level, which eventually improved cooperation. Interestingly, higher status employees are not necessarily the ones who initiate the most humor within groups. Duncan (1985) found this in a small social-network study with six groups.

In conclusion, the four processes described by Cooper (2008) help to explain why humor impacts relationship outcomes in teams. One caveat though is the timing of the humorous comment—as hinted to above. When examining task-oriented management meetings, Consalvo (1989) showed that different phases of problem solving came with different patterns of humor. A second study that points out the importance of timing is the one by Terrion and Ashforth (2002). They observed a leadership training program in a Canadian police college as participants and focused on the development of put-down humor in this temporary group. They found that put-downs followed a certain temporal pattern: group members would first put themselves down, then shared social identities (i.e., the group as a whole), then external groups and finally, other group members. The researchers concluded that this developmental sequence signaled increased trust and inclusion in the group, although they refer to put-down humor, and that it helped to create a common identity and cohesion. Therefore, even more aggressive kinds of humor can be interpreted as benign and can reinforce positive affect if presented at the right time and in the right sequence.

3.5 A Look at the Past: Evolution of Laughter and Humor

In order to understand the interpersonal effects of humor, one must understand how humor and laughter developed over time. Gervais and Wilson (2005) are two biologists who describe how laughter developed as a specific kind of vocalization in our ancestors and how humor was later attached to this vocalization.

So, what exactly are the characteristics of laughter? Several primate species show a distinct facial expression during social play: the so-called open-mouth or "play" face (Preuschoft & van Hoff, 1997). In some apes, this facial expression is accompanied by a distinct vocalization, a panting sound, like Duchenne laughter (Provine, 2000). Interestingly, it is always the same stimuli that elicit this kind of sound in many species and across cultures. These stimuli are (a) unexpected, (b) nonserious, and (c) occur in a social context. Gervais and Wilson (2005) describe these stimuli with the term "non-serious social incongruity" and propose that they explain laughter in nonhuman primates, infants and even adults when they respond to humor. For example, when apes are tickled, they make the same sound as when they are playing, which is similar to human laughter. Tickling is a non-serious stimulation of otherwise vulnerable body parts by another person. Also, a mother who plays peek-a-boo will probably make her baby laugh. And a co-worker telling a funny joke will also see and hear her colleagues laughing. In all three situations, the stimulus that elicits laughter can be described as nonserious social incongruity. Although these stimulus characteristics are the same for all cultures, human laughter is strongly shaped by culture. What kind of humor is appropriate to use and to laugh at varies widely (Lefcourt, 2000).

Laughter developed in our hominid ancestors because it helped them survive in their dangerous environment. This environment probably looked like this (Owren & Bachorowski, 2003): food was rare and predators were numerous, which led to physical and psychological stress. Because survival also required social organization, hominids also experienced social stress. They needed to coordinate group activities and remain together in a hostile environment, exchange resources, negotiate hierarchies, make collective decisions, and interact with members of other groups (Van Vugt & Kameda, 2012). Although group living was complicated, it is an adaptive strategy that increased our ancestor's rate of survival and reproduction. Indeed, this strategy was so successful that humans are "among the most 'groupish' animals" (p. 298).

When times were safe, our hominid ancestors needed a signal to indicate safety. Laughter was just this signal. It is automatic and contagious behavior (Van Vugt & Kameda, 2012), which enables positive emotions to spread quickly throughout a group and which helps to increase the fitness of sender, receiver and group. In the beginning, social play and tickling in safe environments led to laughter. Then hominids generalized stimuli to many other situations that were also based on nonserious social incongruity. As a result, hominids became more playful over time as they found humor in more stimuli. In safe moments, playful hominids could then broaden their perspectives, try out new things, learn a lot and build enduring social relationships with others (according to the Broaden-and-Build Theory of Positive Emotions by Fredrickson, 1998). Similar to Gervais and Wilson (2005), Ramachandran (1998) explained that laughter is a signal to others that a serious situation turns out to be nonserious. Over time, laughter and humor were then co-opted for novel functions, and humans could then use their affect-inducing properties to influence others.

From an evolutionary standpoint, laughter and affect are very closely connected. In general, laughter increases positive mood (Martin, 2001) and decreases negative mood. More specifically, research has shown that humor decreases anxiety, tension, and stress—indicators of negative mood (Berk, 2001). Laughter and affect are particularly relevant in a group context. First, laughter signals positive affect of a sender to receivers (Russell, Bachorowski, & Fernández-Dols, 2003). Second, laughter induces positive affect in others because it is contagious (Owren & Bachorowski, 2003). Therefore, positive affect can spread quickly, unconsciously, and without effort within a group. In summary, laughter is the behavioral component that accompanies a positive emotion that results from nonserious social incongruity (Gervais & Wilson, 2005). It is a medium for emotional contagion. Through laughter, positive emotions spread throughout a group.

So how did fake laughter develop? Biologists and psychologists distinguish two kinds of laughter (Keltner & Bonanno, 1997). Duchenne laughter is elicited by specific stimuli is associated with positive emotions, and has specific physical characteristics. Every human learns how to laugh. Non-Duchenne laughter on the other hand is self-generated, emotionless, and has different physical characteristics than Duchenne laughter. It occurs without humor. The two kinds of laughter arise from the activation of different neural systems in the brain (Wild, Rodden, Grodd, & Ruch, 2003). Non-Duchenne laughter is an imitation of Duchenne laughter. In other words, humans try to use the positive effects of laughter without the appropriate stimulus. It occurs when the speaker aims to smooth the interaction (Vettin & Todt, 2004), shows nervousness (Keltner & Bonanno 1997) or tries to avoid misunderstandings (Vettin & Todt 2004). Kangasharju and Nikko (2009) examined humor and laughter separately in a conversation analysis of several hours of team meetings. They also found that some laughter occurred without humor, but in combination with troubles telling, shame and embarrassment. They reasoned that speakers strategically used laughter in team meetings to show that a topic was difficult and to get over the difficulties.

3.6 A Look at the Present: Research Inspired by Evolutionary Thinking

There is some current research on humor in teams that is more or less directly inspired by evolutionary thinking: one theoretical model about how humor and affect spread in teams, one naturalistic study of groups in bars about how laughter spreads, and one linguistic study about the functions of laughter as distinct from humor. To avoid any misunderstandings, none of these studies were set out to test evolutionary hypotheses. We summarize them under this heading though, because they illustrate evolutionary thinking very well.

The first example is a theoretical model about how humor and affect spread in teams, the "Wheel Model of Humor" by Robert and Wilbanks (2012). It connects humor with affect and spells out how humor evolves into a cyclical and cumulative process in teams over time. The so-called humor wheel starts moving when group members process humor events and experience positive affect. They then display positive affect with their facial expressions and with verbal and nonverbal signs, such as laughter. This positive affect is then transmitted to others via emotional contagion. Because people tend to mimic the behaviors of others, they experience similar emotions (Hatfield, Cacioppo, & Rapson, 1994). Consequently, a collective positive mood can develop in the team.

A cycle of humor may start with one team member saying something humorous. The audience appreciates the comment, experiences positive affect, and displays this experience by laughing. Positive affect in the audience can then bounce back to the sender of the humor. In this fashion, humorous comments or humor events are likely to stimulate more humor events in the teams, which is supported by linguistic research described below. Results of a study examining humor and laughter during team meetings and their relation with team performance also support this reasoning (Lehmann-Willenbrock & Allen, 2014).

According to the wheel model, humor has a cumulative impact. Even minor events may have a large impact because they tend to unfold over time (Frijda, 1993). In the long-run, a humor-supportive climate can develop in a team where humor is accepted and encouraged because it simultaneously conveys serious messages and leads to positive affect. The wheel of humor can certainly stop due to many various circumstances, for example, if the humor fails or is too aggressive. Overall, the wheel model of humor (Robert & Wilbanks, 2012) is a very promising model for future research because it resonates with evolutionary thinking and it explains the complex interpersonal processes regarding humor and affect in teams at the workplace.

The second example is a naturalistic study about how laughter spreads in groups in bars. Dezecache and Dunbar (2012) aimed to learn how many people laugh together spontaneously in naturally occurring groups. For that purpose, they observed social groups in bars in the US and noted (a) group size, (b) conversation subgroup size (that is, how many people took part in a particular conversation by either speaking or listening to the speaker) and (c) laughter subgroup size (that is, how many people laughed together). Their results confirm the upper limit of $n = 4$ of conversation subgroup size (Dunbar, Duncan, & Nettle, 1995). In this particular study, the average conversational subgroup size was 2.9 and the average laughter subgroup size was 2.7. In other words, only relatively few people laughed together at the same time. The authors concluded that laughter is not triggered easily in larger social groups—although laughter is supposed to be contagious. Also, the authors estimated that laughter functions similar to grooming. In a grooming dyad, endorphins are triggered in the groomee. Accordingly, in a laughter group, endorphins may be triggered in all members. Because the "grooming group" for laughter comprises around three individuals, this should—according to the authors—make laughter three times as efficient as grooming. In conclusion, laughter helps humans to increase the size of the group that can be bonded.

The third study is a linguistic study about the functions of laughter that is distinct from humor. It exemplifies the distinction between Duchenne and non-Duchenne laughter well. As a starting point, Warner-Garcia (2014) argues that laughter does not necessarily relate to the content of a message (in other words, to humor in a message), but rather to the relational level of the interaction in order to manage face threats. Previous research has shown that laughter can be used strategically to accomplish certain goals in an interaction (Glenn, 2003). Sometimes, laughter occurs after humorous comments. This would be Duchenne laughter because it is associated with a specific stimulus and associated with positive emotions. Sometimes, though, laughter occurs without any humorous comment. This would then be non-Duchenne laughter, which is self-generated and emotionless, as mentioned above. Speakers sometimes use it to change a serious comment to a laughable comment after the fact (Warner-Garcia, 2014). In these cases, speakers may use laughter in order to be intentionally equivocal about their previous comment. With laughter, they indicate a frame switch from the serious to the nonserious. Warner-Garcia (2014) calls this "coping laughter" and defines it as laughter that is used to manage face-threatening situations. It has four functions—to mitigate face threat, to conceal face-loss, to change frame from the serious to the nonserious and to facilitate topic transition.

Both initiators and respondents can show this kind of laughter. If the initiator of a comment laughs, the person might want to take back a face threat that he or she has just made. If the respondent of a comment laughs, the person might want to diminish a face threat that was just focused on him or her. In both situations, common laughter may indicate that a face threat has been managed successfully, whereas a lack of laughter from others may indicate that the face threat has not been managed successfully and remains bold. Warner-Garcia's research (2014) is particularly interesting because it makes a clear distinction between laughter connected to humor and laughter that occurs without humor and points out the functions of the latter.

3.7 A Look at the Details: Micro-level Research About Humor in Teams

Linguistic studies have focused on the functions of humor on a micro-level. Rather than examining the overall effects of humor during a meeting or even over several meetings, they dissect team conversations and zoom in on single statements. A lot of research in this area originates in Janet Holmes' research group in New Zealand.

In one particularly relevant study, Holmes (2006) examined humor at New Zealand workplaces. She found that one of the most important functions of humor was the maintenance of good relationships with colleagues. More specifically, the entirety of humorous comments reflects the bright and the dark side of humor mentioned above. Humorous comments either supported or contested a previous comment. They often occurred in sequences, meaning that one humorous comment follows another. Sequences were either constructed in collaboration, when one comment built onto another, or in competition, when different speakers tried to take the lead. The first kind of sequence occurred more often in groups that included relatively many women, and the second kind more often in groups that included relatively many men.

The duality of humor also becomes apparent in a linguistic analysis of four intercultural business meetings (Rogerson-Revell, 2007). Humor seemed to be used strategically to include or exclude. On the one hand, humor can mark solidarity. For example in this study, several speakers with converging speech styles constructed humor collaboratively—that is, several humorous comments built onto one another. On the other hand, humor can exert social control. Since it is associated with a style shift, humor is also associated with power. Style shifts create uncertainties because members do not know how to respond. In all cases, humor was associated with a stylistic shift from formal, structured segments to more informal, looser segments. In other words, a shift from serious to playful. In addition, Kangasharju and Nikko

(2009) found that joint laughter helped to close a topic in the conversation and have all participants agree on it. The authors had examined 16 h of meetings from five cross-border meetings. In summary, humor and laughter help to structure a conversation.

Linguistic studies have found two more functions of humor and laughter—helping newcomers in their socialization and subversion. Schnurr and Mak (2009) examined more than 9 hours of authentic discourse collected in three workplaces in Hong Kong and 15 in-depth interviews with newcomers and their colleagues. They assumed that humor helps newcomer socialization because it reflects the norms of a particular workplace and can hint to acceptable and unacceptable behavior (Linstead, 1985). Humor is also subject to norms regarding the kinds of appropriate humor and adequate responses to humor. The researchers found that humor is indeed very important for newcomer socialization because it signals mistakes and teaches newcomers how to handle things appropriately. As long as the newcomer is still learning the ropes and does not understand running jokes, he or she is still not fully part of the team.

Finally, Holmes and Marra (2002) examined how humor can be used subversively among colleagues in two large business organizations. Using critical discourse analysis, they analyzed tape recordings of 12 team meetings and found that subversive humor made up almost 40%. Ironic quips—short, sometimes witty, and often ironic comments about the ongoing action—made up 74% of the subversive humor and were mostly targeted towards the group leader.

3.8 A Note of Caution

Some researchers regard humor as a managerial tool and conduct investigations from a functionalist perspective (Westwood & Johnston, 2013). This perspective on humor led to a number of popular-press books, which are sometimes not based on any empirical results, and to an even greater number of humor consultants. Some managers and employees seem to long for a simple recipe that tells them how humor can improve their relationships at work as well as their performance. This functionalist perspective, however, greatly reduces the complexities of humor (Westwood & Johnston, 2013). Humor can also be disruptive and has the potential to be subversive. It can offer an alternative perspective, a different world view that contrasts current organizational life. The authors state that "humor can, when bounded, be seen as integrative and functionalist, but in other contexts it can also involve a genuine confrontation with the dominant order and undermine and disrupt that order through revealing its paradoxes, inconsistencies and irrationalities" (pp. 238–239). Currently, only few researchers take the subversive potential of humor into account. Holmes and Marra (2002) are among those exceptions.

Two reasons account for a somewhat simplistic view on humor in teams (Westwood & Johnston, 2013). The first one is that the separate disciplines do not speak to each other. Researchers work in departments and publish in journals that belong to one of the following disciplines: psychology, management, communications, linguistics, sociology, biology, and anthropology. Research therefore lacks integration. The second reason is that most research is undertheorized. Most scholars refer to one of the three theoretical positions of incongruity, superiority, and relief in the introductory section of their manuscripts. Yet they do not elaborate on this reasoning any further. Evolutionary theory explaining the development of laughter and humor over time has the potential to unite the different perspectives and disciplines. Such an overarching perspective could better capture the multifaceted nature of humor, its manifestations, forms, and consequences.

3.9 Future Research

What type of research would benefit the study of humor in teams? We propose three domains that would advance research greatly. First, an overarching model about the effects of humor in teams is needed. It would explain what type of humor impacts what type of outcome, and under which circumstances. Such a model would also take into account whether the effects of humor occur at the individual or at the team level (see Tremblay, 2016 for an example) and which role timing plays. From other areas of research, for example self-disclosure, we know how crucial timing is. Currently, we know of only one study that focused on the timing of humorous comments (Terrion & Ashforth, 2002). A new model of humor would take this into account as well.

Second, more research should be geared towards the role of negative and aggressive humor in teams. Although it occurs relatively seldom, it should have a stronger impact on all social and emotional outcomes than positive and friendly humor does. Social psychological research has shown that people process negative information more thoroughly than positive information and that it has a stronger impact (Baumeister, Bratslavsky, Finkenauer, & Vohs, 2001).

Third, longitudinal research is much needed. Although some qualitative studies examined groups over longer amounts of time (e.g., Lynch, 2010), researchers rarely took the development of humor into account. The one exception, mentioned above, is the study by Terrion and Ashforth (2002). Longitudinal research on a micro-level could examine how humor and the spread of positive or negative emotions are tied together. On a more macro-level, it could examine how humor patterns and social outcomes, such as cohesion or differentiation, depend on each other. It could also examine the effects of one and the same humorous comment at different points in time. In summary, the study of humor in teams offers a wide variety of important and interesting research questions that teams of humorous researchers will be able to answer in the future.

3.10 Recommendations for Practice

Which suggestions for humor in teams can we propose without sounding overly simplistic? Lyttle (2007) has already provided specific advice for the workplace, which seems reasonable to us as well: when using humor in teams, one should include everyone in the humorous exchanges. This should increase the chances that humor will unite rather than divide. When using humor about specific persons, one must exercise caution though. For example, Lyttle (2007) suggests using oneself instead of others as a target. When being the "butt of a joke," one must be clear on the boundaries and must openly say when one feels hurt. To this suggestion, we add that feedback in teams about humor is extremely important. A positive humor-supportive climate can only be built if leaders and all team members engage in open conversations about what types of humor they find appropriate and which types are inappropriate. Finally, Lyttle (2007) suggests preparing humorous exchanges, because planning pays off. This might be an opportunity to get the wheel of humor (Robert & Wilbanks, 2012) started, but one then must let go of the wheel and see how spontaneous humor from other team members continues to spin it.

Recommendations for further reading

Cooper, C. (2008). Elucidating the bonds of workplace humor: A relational process model. *Human Relations*, *61*(8), 1087–1115. doi:10.1177/0018726708094861.

Gervais, M., & Wilson, D. S. (2005). The evolution and functions of laughter and humor: A synthetic approach. *The Quarterly Review of Biology*, *80*(4), 395–430. doi:10.1086/498281.

Robert, C., & Wilbanks, J. E. (2012). The wheel model of humor: Humor events and affect in organizations. *Human Relations*, *65*(9), 1071–1099. doi:10.1177/0018726711433133.

References

Baumeister, R., Bratslavsky, E., Finkenauer, C., Vohs, K. (2001). Bad is stronger than good. *Review of general psychology, 5*(4), 323–370. http://doi.apa.org/psycinfo/2001-11965-001.

Berk, R. A. (2001). The active ingredients in humor: Psychophysiological benefits and risks for older adults. *Educational Gerontology, 27,* 323–339. doi:10.1080/036012701750195021.

Bollen, K. A., & Hoyle, R. H. (1990). Perceived cohesion: A conceptual and empirical examination. *Social Forces, 69,* 479–504. doi:10.2307/2579670.

Byrne, D. (1971). *The attraction paradigm.* New York: Academic Press.

Collins, N. L., & Miller, L. C. (1994). Self-disclosure and liking: A meta-analytic review. *Psychological Bulletin, 116*(3), 457. doi:10.1037/0033-2909.116.3.457.

Consalvo, C. M. (1989). Humor in management: No laughing matter. *Humor, 2*(3), 285–297.

Cooper, C. (2008). Elucidating the bonds of workplace humor: A relational process model. *Human Relations, 61*(8), 1087–1115. doi:10.1177/0018726708094861.

Curseu, P. L., & Fodor, O. C. (2016). Humor and group atmosphere: Development of a short scale for evaluating affiliative and aggressive humor in groups. *Team Performance Management: An International Journal, 22*(7/8). doi:10.1108/TPM-04-2015-0022.

Dezecache, G., & Dunbar, R. I. M. (2012). Sharing the joke: The size of natural laughter groups. *Evolution and Human Behavior, 33*(6), 775–779. doi:10.1016/j.evolhumbehav.2012.07.002.

Dunbar, R. I., Duncan, N. D. C., & Nettle, D. (1995). Size and structure of freely forming conversational groups. *Human Nature, 6*(1), 67–78. doi:10.1007/BF02734136.

Duncan, W. J. (1985). The superiority theory of humor at work: Joking relationships as indicators of formal and informal status patterns in small, task-oriented groups. *Small Group Research, 16* (4), 556–564. doi:10.1177/104649648501600412.

Fine, G. A., & De Soucey, M. (2005). Joking cultures: Humor themes as social regulation in group life. *Humor, 18,* 1–22. doi:10.1515/humr.2005.18.1.1.

Fiske, S. T., Cuddy, A. J. C., & Glick, P. (2007). Universal dimensions of social cognition: Warmth and competence. *Trends in Cognitive Sciences, 11*(2), 77–83. doi:10.1016/j.tics.2006.11.005.

Forsyth, D. R. (2006). *Group dynamics* (4th ed.). Belmont, CA: Thomson/Wadsworth.

Fraley, B., & Aron, A. (2004). The effect of a shared humorous experience on closeness in initial encounters. *Personal Relationships, 11,* 61–78. doi:10.1111/j.1475-6811.2004.00071.x.

Fredrickson, B. L. (1998). What good are positive emotions? *Review of General Psychology, 2*(3), 300–319. doi:10.1037/1089-2680.2.3.300.

Frijda, N. H. (1993). Mood, emotion episodes, and emotions. In M. Lewis & J. M. Haviland (Eds.), *Handbook of Emotions* (pp. 381–403). New York: Guilford Press.

Gervais, M., & Wilson, D. S. (2005). The evolution and functions of laughter and humor: A synthetic approach. *The Quarterly Review of Biology, 80*(4), 395–430. doi:10.1086/498281.

Glenn, P. J. (2003). *Laughter in Interaction.* Cambridge: Cambridge University Press.

Gockel, C., & Kerr, N. L. (2015). Put-down humor directed at outgroup members increases perceived—but not experienced—cohesion in groups. *Humor, 28*(2), 205–228. doi:10.1515/humor-2015-0020.

Hackman, J. R. (1986). The psychology of self-management in organizations. In M. S. Pallack & R. O. Perloff (Eds.), *Psychology and Work: Productivity, Change, and Employment* (pp. 89–136). Washington, DC: American Psychological Association.

Hatfield, E., Cacioppo, J. T., & Rapson, R. L. (1994). *Emotional contagion.* New York: Cambridge University Press.

Holmes, J. (2000). Politeness, power and provocation: How humour functions in the workplace. *Discourse Studies, 2*(2), 159–185. doi:10.1177/1461445600002002002.

Holmes, J. (2006). Sharing a laugh: Pragmatic aspects of humor and gender in the workplace. *Journal of Pragmatics, 38*(1), 26–50. doi:10.1016/j.pragma.2005.06.007.

Holmes, J., & Marra, M. (2002). Over the edge? Subversive humor between colleagues and friends. *Humor—International Journal of Humor Research, 15*(1), 65–87. doi:10.1515/humr.2002.006.

Kangasharju, H., & Nikko, T. (2009). Emotions in organizations: Joint laughter in workplace meetings. *Journal of Business Communication, 46*(1), 100–119. doi:10.1177/0021943608325750.

Keltner, D., & Bonanno, G. A. (1997). A study of laughter and dissociation: Distinct correlates of laughter and smiling during bereavement. *Journal of Personality and Social Psychology, 73*(4), 687. doi:10.1037/0022-3514.73.4.687.

Kozlowski, S. W. J., & Ilgen, D. R. (2006). Enhancing the effectiveness of work groups and teams. *Psychological Science in the Public Interest, 7*(3), 77–124. doi:10.1111/j.1529-1006.2006.00030.x.

Lefcourt, R. M. (2000). *Humor: The Psychology of Living Buoyantly.* New York: Plenum Publishers.

Lehmann-Willenbrock, N., & Allen, J. A. (2014). How fun are your meetings? Investigating the relationship between humor patterns in team interactions and team performance. *Journal of Applied Psychology, 99*(6), 1278–1287. doi:10.1037/a0038083.

Linstead, S. (1985). Jokers wild: The importance of humour in the maintenance of organizational culture. *The Sociological Review, 33*(4), 741–767. doi:10.1111/j.1467-954X.1985.tb02447.x.

Lyttle, J. (2007). The judicious use and management of humor in the workplace. *Business Horizons, 50*(3), 239–245. doi:10.1016/j.bushor.2006.11.001.

Lynch, O. (2010). Cooking with humor: In-group humor as social organization. *Humor—International Journal of Humor Research, 23*(2). doi:10.1515/humr.2010.007.

Martin, R. A. (2001). Humor, laughter, and physical health: Methodological issues and research findings. *Psychological Bulletin, 127*(4), 504–519. doi:10.1037//0033-2909.127.4.504.

Martin, R. A., Puhlik-Doris, P., Larsen, G., Gray, J., & Weir, K. (2003). Individual differences in uses of humor and their relation to psychological well-being: Development of the humor styles questionnaire. *Journal of Research in Personality, 37*(1), 48–75. doi:10.1016/S0092-6566(02)00534-2.

Mesmer-Magnus, J., Glew, D. J., & Viswesvaran, C. (2012). A meta-analysis of positive humor in the workplace. *Journal of Managerial Psychology, 27*(2), 155–190. doi:10.1108/02683941211199554.

Meyer, J. C. (2000). Humor as a double-edged sword: Four functions of humor in communication. *Communication Theory, 10*(3), 310–331. doi:10.1111/j.1468-2885.2000.tb00194.x.

Morreall, J. (1991). Humor and work. *Humor-International Journal of Humor Research, 4*(3–4), 359–374. doi:10.1515/humr.1991.4.3-4.359.

Owren, M. J., & Bachorowski, J.-A. (2003). Reconsidering the evolution of nonlinguistic communication: The case of laughter. *Journal of Nonverbal Behavior, 27*(3), 183–200. doi:10.1023/A:1025394015198.

Preuschoft S., & van Hooff J. A. R. A. M. (1997). The social function of "smile" and "laughter": variations across primate species and societies. In U. Segerstråle & P. Molnár (Ed.), *Nonverbal Communication: Where Nature Meets Culture* (pp. 171–189). Mahwah (NJ): Lawrence Erlbaum Associates.

Provine, R. R. (2000). *Laughter: A Scientific Investigation*. New York: Viking.

Ramachandran, V. S. (1998). The neurology and evolution of humor, laughter, and smiling: The false alarm theory. *Medical Hypotheses, 51*(4), 351–354. doi:10.1016/S0306-9877(98)90061-5.

Robert, C., & Wilbanks, J. E. (2012). The wheel model of humor: Humor events and affect in organizations. *Human Relations, 65*(9), 1071–1099. doi:10.1177/0018726711433133.

Robinson, D. T., & Smith-Lovin, L. (2001). Getting a laugh: Gender, status, and humor in task discussions. *Social Forces, 80*(1), 123–158. doi:10.1353/sof.2001.0085.

Rogerson-Revell, P. (2007). Humour in business: A double-edged sword a study of humour and style shifting in intercultural business meetings. *Journal of Pragmatics, 39*(1), 4–28. doi:10.1016/j.pragma.2006.09.005.

Romero, E. J., & Cruthirds, K. W. (2006). The use of humor in the workplace. *Academy of Management Perspectives, 5*, 58–69. doi:10.5465/AMP.2006.20591005.

Romero, E., & Pescosolido, A. (2008). Humor and group effectiveness. *Human Relations, 61*(3), 395–418. doi:10.1177/0018726708088999.

Russell, J. A., Bachorowski, J.-A., & Fernández-Dols, J.-M. (2003). Facial and vocal expressions of emotion. *Annual Review of Psychology, 54*(1), 329–349. doi:10.1146/annurev.psych.54.101601.145102.

Schachter, S. (1959). *The psychology of affiliation*. Stanford, California: Stanford University Press.

Schnurr, S., & Mak, B. (2009). Humor as an indicator of workplace socialization. In V. K. Bhatia, W. Cheng, B. Du-Babcock, & J. Lung (Eds.), *Language for Professional Communication: Research, Practice and Training* (pp. 131–145). Hong Kong: The Hong Kong Polytechnic University. Retrieved from http://www.engl.polyu.edu.hk/RCPCE/documents/LanguageForProfessionalCommunication.pdf#page=131.

Terrion, J. L., & Ashforth, B. E. (2002). From "I" to "we": The role of putdown humor and identity in the development of a temporary group. *Human Relations, 55*(1), 55–88. doi:10.1177/0018726702055001606.

Tramblay, M. (2016). Humor in teams: Multilevel relationships between humor climate, inclusion, trust, and citizenship behaviors. *Journal of Business and Psychology*, 1–16. doi:10.1007/s10869-016-9445-x.

Van Vugt, M., & Kameda, T. (2012). Evolution and groups. In J. M. Levine (Ed.), *Group Processes* (pp. 297–322). New York: Taylor and Francis Group.

Vettin, J., & Todt, D. (2004). Laughter in conversation: Features of occurrence and acoustic structure. *Journal of Nonverbal Behavior, 28*(2), 93–115. doi:10.1023/B:JONB.0000023654.73558.72.

Vinton, K. L. (1989). Humor in the workplace: It is more than telling jokes. *Small Group Behavior, 20*(2), 151–166. doi:10.1177/104649648902000202.

Wanzer, M. B., Booth-Butterfield, M., & Booth-Butterfield, S. (1996). Are funny people popular? An examination of humor orientation, loneliness, and social attraction. *Communication Quarterly, 44*(1), 42–52. doi:10.1080/01463379609369999.

Warner-Garcia, S. (2014). Laughing when nothing's funny: The pragmatic use of coping laughter in the negotiation of conversational disagreement. *Pragmatics, 24*(1), 157–180. doi:10.1075/prag.24.1.07war.

Westwood, R., & Johnston, A. (2013). Humor in organization: From function to resistance. *Humor—International Journal of Humor Research, 26*(2), 219–247. doi:10.1515/humor-2013-0024.

Wild, B., Rodden, F. A., Grodd, W., & Ruch, W. (2003). Neural correlates of laughter and humour. *Brain, 126*(10), 2121–2138. doi:10.1093/brain/awg226.

Wilkinson, C. E., Rees, C. E., & Knight, L.V. (2007). From the heart of my bottom: Negotiating humor in focus group discussions. *Qualitative Health Research, 17*(3), 411–422.

Wrightsman, L. (1959). *The effects of small-group membership on level of concern* (Unpublished doctoral dissertation). University of Minnesota.

Chapter 4
Humor in Leadership: How to Lead People with Humor

Christine Gockel and Laura Vetter

Abstract A leader may use humor for a variety of relational goals in a hierarchical relationship. Humor can be used to create cohesion and strengthen solidarity with subordinates, but also to create divisions between them and increase a leader's status. The duality of humor functions becomes especially apparent in the context of leader-subordinate relationships. In this chapter, we will describe how perceptions of leader humor and leader effectiveness go hand in hand, partly due to implicit personality theories. We will show that the effects of leader humor are stronger in some tasks and for some persons than others, and that the effects of general leader behaviors such as transactional and transformational leadership in part depend on leader humor use. We will explain various response strategies that enable listeners to acknowledge humor and power differences simultaneously. Finally, we will close by pointing out differences in humor use between female and male leaders.

Keywords Leadership · Leader humor · Transactional and transformational leadership · LMX · Leader perception · Leader effectiveness · Subordinate reactions · Gender

4.1 Introduction

Humor is often advertised for leaders—on the web, in books and in presentations. It is supposed to give leaders a competitive edge when motivating employees. Consultants purport to know exactly which type of humor brilliant leaders use. So they draw the conclusion that any leader can also become a brilliant leader by using certain kinds of humor. However, things are certainly not that simple. Leader humor does have effects on subordinates, yet they vary based on the task, the type of humor and the relationship between leader and subordinate among other factors. In

The original version of this chapter was revised: See the "Chapter Note" section at the end of this chapter for details. The erratum to this chapter is available at https://doi.org/10.1007/978-3-319-65691-5_9

T. Scheel and C. Gockel, *Humor at Work in Teams, Leadership, Negotiations, Learning and Health*, SpringerBriefs in Psychology,
DOI 10.1007/978-3-319-65691-5_4

this chapter, we attempt to shed some light on leader humor and to point out what we know and do not know in this area.

Leadership is generally considered to be an influence process. The goal is to make others "understand and agree about what needs to be done and how to do it" (Yukl, 2009, p. 8). Early research about leader humor accordingly described humor as a tool in order to get things done (Malone, 1980). Humor was also regarded as "a virtually undeveloped resource that can contribute to enhancing the satisfaction and productivity of human beings at work" (Malone, 1980, p. 360). Early articles about leader humor described its positive effects and provided suggestions for leaders. The underlying assumption seemed to be that the appropriate use of humor would help one to build a team of highly motivated and cohesive members and would eventually improve performance (Crawford, 1994; Duncan, 1982).

Below, we provide an overview of the functions of leader humor, describe how leader humor is related to a positive perception of leaders, point out how complex the effects of leader humor are, put a special focus on the relationship between leader and subordinate, explain how subordinates can respond to leader humor and, finally, describe how female and male leaders differ in their humor usage. We will close by pointing out avenues for future research and provide suggestions for leaders who wish to capitalize on the positive effects of humor.

4.2 Functions of Humor Use by Leaders

The often-cited notion of humor as a double-edged sword (e.g., Collinson, 2002; Malone, 1980; Meyer, 2000) may apply especially to its functions in relation to leadership. A leader's use of positive humor has been associated with enhanced subordinate job performance, reductions in subordinate work withdrawal and improvements in workgroup cohesion (Mesmer-Magnus, Glew, & Viswesvaran, 2012). Whereas a leader's use of self-enhancing and affiliative humor styles is positively related to subordinates' psychological well-being (Kim, Lee, & Wong, 2016), aggressive humor has been related to employees' physical and psychological stress (Evans & Steptoe-Warren, 2015; Huo, Lam, & Chen, 2012), and negatively related to their psychological well-being (Kim et al., 2016).

Creating cohesion, strengthening solidarity, and emphasizing collegiality are relational outcomes of humorous leadership behavior (Holmes & Marra, 2006). Employing ethnographic fieldwork in a mental healthcare setting, Griffiths (1998) found that psychiatrists engaged in humorous behavior to diminish authority and to emphasize a "common ground" with the team. One possibility to de-emphasize status distinctions within the leader–subordinate relationship was the use of self-deprecating humor by making oneself the target of the joke. A leader's use of affiliative and moderate self-defeating humor may facilitate interpersonal interactions (Romero & Cruthirds, 2006) and may minimize social distance by engaging in joking behavior (Duncan, 1984). Self-enhancing and affiliative humor styles have been negatively associated with social distance, and aggressive humor has been positively associated with social distance (Kim et al., 2016).

Humor may be used as a repressive discourse device, meaning as a disguise for a less acceptable message (Holmes, 2000). After being asked by his manager to speed up the team and increase pressure, the subordinate complains that "everyone has been running around like crazy men since our phone call this morning" (Holmes, 2000, p. 175). The manager laughingly remarks "not altogether a bad thing" (p. 175), thus allowing for humor to provide a cover for a remark that may otherwise be considered unreasonably oppressive (Holmes, 2000). Teasing or mocking lower status employees may assist in gaining behavioral compliance (Dwyer, 1991) and in controlling the behavior of subordinates (Holmes, 2007). Humor may be used in constructing a leadership identity with teasing being one way to portray oneself as an effective and competent leader (Schnurr, 2009).

Humor may serve a leader's need to maintain face as well as to assist in saving a subordinate's face. By analyzing recorded workplace interactions at business meetings, Holmes and Marra (2006) found indicators for both. When two advisors compared their written evaluations, the more senior and experienced advisor commented on the written evaluation of his junior colleague by saying "and apart from that, I've just got what you've got, but in a lot less words" (Holmes & Marra, 2006, p. 129). This comment was followed by laughter from both sides. Here, the senior colleague conveyed a clear message that the report by his junior colleague was too wordy, but attenuated its negative impact through the use of humor, which also serves the subordinate's face needs. Humor also serves a leader's need to a dignified profile when he or she makes an error. In another incident, a document, which was produced by a leader contained an error, which elicited a humorous comment by the leader—"I find it really hard being perfect at everything" (Holmes & Marra, 2006, p. 130).

Leaders' use of humor has been found to inspire subordinates to find creative and innovative solutions to complex problems (Dixon, 1980). Humor can make it easier to introduce and to exchange new ideas in a low-risk manner, to experiment with potentially risky new behaviors and to engage in constructive conflicts (Barsoux, 1996; Romero & Pescosolido, 2008), with people enjoying higher status being able to use humor to end conflicts (Norrick & Spitz, 2008). Eliciting laughter during conflict assists in committing a group to one another and to challenge them to play, which can ultimately enhance problem-solving (Consalvo, 1989). Self-disparaging humor has been perceived as especially effective at relieving tension, summarizing group member opinions and encouraging participation (Smith & Powell, 1988). Although a leader's humor can promote commitment and group cohesiveness (Avolio, Howell, & Sosik, 1999; Francis, 1994), it can also create divisions among subordinates (Dwyer, 1991).

The variety of humor functions seems to offer much potential for enhancing one's leadership effectiveness, but also for diminishing it. Using positive humor appears more likely to lead to beneficial leadership outcomes than using negative humor. But all leaders should be aware that there is no "one size fits all" approach to integrate humor into their behavior, let alone a guarantee that humor will work in the way in which it is intended. Managers who try to manufacture humor might actually suppress it, and managers who suppress humor might actually provoke it (Collinson, 2002).

4.3 Perception of Humorous Leaders

Leader humor can serve a variety of functions and can have several positive and some negative effects, as demonstrated above. When leadership scholars and humor researchers started to examine leader humor in empirical studies, they began to do so by focusing on the perception of leaders. Many early studies were based on the assumption that humorous leaders are regarded to be more effective and that their subordinates feel more satisfied. These studies are based on correlational survey data with participants indicating how they perceive their leader in terms of humor and other characteristics. Five specific results suggest the following relationships:

First, leaders who are ascribed a good sense of humor are also attributed many other positive attributes such as effectiveness, intelligence, friendliness, and positive task and relationship behavior (Decker, 1987; Decker & Rotondo, 2001). Second, leaders with a high humor orientation, which refers to a predisposition to use humorous communication during interactions, are more liked (Rizzo, Wanzer, & Booth-Butterfield, 1999). Third, these leaders are also perceived to be more responsive, which means that they listen, try to understand and are sensitive (Campbell, Martin, & Wanzer, 2001). Fourth, subordinates of these leaders experience higher job satisfaction (Hurren, 2006, who examined principals as leaders in schools). And finally, fifth, leaders who use negative humor are perceived to show fewer task and relationship behaviors (Decker & Rotondo, 2001).

One may also turn around this thinking and examine whether "good" and "bad" leaders are associated differently with humor. This is exactly what Priest and Swain (2002) did. They conducted two studies in the military and asked their participants to think of a "good" or a "bad" leader. Participants then rated the leader they had in their minds on several characteristics—among them was humorous behavior. Good leaders were described as having a warm, competent and benign humorous style when compared to bad leaders. For example, they were said to "use good-natured jest to put others at ease" whereas the "bad" leaders were said to "poke fun at the naïve or unsophisticated" or to be "unable to laugh at personal failings." These effects were even found when controlling for differences in rated leader effectiveness.

All of the previously mentioned studies are based on correlational data and prohibit cause-and-effect conclusions. One lab experiment, however, tried to tease apart the relationship (Hoption, Barling, & Turner, 2013). In a vignette study, 155 participants were provided with a select situation in which a project manager at an inaugural project meeting introduced a new recruit named Pat. At the end of the vignette, participants read one out of four different statements: "I am so glad that Pat took this job…" (1) "despite knowing all about me!" (self-deprecating humor), (2) "despite knowing all about you!" (aggressive humor), (3) "despite knowing all about us!" (ingroup deprecating humor) and (4) without any additional comments (no humor condition). After reading the vignette, participants rated the extent to which the project manager showed transformational leadership behaviors. Results indicate that leaders who used self-deprecating humor (as compared to those using aggressive humor) were rated higher on individualized consideration, which is one facet of transformational leadership. This means that a leader is attentive and sensitive to subordinates' individual needs and skills. The finding suggests that individualized consideration could also be demonstrated by putting oneself last and by minimizing one's superiority through the use of humor. Recognizing and laughing at one's own shortcomings may be a way to enhance perceptions of transformational leadership by demonstrating egalitarianism at the workplace (Hoption et al., 2013).

All empirical results about the perception of leaders and the correspondent attribution of personality characteristics could be based on so-called implicit personality theories (e.g., Kenney, Schwartz-Kenney, & Blascovich, 1996). Humans associate specific characteristics with other specific characteristics. For example, a mother might be ascribed a warm and caring nature and a person with glasses might be ascribed high intelligence. Likewise, a humorous leader might be ascribed sympathy and effectiveness and an effective leader might be ascribed a high sense of humor. Though these associations do not tell us anything about actual behaviors. It remains to be seen how strongly humorous leaders actually influence subordinate outcomes and whether effective leaders actually use more humor in their communications.

4.4 The Complexity of Effects

Many older studies focused on direct associations between leader humor and subordinate outcomes. More recent studies have acknowledged that the associations are not so simple and paint a more complex picture. They are based on the assumption that the relation between leader humor and subordinate outcomes is dependent on specific circumstances. In statistical terms, the relation between leader humor and subordinate outcomes is moderated by specific variables. Another assumption is that these moderating effects can be found more easily for socio-emotional subordinate outcomes than for performance because leader humor generally affects socio-emotional outcomes more strongly than performance (Hughes & Avey, 2009).

One of the first studies that examined moderating effects focused on subordinate tenure. The hypothesis was that the effects of leader humor would vary based on how long an employee had been in an organization (Gkorezis, Hatzithomas, & Petridou, 2011). This study examined empowerment as subordinate outcome. Empowerment refers to intrinsic task motivation and consists of four facets, namely meaning, competence, self-determination and impact (Spreitzer, 1995). Meaning refers to the value of a work goal in relation to one's own ideals. Competence refers to one's self-efficacy. Self-determination refers to the feeling of having a choice in starting actions. Impact refers to the degree to which an individual can influence important work outcomes. To test their hypothesis, the authors collected cross-sectional questionnaire data in four US dinner houses and measured leader's use of positive and negative humor, subordinate empowerment and tenure in months. First, Gkorezis et al. (2011) found two direct effects. The more positive humor a leader used, the more empowered the employee felt. And the more negative humor a leader used, the less empowered the employee felt. Second, they found the expected moderating effect. The relationship between positive humor and empowerment was especially strong for employees with short tenure. In other words, the newcomers benefitted more from positive humor than the old-timers. Additionally, the relationship between negative humor and empowerment was especially strong for employees with long tenure. In other words, the old-timers suffered more from negative humor than the newcomers. We believe that this effect may have occurred because the effects of negative humor are cumulative and build up over time. One might overhear a leader's negative humor comment, which is supposed to be funny, once or twice. But if one hears such comments every day, one may perceive some underlying problems and may eventually take the supposedly funny comments very seriously.

Another study that focused on boundary conditions of leader humor use is the one by Pundt (2015). One hundred and fifty employees participated in his survey study. Humorous leader behavior was only related to innovative behavior (as rated by the employee) if the task called for such behavior—that is, if creative requirements were high. Otherwise, humorous leader behavior was not related to innovative subordinate behavior. Interestingly, this effect occurred above and beyond the effects of transformational leadership and leader–member exchange, which refers to the quality of the relationship between leader and subordinate.

The previous studies examined the circumstances under which leader humor impacts subordinate outcomes and focused on tenure and task requirements. Other studies, however, focused on the effects of general leader behavior and took humor as one special circumstance into account. That means that these studies also acknowledge the complexity of the relationships, yet they have a slightly different take on them.

A cross-sectional study that was conducted in a financial institution by Avolio et al. (1999) examined how the use of humor moderates the effects of transformational, contingent reward and laissez-faire leadership on performance. Data were collected from 115 leaders and their 322 respective subordinates, who were all asked to assess their manager's leadership behavior and their use of humor. Transformational leadership was more positively related to unit performance for leaders who used humor at a high rate (relative to low rate). Contingent reward leadership was more negatively associated with performance when leaders used humor more often. Because of the radical changes in the financial service industry back then, the use of humor by leaders in relation to setting goals and target objectives may have been perceived as insufficient to address the serious changes (Avolio et al., 1999).

A more recent study was conducted in schools (Vecchio, Justin, & Pearce, 2009). Here, principals were examined as leaders and teachers as subordinates. In a questionnaire study, 179 principals rated a teacher's performance. The respective teacher rated the use of their principal's contingent personal reward (i.e., a set of behaviors focusing on clear exchanges between leader and subordinate; Bass, 1985) and their use of humor. In general, the more contingent personal reward the principal used, the better the teacher performed. This relation was stronger when the principal used less humor and weaker if the principal used more humor. We believe that this might be a fit issue. Humor and the use of contingent personal rewards may not go well together. A leader who uses humor, which is by nature ambiguous, and at the same time tries to motivate with contingent reward, which needs to be unambiguous by definition, may simply confuse subordinates and may therefore not be able to influence performance well.

The last study that examined the complexity of relationships focused on transformational leadership, which inspires subordinates to change based on a clear vision (Bass, 1985). The researchers (Hughes & Avey, 2009) collected data from 316 employees at two points in time one week apart. For their analyses, they split the sample into halves: the first half of the employees had reported to have leaders who used humor relatively often and the second half had reported to have leaders who used humor relatively seldom. When leaders often used humor, the following was found: The more transformational leadership behaviors leaders showed, the higher the employees rated their trust and affective commitment. In contrast, when leaders only seldomly used humor, transformational leadership was not associated with trust and affective commitment. The author's explanation is that if a leader is confident enough to joke about certain situations, subordinates feel reassured and transformational leadership behavior can play out to its full potential.

In summary, the effects of leader humor are stronger in some tasks and for some persons than others. The effects of general leader behaviors depend in part on leader humor use. Humor seems to fit transformational leadership because it enhances its positive effects. Yet it does not seem to fit transactional leadership because it diminishes its positive effects. The interplay between leader behavior, leader humor, task requirements, subordinate characteristics, and situational circumstances is very complex and thus provides a promising arena for future research.

4.5 The Relationship Between Leader and Subordinate

The variety of humor functions encompasses numerous socio-emotional processes. It is therefore plausible that leader humor should have a strong impact on the relationship between leaders and subordinates. Previous research has already shown that humor substantially influences the quality of leader–subordinate relationships (Cooper, 2008; Wisse & Rietzschel, 2014), which in turn is vital in shaping employee attitudes, such as organizational commitment, job satisfaction, and well-being (Epitropaki & Martin, 2005). Thus, leader-member exchange

(LMX) theory, which focuses on the separate dyadic relationships between a leader and each subordinate, is of special importance in this context. By varying their interactions across subordinates, leaders determine the relationship quality (Dulebohn, Bommer, Liden, Brouer, & Ferris, 2012), which may range from one that is strictly based on employment contract (low LMX) to one that includes mutual trust, respect, liking and reciprocal influence (high LMX; Dansereau, Graen, & Haga, 1975; Liden & Maslyn, 1998). LMX is comprised of four dimensions: affect (liking one another), contribution (task-related behavior), loyalty (expression of public support for the goals and the personal character of the other member) and professional respect (perception of knowledge, competence, skills; Greguras & Ford, 2006; Liden & Maslyn, 1998).

Considering that different humor styles (affiliative, self-enhancing, aggressive, and self-defeating) can either have a positive or negative effect on organizational outcomes, this may also apply to a leader's use of humor styles. For example, affiliative humor as a positive form of humor may be used to amuse other people in order to reduce interpersonal tension, whereas aggressive humor, as a rather negative form of humor, may be intended to mock other people in order to elevate one's self (Pundt & Herrmann, 2015; Romero & Arendt, 2011). A leader's positive humor has been found to be positively related to LMX (Gkorezis, Petridou, & Xanthiakos, 2014), with its dimensions "affect" and "professional respect" being significantly related to a leader's humor expression (Cooper, 2004).

Pundt and Herrmann (2015) provide a closer look at the association between leader humor and LMX. In a 2-wave study, they investigated the relation of a leader's affiliative and aggressive humor to LMX as perceived by subordinates. Results indicated that affiliative and aggressive humor are related to LMX. Subordinates whose leaders frequently used affiliative humor rated their relationship with their leaders as better than subordinates whose leaders used affiliative humor less frequently. In contrast, subordinates whose leaders used aggressive humor frequently rated their relationships with their leaders worse than subordinates whose leaders used aggressive humor less frequently. Identification with the leaders mediated the relationships between affiliative leader humor and LMX. In this context, humor is seen as an offer for relational identification, which is viewed as a precondition for the development of a positive relationship in terms of trust (Pundt & Herrmann, 2015; Sluss & Ashforth, 2007).

In contrast to previous research, Wisse and Rietzschel (2014) found no evidence for the impact of leaders' humor style on subordinates' perceived relationship quality. They assessed leaders' and subordinates' self-reported humor styles and the extent to which subordinates perceived a high LMX relationship with their leader. The authors assumed that the perceptions of a leader's humor styles may actually be more important than the leader's actual humor styles in the prediction of relationship quality. With regard to the role of similarities in humor styles and their association with relationship quality, it was found that leaders' self-defeating humor was linked to higher LMX when subordinates' self-defeating humor was also high (Wisse & Rietzschel, 2014). The effects of similarity in self-defeating humor style were especially pronounced for the LMX sub-dimensions of affect, professional respect and loyalty, but not significant for contribution. This indicates that similarity effects draw rather on affective aspects than exchange-related aspects of the leader–subordinate relationship (Cooper, 2008; Wisse & Rietzschel, 2014).

Humor styles per se, unlike other aspects of humor such as frequency, may not be as important for the relationship between leaders and subordinates (Wisse & Rietzschel, 2014). A study by Robert, Dunne and Iun (2016) found that subordinates' job satisfaction was impacted by the perceived quality of the leader–subordinate relationship, and not by leaders' use of affiliative or aggressive humor. The authors argued that, when subordinates evaluate their relationships with their supervisors as positive, they are more likely to interpret the leaders' humor as positive—regardless of the leaders' self-reported use of aggressive or affiliative humor. On the other hand, a negative relationship can lead employees to perceive a leader's humor as rather negative, even when its use is intended to be positive (Robert et al., 2016). Employees may feel that the use of humor is inappropriate or that it only serves as a distraction (Avolio et al., 1999), or even as a leadership tactic of ingratiation (Cooper, 2005). Thus, leader humor seems to be in the ears of the listener, and not so much in the mouth of the speaker.

4.6 Subordinate Reactions to Leader Humor

Humor is ambiguous by nature. Its effects seem to be based more on the kind of relationship between leader and subordinate and not so much on the actual type of humor used (Robert et al., 2016). In order to fully understand the effects of leader humor on subordinates, one needs to examine how subordinates react to humorous comments in situ. Linguistic research that examines humor effects on a micro-level gives some hints about how subordinates deal with ambiguous humor.

The most interesting humorous instances are those that are maximally ambiguous, when listeners do not know to what extent the message is meant seriously and when it contains a potential face threat. Two types of humor that are particularly ambiguous are teasing and self-denigrating humor. Teasing refers to comments about the listener that are potentially aggressive and simultaneously contain cues signaling that the comment is not meant seriously. For example, when a leader says to a team member "Wow! Now that you have finally found the document, you should treat the team to dinner." Self-denigrating humor refers to comments about the speaker him- or herself. They are also potentially aggressive and contain cues that signal that the comment is not meant seriously, for example, when a leader says the following about herself: "I've got this terrible reputation for being a technical klutz." In both instances, it seems important for listeners in a relationship with power differences to acknowledge the humor, to remain polite and not question the power differences, and to maintain face (Schnurr & Chan, 2011).

A linguistic study examined how subordinates react to leaders' teasing and self-denigrating humor (Schnurr & Chan, 2011). The researchers analyzed data from workplace interactions in New Zealand and Hong Kong and used both one-on-one interactions and large formal meetings. Their results of specific examples indicate that listeners used a variety of response strategies. Most listeners laughed, which indicates that they understood the comment as humorously. Specifically, after teasing, listeners either played along with the humor, blamed someone else, teased back or responded to the criticism. After self-denigrating humor, listeners played along, teased back, offered alternative explanations, expressed agreement or did not respond. Overall, there are a variety of response strategies that enable listeners to acknowledge the humor and the power differences simultaneously. The choice of response seemed to depend on several factors on different levels such as norms in the workplace and the larger sociocultural context (Schnurr & Chan, 2011).

4.7 Leader Humor and Gender

Leadership and humor still seem to have one widespread perception in common—they are often associated with masculinity (Crawford, 1995; Hearn & Parkin, 1986). Thus, the notion of a humorous female leader may sound like a bad joke to some people. Empirical research has found substantiated evidence for gender differences in the use of humor (see also Chap. 8 in this book). Whereas women are much more likely to use humor for the specific function of forming or maintaining solidarity, men are more likely to use humor for the general function of increasing solidarity and status and performing positive work on their personal identity (Hay, 2000).

With regard to humor styles (affiliative, aggressive, self-enhancing and self-defeating), males score significantly higher than females in all styles and they report a much greater tendency to engage in aggressive forms of humor (Martin, Puhlik-Doris, Larsen, Gray, & Weir, 2003). Gender differences in humor use have also been found within a workplace setting, with contesting and challenging humor being generally perceived to be more masculine whereas collaborative and supportive humor is considered to be more feminine (Holmes, 2006a, b).

It has been suggested that women have a lower propensity to use humor in professional situations (Cox, Read, & Van Auken, 1990) and that they are encouraged to respond to humor rather than creating it (Crain, 1981). These suggestions are contradicted by analyses based on the amount of initiated humor in business meetings that were either chaired by women or men and that included up to 17 participants (Holmes, Burns, Marra, Stubbe, & Vine, 2003). In both mixed-gender and single-gender meetings, the overall amount of humor initiated by female chairs was greater than the amount initiated by their male counterparts. Compared to individual participants, the women who were in leadership positions in these meetings, the chairs and managers, contributed more to the overall amount of humor (Holmes et al., 2003). Female and male chairs' use of humor in business meetings was also investigated by Mullany (2004) who focused on the role of humor as a linguistic politeness device in order to gain compliance from subordinates. Although only female leaders were found to use repressive humor as a mitigation tactic, both female and male chairs most commonly used mitigation tactics other than humor. Nonetheless these findings suggest that the use of repressive humor as a strategy is favored by female chairs and may be part of a wider gender patterning (Mullany, 2004).

A more detailed look at women's uses of humor in order to portray themselves as effective leaders was undertaken by Schnurr (2008). She analyzed conversational data of female leaders in a predominantly masculine environment (IT) with a multi-method approach and included interviews and participant observation. Findings indicate that women use humor to display masculine and feminine leadership behaviors as well as to exhibit gender stereotypes. A female leader who laughingly tells her subordinates that she has to send a particular email off, because "if we don't we're in the poo" releases stress and tension in a rather masculine manner while maintaining a feminine style by using the inclusive pronoun "we" as well as using the rather weak expletive "poo" (Schnurr, 2008, p. 305). Thus, humor enables the leader to display leadership behavior associated with masculinity while preventing her from being judged negatively as "unfeminine." A female leader who teasingly remarks in a slightly challenging tone that "you'd better do a quick programming course, Errol" (p. 308) expresses criticism to her colleague for not being able to help with a project that involves much programming, while simultaneously maintaining a good relationship by minimizing the potential negative impact of this remark. The transactional and relational functions of humor assist in displaying authority and power—stereotypically masculine behaviors—while simultaneously maintaining a leader's femininity. A leader may use self-denigrating humor to construct a stereotypical feminine identity and challenge the masculine norms (Schnurr, 2008). For example, a leader who states that she has a reputation for being a "technical klutz" (p. 310) is playing down her status and authority and makes use of the stereotype of a technophobic woman. The examples cited here demonstrate how using humor as a female leader in a male dominated profession can become part of an effective leadership style (Schnurr, 2008).

Female and male leaders not only use humor differently; their humor also has different effects. Decker and Rotondo (2001) investigated how gender moderates the relationship between humor and leader behavior and effectiveness. Although female managers were reported to use less positive humor than their male counterparts, they were rated higher on relationship behavior and effectiveness. Although male managers were reported to use more negative humor than their female counterparts, they were rated higher on relationship behavior and effectiveness. It appears that in comparison to men, women are more severely "penalized" when using negative humor and more "rewarded" when using positive humor (Decker & Rotondo, 2001, p. 460). The authors speculated that women who use humor are rather surprising and not perceived as the norm. Whereas the use of positive humor enhances a female leader's ability to communicate effectively and to create a better working environment, her use of negative humor may be perceived as a more serious offense than that of male leaders.

4.8 Future Research

A leader may use humor for a variety of relational goals that can become of special importance in a hierarchical relationship. Humor can be used to create cohesion and strengthen solidarity with subordinates, but can also create divisions between them. Its use can emphasize but also diminish a leader's status and authority. Humor can be employed to reduce face threat and soften critical comments, but also to control subordinates' behavior. A leader's humor may contribute to the well-being of employees and increase job satisfaction, but may also lead to increased strain. Thus, the duality of humor functions becomes especially apparent in the context of leader–subordinate relationships. With regard to task-related outcomes, a leader's humor can inspire creative and innovative behavior in subordinates and can have an impact on their intrinsic task motivation.

Leaders who are ascribed a good sense of humor may be perceived as more likeable and responsive and be attributed a positive task and relationship behavior. A leader's humor may enhance perceptions of transformational leadership behavior. Subordinates' perception may also play an important role with regard to the leader's gender, considering that female managers, who have been reported to use less positive humor than their male counterparts, were rated higher on relationship effectiveness and behavior. A leader's choice of humor style may also affect subordinates' perceived relationship quality. Subordinates whose leaders frequently use affiliative humor rate their relationship as better, whereas subordinates whose leaders use aggressive humor frequently rate their relationships with their leaders as worse. On the other hand, the leader–subordinate relationship may determine how subordinates interpret leader humor.

There are a variety of response strategies to humor that enable listeners to acknowledge the humor as well as the power differences. Reactions may range from laughing, playing along with the humor, blaming others, teasing back and expressing agreement, to not responding at all.

Although empirical research about leader humor has greatly increased our understanding about this phenomenon, several avenues for future research are very promising. We see four different ways of thinking and doing research that should increase our understanding even more.

First, it is important to develop an overarching model regarding the effects of leader humor. It should attempt to explain which kinds of humor affect which subordinate socio-emotional and performance outcomes. Such a model should also include moderators regarding leader characteristics, subordinate characteristics, task and situational demands, and the wider organizational context. An overarching model would systematically summarize previous research, guide future research and help to integrate new research findings.

Second, research needs to move from correlational survey methods which assess associations at one point in time to different methods. Experiments in laboratories and the field would clearly tell us about causes and effects. Longitudinal research methods (e.g., based on diary methods) would help us to understand how leader humor and its effects develop over time and to what extent the effects are cumulative.

Third, research must take into account the more negative kinds of humor (such as aggressive humor). Most previous research is based on the assumption that positive humor has positive effects and does not contrast positive with negative humor. Taking into account the dark side of humor would more adequately reflect the double-edged sword of leader humor and point out potentially ironic effects of humor, such as positive outcomes after aggressive humor.

Further research that employs cluster analysis can provide more insights into the ratio of positive and negative humor and its outcomes. Results of a recent study that employed this method suggest that using aggressive humor may only be of negative consequence if it is not accompanied by affiliative humor (Evans & Steptoe-Warren, 2015).

Fourth, research should focus more strongly on the dyad between leader and subordinate. Humor always needs a speaker and a listener, and the effects of humor can only play out within a dyad (or within a larger team). Previous research has mostly examined the subordinate perspective and has neglected the leader perspective. A closer look at the dyadic relationship helps us grasp how leader humor is understood and misunderstood and how a fit in humor styles and other characteristics impact humor effects.

4.9 Recommendations for Practice

Even though we already know a lot about leader humor, there is still no simple recipe for leaders on how to use humor. And there never will be. Before providing specific suggestions, we would like to point out that effective leadership can never be substituted with humor. Humor is one out of many communicative tools that leaders can use to motivate subordinates. That being said, it should also be clear that leaders do not have to use humor in order to be effective. There are numerous other ways of motivating employees.

Leaders can use humor in order to create a humor-supportive climate in which humor is not only accepted, but encouraged and enhances positive affect (Robert & Wilbanks, 2012). Positive affect may in turn increase creative performance, which is particularly relevant for creative and innovative tasks. Possible ways of creating such a climate are actively using humor and encouraging other team members to use humor as well; making fun of oneself to show that one does not take oneself too seriously; using humor to communicate one's imperfections in order to motivate others in practicing self-criticism; and finally encouraging open feedback when people feel that they were made fun of inappropriately or feel hurt by humor.

Before creating such a humor-encouraging climate, leaders need to consider their relationships with their subordinates. A negative relationship can lead employees to perceive a leader's humor as rather negative, even when its use is intended to be positive. Thus, leaders who want to engage in humorous behavior with their employees should assess first whether the relationship quality will support their use of humor. An already poor leader–subordinate relationship may not be a good foundation for humorous overtures, whereas a high trust relationship seems to increase the effectiveness of a leader's humor (Kim et al., 2016).

Recommendations for further reading

Hoption, C., Barling, J., & Turner, N. (2013). "It's not you, it's me": Transformational leadership and self-deprecating humor. *Leadership & Organization Development Journal, 34*(1), 4–19. doi:10.1108/01437731311289947.

Robert, C., Dunne, T. C., & Iun, J. (2016). The impact of leader humor on subordinate job satisfaction: The crucial role of leader-subordinate relationship quality. *Group & Organization Management, 41*(3), 375–406. doi:10.1177/1059601115598719.

Wisse, B., & Rietzschel, E. (2014). Humor in leader-follower relationships: Humor styles, similarity and relationship quality. *Humor: International Journal of Humor Research, 27*(2), 249–269. doi:10.1515/humor-2014-0017.

References

Avolio, B. J., Howell, J. M., & Sosik, J. J. (1999). A funny thing happened on the way to the bottom line: Humor as a moderator of leadership style effects. *The Academy of Management Journal, 42*(2), 219–227. doi:10.2307/257094.

Barsoux, J.-L. (1996). Why organisations need humour. *European Management Journal, 14*(5), 500–508. doi:10.1016/0263-2373(96)00044-8.

Bass, B. M. (1985). *Leadership and performance beyond expectations*. New York , London: Free Press.

Campbell, K. L., Martin, M. M., & Wanzer, M. B. (2001). Employee perceptions of manager humor orientation, assertiveness, responsiveness, approach/avoidance strategies, and satisfaction. *Communication Research Reports, 18*(1), 67–74. doi:10.1080/08824090109384783.

Collinson, D. L. (2002). Managing humour. *Journal of Management Studies, 39*(3), 269–288. doi:10.1111/1467-6486.00292.

Consalvo, C. M. (1989). Humor in management: No laughing matter. *Humor—International Journal of Humor Research, 2*(3), 285–297. doi:10.1515/humr.1989.2.3.285.

Cooper, C.D. (2004). *Did you hear the one about humor and leadership? A field study of supervisor humor and leader–member exchange quality*. Paper presented at the annual meeting of the Academy of Management, New Orleans, LA.

Cooper, C. D. (2005). Just joking around? Employee humor expression as an ingratiatory behavior. *Academy of Management Review, 30*(4), 765–776. doi:10.5465/AMR.2005.18378877.

Cooper, C. D. (2008). Elucidating the bonds of workplace humor: A relational process model. *Human Relations, 61*(8), 1087–1115. doi:10.1177/0018726708094861.

Cox, J. A., Read, R. L., & Van Auken, P. M. (1990). Male-female differences in communicating job-related humor: An exploratory study. *Humor: International Journal of Humor Research, 3* (3), 287–295. doi:10.1515/humr.1990.3.3.287.

Crain, S. (1981). At work, it pays to be funny. *Family Weekly*.

Crawford, C. B. (1994). Theory and implications regarding the utilization of strategic humor by leaders. *Journal of Leadership & Organizational Studies, 1*(4), 53–68. doi:10.1177/107179199400100406.

Crawford, M. (1995). Talking Difference: On Gender and Language. SAGE.

Dansereau, F., Graen, G., & Haga, W. J. (1975). A vertical dyad linkage approach to leadership within formal organizations. *Organizational Behavior and Human Performance, 13*(1), 46–78. doi:10.1016/0030-5073(75)90005-7.

Decker, W. H. (1987). Managerial humor and subordinate satisfaction. *Social Behavior & Personality: An International Journal, 15*(2), 225–232. doi:10.2224/sbp.1987.15.2.225.

Decker, W. H., & Rotondo, D. M. (2001). Relationships among gender, type of humor, and perceived leader effectiveness. *Journal of Managerial Issues, 13*(4), 450–465.

Dixon, N. F. (1980). Humor: A cognitive alternative to stress? In I. G. Sarason & C. D. Spielburger (Eds.), *Stress and Anxiety* (Vol. 7, pp. 281–289)., Hemisphere DC: Washington.

Dulebohn, J. H., Bommer, W. H., Liden, R. C., Brouer, R. L., & Ferris, G. R. (2012). A meta-analysis of antecedents and consequences of leader-member exchange integrating the past with an eye toward the future. *Journal of Management, 38*(6), 1715–1759. doi:10.1177/0149206311415280.

Duncan, W. J. (1982). Humor in management: Prospects for administrative practice and research. *The Academy of Management Review, 7*(1), 136–142. doi:10.2307/257259.

Duncan, W. J. (1984). Perceived humor and social network patterns in a sample of task-oriented groups: A reexamination of prior research. *Human Relations, 37*(11), 895–907. doi:10.1177/001872678403701102.

Dwyer, T. (1991). Humor, power, and change in organizations. *Human Relations, 44*(1), 1–19. doi:10.1177/001872679104400101.

Epitropaki, O., & Martin, R. (2005). From ideal to real: A longitudinal study of the role of implicit leadership theories on leader-member exchanges and employee outcomes. *Journal of Applied Psychology, 90*(4), 659–676. doi:10.1037/0021-9010.90.4.659.

Evans, T. R., & Steptoe-Warren, G. (2015). Humor style clusters: Exploring managerial humor. *International Journal of Business Communication*. x, s-y. doi:10.1177/2329488415612478.

Francis, L. E. (1994). Laughter, the best mediation: Humor as emotion management in interaction. *Symbolic Interaction, 17*(2), 147–163. doi:10.1525/si.1994.17.2.147.

Gkorezis, P., Hatzithomas, L., & Petridou, E. (2011). The impact of leader's humor on employees' psychological empowerment: The moderating role of tenure. *Journal of Managerial Issues, 23* (1), 83–95.

Gkorezis, P., Petridou, E., & Xanthiakos, P. (2014). Leader positive humor and organizational cynicism: LMX as a mediator. *Leadership & Organization Development Journal, 35*(4), 305–315. doi:10.1108/LODJ-07-2012-0086.

Greguras, G. J., & Ford, J. M. (2006). An examination of the multidimensionality of supervisor and subordinate perceptions of leader-member exchange. *Journal of Occupational and Organizational Psychology, 79*(3), 433–465. doi:10.1348/096317905X53859.

Griffiths, L. (1998). Humour as resistance to professional dominance in community mental health teams. *Sociology of Health & Illness, 20*(6), 874–895. doi:10.1111/1467-9566.00133.

Hay, J. (2000). Functions of humor in the conversations of men and women. *Journal of Pragmatics, 32*(6), 709–742. doi:10.1016/S0378-2166(99)00069-7.

Hearn, J., & Parkin, P. W. (1986). Women, men, and leadership: A critical review of assumptions, practices, and change in the industrialized nations. *International Studies of Management & Organization, 16*(3–4), 33–60. doi:10.1080/00208825.1986.11656433.

Holmes, J. (2000). Politeness, power and provocation: How humour functions in the workplace. *Discourse Studies, 2*(2), 159–185. doi:10.1177/1461445600002002002.

Holmes, J. (2006a). *Gendered Discourse in the Workplace*. Oxford: Blackwell.

Holmes, J. (2006b). Sharing a laugh: Pragmatic aspects of humor and gender in the workplace. *Journal of Pragmatics, 38*(1), 26–50. doi:10.1016/j.pragma.2005.06.007.

Holmes, J. (2007). Making humour work: Creativity on the job. *Applied Linguistics, 28*(4), 518–537. doi:10.1093/applin/amm048.

Holmes, J., Burns, L., Marra, M., Stubbe, M., & Vine, B. (2003). Women managing discourse in the workplace. *Women in Management Review, 18*(8), 414–424. doi:10.1108/09649420310507505.

Holmes, J., & Marra, M. (2006). Humor and leadership style. *Humor—International Journal of Humor Research, 19*(2), 119–138. doi:10.1515/HUMOR.2006.006.

Hoption, C., Barling, J., & Turner, N. (2013). "It's not you, it's me": Transformational leadership and self-deprecating humor. *Leadership & Organization Development Journal, 34*(1), 4–19. doi:10.1108/01437731311289947.

Hughes, L. W., & Avey, J. B. (2009). Transforming with levity: Humor, leadership, and follower attitudes. *Leadership & Organization Development Journal, 30*(6), 540–562. doi:10.1108/01437730910981926.

Huo, Y., Lam, W., & Chen, Z. (2012). Am I the only one this supervisor is laughing at? Effects of aggressive humor on employee strain and addictive behaviors. *Personnel Psychology, 65*(4), 859–885. doi:10.1111/peps.12004.

Hurren, B. L. (2006). The effects of principals' humor on teachers' job satisfaction. *Educational Studies, 32*(4), 373–385. doi:10.1080/03055690600850321.

Kenney, R. A., Schwartz-Kenney, B. M., & Blascovich, J. (1996). Implicit leadership theories: Defining leaders described as worthy of influence. *Personality and Social Psychology Bulletin, 22*(11), 1128–1143. doi:10.1177/01461672962211004.

Kim, T.-Y., Lee, D.-R., & Wong, N. Y. S. (2016). Supervisor humor and employee outcomes: The role of social distance and affective trust in supervisor. *Journal of Business and Psychology, 31* (1), 125–139. doi:10.1007/s10869-015-9406-9.

Liden, R. C., & Maslyn, J. M. (1998). Multidimensionality of leader-member exchange: An empirical assessment through scale development. *Journal of Management, 24*(1), 43–72. doi:10.1177/014920639802400105.

Malone, P. B., III. (1980). Humor: A double-edged tool for today's managers? The Academy of Management Review, *5*(3), 357–360. doi:10.5465/AMR.1980.4288842.

Martin, R. A., Puhlik-Doris, P., Larsen, G., Gray, J., & Weir, K. (2003). Individual differences in uses of humor and their relation to psychological well-being: Development of the Humor Styles Questionnaire. *Journal of Research in Personality, 37*(1), 48–75. doi:10.1016/S0092-6566(02)00534-2.

Mesmer-Magnus, J., Glew, D. J., & Viswesvaran, C. (2012). A meta-analysis of positive humor in the workplace. *Journal of Managerial Psychology, 27*(2), 155–190. doi:10.1108/02683941211199554.

Meyer, J. C. (2000). Humor as a double-edged sword: Four functions of humor in communication. *Communication Theory, 10*(3), 310–331.

Mullany, L. (2004). Gender, politeness and institutional power roles: Humour as a tactic to gain compliance in workplace business meetings. *Multilingua, 23*(1–2), 13–37.

Norrick, N. R., & Spitz, A. (2008). Humor as a resource for mitigating conflict in interaction. *Journal of Pragmatics, 40*(10), 1661–1686. doi:10.1016/j.pragma.2007.12.001.

Priest, R. F., & Swain, J. E. (2002). Humor and its implications for leadership effectiveness. *Humor, 15*(2), 169–189. doi:10.1515/humr.2002.010.

Pundt, A. (2015). The relationship between humorous leadership and innovative behavior. *Journal of Managerial Psychology, 30*(8), 878–893. doi:10.1108/JMP-03-2013-0082.

Pundt, A., & Herrmann, F. (2015). Affiliative and aggressive humour in leadership and their relationship to leader-member exchange. *Journal of Occupational and Organizational Psychology, 88*(1), 108–125. doi:10.1111/joop.12081.

Rizzo, B. J., Wanzer, M. B., & Booth-Butterfield, M. (1999). Individual differences in managers' use of humor. Subordinate perceptions of managers' humor. *Communication Research Reports, 16*(4), 360–369. doi:10.1080/08824099909388737.

Robert, C., Dunne, T. C., & Iun, J. (2016). The impact of leader humor on subordinate job satisfaction: The crucial role of leader-subordinate relationship quality. *Group & Organization Management, 41*(3), 375-406. doi:10.1177/1059601115598719.

Robert, C., & Wilbanks, J. E. (2012). The wheel model of humor: Humor events and affect in organizations. *Human Relations, 65*(9), 1071–1099. doi:10.1177/0018726711433133.

Romero, E. J., & Arendt, L. A. (2011). Variable effects of humor styles on organizational outcomes. *Psychological Reports, 108*(2), 649–659. doi:10.2466/07.17.20.21.PR0.108.2.649-659.

Romero, E. J., & Cruthirds, K. A. (2006). The use of humor in the workplace. *The Academy of Management Perspectives, 20*(2), 58–69.

Romero, E. J., & Pescosolido, A. (2008). Humor and group effectiveness. *Human Relations, 61*(3), 127–149. doi:10.1177/0018726708088999.

Schnurr, S. (2008). Surviving in a man's world with a sense of humour: An analysis of women leaders' use of humour at work. *Leadership, 4*(3), 299–319. doi:10.1177/1742715008092363.

Schnurr, S. (2009). Constructing leader identities through teasing at work. *Journal of Pragmatics, 41*(6), 1125–1138. doi:10.1016/j.pragma.2008.10.002.

Schnurr, S., & Chan, A. (2011). When laughter is not enough. Responding to teasing and self-denigrating humour at work. *Journal of Pragmatics, 43*(1), 20–35. doi:10.1016/j.pragma.2010.09.001.

Sluss, D. M., & Ashforth, B. E. (2007). Relational identity and identification: Defining ourselves through work relationships. *Academy of Management Review, 32*(1), 9–32. doi:10.5465/AMR.2007.23463672.

Smith, C. M., & Powell, L. (1988). The use of disparaging humor by group leaders. *Southern Speech Communication Journal, 53*(3), 279–292. doi:10.1080/10417948809372729.

Spreitzer, G. M. (1995). Psychological empowerment in the workplace: Dimensions, measurement, and validation. *Academy of Management Journal, 38*(5), 1442–1465. doi:10.2307/256865.

Vecchio, R. P., Justin, J. E., & Pearce, C. L. (2009). The influence of leader humor on relationships between leader behavior and follower outcomes. *Journal of Managerial Issues, 21*(2), 171–194.

Wisse, B., & Rietzschel, E. (2014). Humor in leader-follower relationships: Humor styles, similarity and relationship quality. *Humor, 27*(2), 249–269. doi:10.1515/humor-2014-0017.

Yukl, G. A. (2009). *Leadership in Organizations* (7th ed.). Upper Saddle River, N.J: Pearson.

Chapter 5
Humor in Negotiations: How to Persuade Others with Humor

Christine Gockel

Abstract Negotiations are a very common business activity. The power of humor in negotiations lies in its capacity to be used competitively and cooperatively simultaneously. It thus helps negotiators to be tough on the issue and soft on the people. In this chapter, we will present general functions of humor in negotiations and explain which linguistic cues signal humor. We will then describe an important experimental study involving a pet frog that shows how humor can lead to financial concessions. Other research rather focused on softer, socio-emotional negotiation outcomes. We will then explain how one's own characteristics (such as power) and one's partner's characteristics influence the amount and type of humor used. Because humor can change both positive and negative moods, we will present relevant findings on the influence of affect in negotiations. We will close by pointing out how humor works in online negotiations.

Keywords Negotiation · Humor · Linguistic cues · Concession · Transition · Power · Positive affect · Anger · Online negotiation

5.1 Introduction

One of the most common activities in business is negotiation. It is difficult to think of any business transaction that is not connected to some sort of negotiation (Engle, Elahee, & Tatoglu, 2013). Managers and employees engage in negotiations on a day-to-day basis to further their tasks and to build and change relationships.

In a negotiation, parties with nonidentical preferences allocate resources in a decision-making process (Bazerman & Carroll, 1987). The basic assumption about negotiators is that they have at least two goals: to pursue the issue at stake and to maintain the relationship with the other party (Adelswärd & Öberg, 1998).

The original version of this chapter was revised: See the "Chapter Note" section at the end of this chapter for details. The erratum to this chapter is available at https://doi.org/10.1007/978-3-319-65691-5_9

T. Scheel and C. Gockel, *Humor at Work in Teams, Leadership, Negotiations, Learning and Health*, SpringerBriefs in Psychology,
DOI 10.1007/978-3-319-65691-5_5

Two humor functions closely relate to these goals: to convey aggressive messages and to facilitate communication (Graham, Papa, & Brooks, 1992). Therefore, these two humor functions might be used to criticize the other party's position and to facilitate the negotiation (Bonaiuto, Castellana, & Pierro, 2003). In other words, the power of humor in negotiations lies in its capacity to be used competitively and cooperatively simultaneously (Vuorela, 2005).

The kind of humor that has been examined in negotiations usually refers to humorous comments instead of stable personality characteristics regarding the perception or production of humor. Therefore, in this chapter, when mentioning humor, we will refer to humorous comments, i.e., remarks that are meant to be nonfactual and nonserious (Banitz, 2005). Researchers have focused mostly on verbal as compared to nonverbal humor in negotiations. Humorous comments are perceived as such when they involve two (somewhat) opposing semantic scripts (Banitz, 2005). An example is the following comment during a sales negotiation: "Well, my final offer is $1000 and I'll throw in my pet frog." These comments combine two seemingly contradictory ideas, a final monetary offer and a pet frog, and are thus perceived as funny (see also Raskin's Semantic Script Theory of Humor, SSTH, 1985).

5.2 General Functions of Humor in Negotiations

Much has been written about the functions of humor in negotiations, but not much has been examined empirically. From a theoretical point of view, humor should be useful in negotiations. It helps speakers to handle problematic situations (e.g., refusing an offer) while maintaining politeness because it helps to say what one means without spelling it out (Mulkay, Clark, & Pinch, 1993). A negotiator can quickly deny responsibility for what he or she just said and can throw in a new and wild idea while obliging the recipient to respond kindly. A powerful conversational norm requires humor recipients to respond with laughter or smiles when noticing that a statement is meant to be humorous (Mulkay et al., 1993). The norm prescribes recipients to keep serious objections to themselves and helps to forestall criticism (Mulkay et al., 1993).

Humor in negotiations can help to avoid difficult items: By replying humorously to serious concerns, one can show that one does not take the other party's concerns seriously (Vuorela, 2005). The duality of humor in negotiations is expressed in the fact that one can express frustration and discontent while saving face (aggressive function) and release tension after difficult agenda items (cooperative function; Vuorela, 2005). In summary, although humorous exchanges appear to be spontaneous, they have important functions.

5.3 Specific Functions of Humor in Negotiations

A more fine-grained view on the functions of humor in negotiations is provided by linguists. They systematically analyze specific humorous comments in negotiations, examine those comments preceding and following the humor, and draw conclusions on how humor changes the course of a negotiation. One such study was conducted by Bonaiuto et al., (2003). They assumed that someone else's proposal can be challenged or criticized through a humorous comment. The researchers describe these kinds of humorous comments as "de-legitimizing" comments and aimed to learn how humor is used in a group with a negotiation task. In their study of four groups (of four students each), all sequences that contained laughter were analyzed. Laughter was defined as a sign of humor that can be perceived by all members of the group.

In their sample, all sequences containing laughter followed these steps: First, Person A made a request, then Person B responded humorously, and then one or more group members laughed. After that, five different kinds of reactions/functions could be observed:

- A redefined the original request. Often the new request was more modest (The researchers labeled this as "straight redefinition").
- A replied to the humorous comment, B specified the comment by turning into serious mode, and A redefined the request. Again, often the new request was more modest ("redefinition through reformulation").
- A specified the original request ("argumentation"—this was the most frequent case).
- A protested, B apologized or took back the humorous comment ("protest").
- A showed minimal or no acknowledgement of the humorous comment and restated the original request ("no acknowledgement").

In summary, in all examined cases, humor was used to delegitimize another's request. The list of five reactions can be placed along a continuum from the most to the least effective in the negotiation (from the point of view of the speaker of the humorous comment). The first two reactions lead to changes in the request, whereas the last two have no positive outcome for the speaker of the humorous comment. It seems as though humor helps to state criticisms in a safe way—when issues are emotionally charged or positions are socially unacceptable (Attardo, 1994). The researchers had originally proposed that humor could also be used to legitimize one's own request. Because this did not occur very often, they did not integrate this case into their list.

Maemura and Horita (2012) add more specific reactions to this list. In their research, they also used the classification scheme by Bonaiuto and colleagues (2003). Their aim had also been to learn what the relationship between humor/laughter and the negotiation process is. They recorded and transcribed a set of discussions and found that laughter at the end of a chain of arguments did allow for a new issue. It seems as though humor and laughter help to change the content and process of the negotiation. Therefore, they might help negotiators to stop circular argumentation and to break out of deadlocks.

An important limitation of these two studies is that they consider only humorous sequences that are followed by laughter. As mentioned above, laughter can be a strong verbal cue for humor, but it does not necessarily indicate humor. Thus, it is important to have a closer look at the specific cues indicating humor in negotiations.

5.4 Verbal Signs for Humor in Negotiations

How does one know that a comment in a negotiation is meant humorously and not seriously? Banitz (2005) attempted a linguistic description of humor in the business context. Her goal was to find linguistic markers that signaled humorous comments or instances. The target groups for her research findings were second-language speakers because it is especially difficult for them to recognize and appropriately use humor in business conversations. They may not pick up on nonverbal and verbal cues for humor because these cues might be different in their native language. Therefore, misunderstandings are likely to happen.

Banitz (2005) analyzed videos of business speeches, negotiations, and meetings. Her analysis and a careful review of the literature yielded a description of three kinds of linguistic cues for humor.

First, semantic cues for humor, which refer to the content of a comment, are a play of words or the ambiguity of a meaning (for example "Uncles don't like their wives to take money out of their pockets, because they don't like to have AUNTS in their pants," Nilsen, 1970, p. 55). They can also be typical opening phrases such as "Did you hear the one about…". Second, syntactic cues, which refer to the structure of a comment, can be syntactic formulae (for example "An afternoon snack: the pause that refleshes," Hempelmann, 2003, p. 119), ungrammaticality, or syntactic ambiguity (for example "The roosters do the crowing, but the HENCE lay the eggs," Hempelmann, 2003, p. 123). Third, phonological cues, which refer to the sound of a comment, are a change from the default, changes in pitch, an inappropriate sound or a pause before a comment.

These three linguistic cues do not seem to be sufficient to recognize humor in a conversation. People often seem to rely on more obvious cues such as facial cues and laughter (This is also true for humor researchers). Relying on laughter to recognize humor is problematic though because laughter often occurs following comments that are not meant to be humorous (Provine, 2000; see also Chap. 3 about teams). Speakers often start a round of laughter by starting to laugh themselves. This kind of behavior serves many functions such as gaining approval, but is not humor in a strict sense. As explained in Chap. 3, speakers sometimes use laughter after serious, non-humorous comments in order to withdraw their statement.

5.5 Timing of Humor and Laughter in Negotiations

The frequency of humor and laughter certainly changes throughout a negotiation. Thus, it is important to find out when humor and laughter occur most often, and if their occurrence is connected to changes in the course of the negotiation. Adelswärd and Öberg (1998) focused on this issue in their research. They examined three international negotiations between native and non-native English speakers, transcribed them, and analyzed all sequences that contained laughter. Previous research (Öberg, 1995) had shown that three typical steps in a negotiation, namely information exchange, discussion, and decision, usually end with more informality. Thus, laughter should occur when negotiators transition from one step to the next.

This is exactly what the researchers found. 60% of all laughter events occurred at topic boundaries. "The laughter puts a parentheses (…) around a moment in the 'real' negotiation and serious business is temporarily suspended" (Adelswärd & Öberg, p. 421). It functions as a "time-out" and helps to structure the negotiation.

Although it puts a halt to the negotiation, laughter often occurrs in connection with the issues under negotiation. Adelswärd and Öberg (1998) reason that it signals a certain amount of ambiguity such as "the issue is important and sensitive." This implies that negotiators need to talk about the issue, but that it is also difficult to talk about it. Because humor and laughter seem to lend structure to a negotiation and imply how important an issue is, it is crucial to find out which effects they have on important negotiation outcomes.

5.6 Humor and Negotiation Outcomes

Can humor make you money in a negotiation? The first to examine how humor influences financial concessions were O'Quin and Aronoff (1981). They assumed that a humorous comment by the seller in a sales negotiation should lead to higher financial concessions from the buyer. In a lab experiment, a confederate always played the role of seller. In the humor condition, the seller said, toward the end of the negotiation, "Well, my final offer is $xxx and I'll throw in my pet frog." In the non-humor condition, the last part of the sentence was not mentioned. Participants in the humor condition made a bigger proportional financial concession than participants in the non-humor condition. They also liked the task more (but did not like their partner more). The authors propose a potential reason for the financial concession: They believe that the situation becomes less important through humor. And this, in turn, leads to greater compliance.

Apart from financial concessions, which other effects can humor have in negotiations? Bergeron and Vachon (2008) examined humor in financial selling encounters. They hypothesized that the perception of having a sense of humor should positively affect relational outcomes. Financial advisors and their clients were asked to fill out questionnaires. The authors measured humor with two items:

"… is a humoristic individual" and "…told a few jokes and made me laugh." They thereby measured the attribution of sense of humor instead of humor during the negotiation like most other studies.

Attributed sense of humor was associated with positive outcomes other than financial ones (Bergeron & Vachon, 2008). The more humor clients perceived in their financial advisor, the higher they rated trust, service quality, satisfaction, the stronger their purchase intention, word-of-mouth intentions, and the less risk they perceived. Because data were collected in a cross-sectional study, no causal relations could be examined. Also, because data were collected after the negotiation, the overall positive results could be explained with the halo effect. In other words, the client's overall positive impression of the financial advisor may have been based on the perception of one single positive characteristic.

Humor is not only important in negotiations because it can lead to financial concessions and a positive impression. We believe it has far-reaching consequences aside from those mentioned above. Humor can strongly influence affect, and affect in turn can strongly influence negotiation outcomes. In our brief discussion, we focus on positive mood and anger as a specific negative emotion because they have been shown to be important in negotiations.

Regarding positive mood, the broaden-and-build theory of positive emotions (Fredrickson, 1998, 2001) can help to explain the relationship between humor and positive outcomes in negotiations. Its main premise is that positive emotions "broaden people's momentary thought-action repertoires and build their enduring personal resources" (Fredrickson, 1998, p. 219). One effect of positive emotions is that they broaden the scope of attention, cognition, and action (Fredrickson, 1998). For example, for the positive emotion of joy, Fredrickson (1998) proposes a readiness to engage in new opportunities. For the positive emotion of interest, she proposes a readiness to explore and deepen the experience with a target of interest. Ample research by Isen and her colleagues (Isen, 1990; Isen, Daubman, & Nowicki, 1987; Ziv, 1976) shows how positive emotions impact cognition and that they can, for example, positively influence creative thinking. In negotiations, positive emotions should also increase the likelihood of coming up with creative solutions. Another effect of positive emotions is that they help to create social bonds between people as a personal resource. Sharing positive emotions, as signaled with smiles or laughter, helps to create enduring bonds with others (Fredrickson, 1998, 2001). This can help maintain a positive relationship with one's negotiation partner.

When examining emotions in negotiations, it is also important to focus on negative emotions—because they can arise quickly. The negative emotion that has been examined most often in this context is anger. Anger influences how one perceives the self and one's partner and which choices one makes in a negotiation. Angry persons feel more certain about the course of events and a sense of personal control (Frijda, Kuipers, & ter Schure, 1989; Lerner & Keltner, 2001). They tend to evaluate others in a negative light (DeSteno, Dasgupta, Bartlett, & Cajdric, 2004); specifically, they regard others as less trustworthy (Dunn & Schweitzer, 2005). When situations are ambiguous, as it can often be the case in negotiations, angry persons tend to attribute higher responsibility to other parties and tend to blame others (Quigley & Tedeschi, 1996). In general, they have the drive to take action against others (Mackie, Devos, & Smith, 2000). Anger should thus make it extremely difficult to reach agreement. All humorous comments that may potentially invoke anger should better be avoided in negotiations.

5.7 Humor Producers in Negotiations

Who is most likely to use humor in negotiations? Early research has focused mostly on power as a characteristic. More recent research has examined humor styles and taken into account the dyadic interplay between the characteristics of two negotiation partners.

Regarding the effects of power on humor production, two positions have been put forward and two different results have been found. Mulkay et al. (1993) assumed that humor helps negotiators in dealing with difficulties during the interaction. These difficulties arise due to negotiators' positions or the structure of the interaction. Mulkay and colleagues (1993) therefore reason that negotiators in the subordinate position with less power should use humor more often. They conducted a case study and examined a videotaped interaction in a photo shop. In this sales interaction, the seller made several offers, which the buyer declined humorously—perhaps to not disrupt the course of the conversation. Specific examples showed that at problematic instances, the buyer refused the seller's offer humorously, the seller appeared to recognize the criticism and responded accordingly, but not in a serious mode. The seller seemed to decipher the implicit meaning in the humorous remark, which often contradicted the literal meaning. The researchers concluded that negotiators with less power are more likely to use humor than negotiators with more power.

Vuorela (2005), on the other hand, reasoned that negotiators with power should start and end humorous exchanges more often than negotiators with less power. She examined two negotiation types: the internal meeting of a sales team and a negotiation between sellers and potential buyers. She used audio recordings of the meetings (16 h total) and coded humor in the recordings according to type and subject. In her study, project leaders who held power initiated humorous exchanges more often than those group members with less power. She reasoned that, although humor seemed to appear spontaneously in these meetings, it had important functions. In conclusion, the question remains as to what degree power influences negotiators to produce humor in negotiations. The diverging results indicate that moderating variables might play a role. These could be the type of negotiation, the size of the power distance, or the timing of the comment. Because results have been ambiguous, more research is needed in this area.

When examining the persons who produce humor in a negotiation, it is not only important to take into account the characteristics of a speaker, but also of a listener. Depending on a negotiation partner, one may either be inspired or rather scared to use humor. To date, there is no research in this area in the business context.

However, research in the area of close relationships, specifically about how romantic partners negotiate with each other, might give a hint and show the complex interplay.

Winterheld, Simpson and Orina (2013) examined how stable dispositions could explain how romantic partners use and respond to humor. They invited 96 couples who were in long-term relationships into their lab. Partners filled out questionnaires first and then engaged in a conflict resolution discussion. In other words, couples needed to discuss an unresolved relationship problem. The researchers then coded the videotaped discussions according to the function model of humor styles (Martin, Puhlik-Doris, Larsen, Gray, & Weir, 2003). For each humorous comment, they coded if it was (a) directed at the self or the partner and (b) benign or detrimental to well-being. Thus, the researchers distinguished between affiliative (other-directed, benign), aggressive (other-directed, detrimental), self-enhancing (self-directed, benign), and self-defeating (self-directed, detrimental) humor.

They found that stable dispositions indeed influenced the production of humor. Partners with high scores in attachment anxiety, who worry that their partner may not be available in times of need, produced more self-defeating humor. This might be due to the fact that they tend to focus on their own distress in times of conflict. Partners with high scores in attachment avoidance, who generally strive to maintain self-reliance, produced less affiliative and more aggressive humor. This could be due to them trying to prevent vulnerabilities in times of conflict (Martin et al., 2003).

Humor use, however, was not only predicted by one's own stable dispositions, but also by the partner's dispositions as well. The more distressed the partner was during the discussion, the more affiliative and the less aggressive humor their partners used. This was only found when the partner also had high scores in attachment anxiety. It was not found when scores were low.

Stable dispositions also predicted reactions to partner's humor use. Partners were more satisfied and laughed more during the discussion when their partners used more affiliative humor. They were less satisfied when their partners used more aggressive humor. These effects were moderated by other variables such as one's own distress and one's own stable characteristics. In summary, this study shows that both humor use and reactions to humor depend on several factors—an individual's characteristics, the partner's characteristics and on features of the relationship (Winterheld et al., 2013). It therefore points to the complex interplay of contributing factors and it may inspire researchers examining negotiations in the business context.

5.8 Characteristics of Online Negotiations

Most business transactions are connected to some sort of negotiation. Because the use of information technology media, such as email, is now standard in business and consumer transactions, the number of online negotiations has increased dramatically. However, it is impossible to find reliable estimates about how often online negotiations occur (Nadler & Shestowsky, 2006).

Which changes occur when people negotiate online versus face-to-face (FTF)? In online negotiations, the "social bandwidth" becomes narrower because many cues that are in the words themselves are lost. This pertains to verbal and nonverbal cues. One cannot see when a negotiation partner lifts his eyebrows while replying to an offer online, and one cannot hear changes in the partner's voice when all comments are written. Thus, negotiators may easily fail to detect humorous comments as such and may perceive the partner to exaggerate or to lie (see also Sect. 8.2 on Virtuality).

Previous research in the area of online communication has shown that senders of funny emails tend to overestimate the receiver's ability to decipher the meaning of their message (Kruger, Epley, Parker, & Ng, 2005). This could be due to increased difficulties in perspective-taking during online communication because nonverbal cues are absent. Also, it is more difficult to develop trust and easier to break trust in online negotiations in comparison with FTF negotiations (Naquin & Paulson, 2003).

Two studies by Kurtzberg, Naquin, and Belkin (2009) shed light on the impact of humor in online negotiations. The researchers assumed that negotiators, who use humor to introduce themselves, build trust with their partner. Both studies followed the same procedure and used an integrative negotiation. In an integrative negotiation, it is possible to produce better outcomes together than either party could reach alone. In this kind of negotiation, cooperation benefits both parties. In the experimental condition, negotiators sent an email to their partner with a funny Dilbert cartoon about negotiating. In the control condition, they did not send a cartoon.

The results of the first study showed that when the negotiation started with a cartoon (as compared to no cartoon), the joint outcomes of the negotiation were higher. More detailed analyses indicated that the effect occurred because negotiators were more likely to discover compatible issues. The authors suggest that this may be based on an increase in trust. The humorous email was not only beneficial for joint outcomes, but also for individuals sending this email as well—their individual payoff was greater than the payoff of the cartoon recipients (Kurtzberg et al., 2009).

The second study examined the effect of introductory humor on initial offers in a negotiation. Results showed that when the negotiation started with a cartoon (again as compared to no cartoon), the first offer was more likely to be in the bargaining zone where both negotiators are likely to make gains (Kurtzberg et al., 2009). Overall, there seem to be more concessions to negotiators who introduce humor. Why is this the case? The addressee of the humor might want to reciprocate by being kind—after all, it is difficult to spontaneously reciprocate by making another humorous comment.

5.9 A Brief Note of Caution

Previous theories and research have painted a quite positive picture of humor in negotiations. Many have pointed out that humor is a friendly gesture that helps to smooth the interaction and can build rapport between negotiators. To date, there is no research about the use of humor in negotiations between enemies who have a long history of resentment. Research about friendly gestures in the context of enemy relationships indicates that humor, even friendly humor, may not always have beneficial effects, but can terribly backfire. Menon, Sheldon and Galinsky (2014) showed in three lab studies that friendly gestures and comments can agitate and confuse the recipient. It seems as though if the atmosphere is hostile, an attempt to lighten the atmosphere and to build trust can backfire. Thus, if the relationship or the negotiation cannot be avoided, it seems wise to avoid humor in these kinds of relationships. Also, in culturally diverse settings, which might have very vague norms about the appropriateness of humor, it is advisable to be cautious when using humor.

5.10 Future Research

The research on humor in negotiations has just started and currently leaves a lot of room for exciting future research questions and studies. We would like to highlight three separate issues that seem promising to us.

The first issue is a clear distinction between outcomes for individuals and for the dyad in both distributive and integrative negotiations. Most research has focused on individual-level outcomes and has neglected dyadic outcomes. Psychological theories suggest that positive forms of humor should especially improve dyadic outcomes in integrative negotiations. The reasoning is as follows: If humorous comments increase negotiators' positive mood, they should be much more likely to find creative solutions based on their broadened cognitive focus. This is what the broaden-and-build theory of positive emotions (Fredrickson, 1998) suggests. Thus, it seems advisable to focus on integrative solutions as outcomes in future research next.

The second issue is a theoretical one. All negotiations take place between at least two people. However, researchers have mostly focused on individual predictors and individual outcomes and have neglected the complex interplay between parties. One's humor in a negotiation does not only depend on one's own characteristics, but is also strongly influenced by one's partner's outcomes as well. Research in close relationships usually focuses on both partners and has developed adequate methods to study the resulting interactions. The study done by Winterheld and colleagues (2013) is a great example. We hope that its basic assumptions and methods inspire future research on humor in negotiations.

The third issue is a methodological one. Researchers who have studied humor in experimental settings usually contrast a humor with a non-humor condition. They then conclude that humor has positive effects. However, it would be more interesting to know if humor as compared to direct comments still has these positive effects. Direct comments are those comments that have the same content as humorous comments, but no linguistic cues indicating that the comment is meant to be funny. This kind of comparison would enable us to know if there is something specific about the humor or if the positive effects are mainly due to the content of the message.

5.11 Recommendations for Practice

Which suggestions about humor in negotiations can we safely propose? Forester (2004) already presented suggestions with respect to the use of humor in negotiations (in participatory, conflict-ridden settings). He points out that humor is important and that one should try to use it in critical moments. There is a risk associated with being too serious, and that is to cycle down. One negative statement follows another, the atmosphere becomes heavier, and accusations build upon one another; this can feel "like a reverse tornado" (Forester, 2004, p. 231). Humor could break this cycle and change the atmosphere. However, if the atmosphere is already toxic, humor can backfire, and it seems wise to refrain from using it.

In less tense situations, positive forms of humor can create positive impressions and help to increase positive affect. This, in turn, encourages divergent and creative thinking and helps negotiators to come up with new solutions that are beneficial for all parties involved.

Recommendations for further reading

Bonaiuto, M., Castellana, E., & Pierro, A. (2003). Arguing and laughing: The use of humor to negotiate in group discussions. *Humor - International Journal of Humor Research, 16*(2), 183–223. doi:10.1515/humr.2003.010.

Kurtzberg, T. R., Naquin, C. E., & Belkin, L. Y. (2009). Humor as a relationship-building tool in online negotiations. *International Journal of Conflict Management, 20*(4), 377-397. doi:10.1108/10444060910991075.

Mulkay, M., Clark, C., & Pinch, T. (1993). Laughter and the profit motive: The use of humor in a photographic shop. *Humor—International Journal of Humor Research, 6*(2), 163–193. doi:10.1515/humr.1993.6.2.163.

References

Adelswärd, V., & Öberg, B.-M. (1998). The function of laughter and joking in negotiation activities. *Humor, 11*(4), 411–430. doi:10.1515/humr.1998.11.4.411.

Attardo, S. (1994). *Linguistic theories of humor* (Vol. 1). Berlin: Walter de Gruyter.

Banitz, B. (2005, August). *Funny business: Verbal humor in business negotiation and English-as-a-second-language-speaker* (Dissertation). Purdue University, US. Retrieved from http://docs.lib.purdue.edu/dissertations/AAI3191422/.

Bazerman, M. H., & Carroll, J. S. (1987). Negotiator cognition. *Research in Organizational Behavior, 9,* 247–288.

Bergeron, J., & Vachon, M. (2008). The effects of humour usage by financial advisors in sales encounters. *International Journal of Bank Marketing, 26*(6), 376–398. doi:10.1108/02652320810902424.

Bonaiuto, M., Castellana, E., & Pierro, A. (2003). Arguing and laughing: The use of humor to negotiate in group discussions. *Humor—International Journal of Humor Research, 16*(2), 183–223. doi:10.1515/humr.2003.010.

DeSteno, D., Dasgupta, N., Bartlett, M. Y., & Cajdric, A. (2004). Prejudice from thin air the effect of emotion on automatic intergroup attitudes. *Psychological Science, 15*(5), 319–324.

Dunn, J. R., & Schweitzer, M. E. (2005). Feeling and believing: The influence of emotion on trust. *Journal of Personality and Social Psychology, 88*(5), 736–748.

Engle, R. L., Elahee, M. N., & Tatoglu, E. (2013). Antecedents of problem-solving cross-cultural negotiation style: Some preliminary evidence. *Journal of Applied Management and Entrepreneurship, 18*(2), 83.

Forester, J. (2004). Responding to critical moments with humor, recognition, and hope. *Negotiation Journal, 20*(2), 221–237. doi:10.1111/j.1571-9979.2004.00019.x.

Fredrickson, B. L. (1998). What good are positive emotions? *Review of General Psychology, 2,* 300–319.

Fredrickson, B. L. (2001). The role of positive emotions in positive psychology: The broaden-and-build theory of positive emotions. *American Psychologist, 56,* 218–226.

Frijda, N. H., Kuipers, P., & ter Schure, E. (1989). Relations among emotion, appraisal, and emotional action readiness. *Journal of Personality and Social Psychology, 57*(2), 212–228.

Graham, E. E., Papa, M. J., & Brooks, G. P. (1992). Functions of humor in conversation: Conceptualization and measurement. *Western Journal of Communication (Includes Communication Reports), 56*(2), 161–183. doi:10.1080/10570319209374409.

Hempelmann, C. F. (2003). *Paranomasic puns: Target recoverability towards automatic generation* (Unpublished doctoral dissertation). Purdue University, West Lafayette, Indiana.

Isen, A. M. (1990). The influence of positive and negative affect in cognitive organization: Some implications for development. In N. Stein, B. Leventhal, & T. Trabasso (Eds.), *Psychological and biological approaches to emotion* (pp. 75–94). Hillsdale, NJ: Erlbaum.

Isen, A. M., Daubman, K. A., & Nowicki, G. P. (1987). Positive affect facilitates creative problem solving. *Journal of Personality and Social Psychology, 52,* 1122–1131.

Kruger, J., Epley, N., Parker, J., & Ng, Z.-W. (2005). Egocentrism over e-mail: Can we communicate as well as we think? *Journal of Personality and Social Psychology, 89*(6), 925.

Kurtzberg, T. R., Naquin, C. E., & Belkin, L. Y. (2009). Humor as a relationship-building tool in online negotiations. *International Journal of Conflict Management, 20*(4), 377–397. doi:10.1108/10444060910991075.

Lerner, J. S., & Keltner, D. (2001). Fear, anger, and risk. *Journal of Personality and Social Psychology, 81*(1), 146–159.

Maemura, Y., & Horita, M. (2012). Humour in negotiations: A pragmatic analysis of humour in simulated negotiations. *Group Decision and Negotiation, 21*(6), 821–838. doi:10.1007/s10726-011-9251-9.

Mackie, D. M., Devos, T., & Smith, E. R. (2000). Intergroup emotions: Explaining offensive action tendencies in an intergroup context. *Journal of Personality and Social Psychology, 79*(4), 602–616.

Martin, R. A., Puhlik-Doris, P., Larsen, G., Gray, J., & Weir, K. (2003). Individual differences in uses of humor and their relation to psychological well-being: Development of the Humor Styles Questionnaire. *Journal of Research in Personality, 37*(1), 48–75.

Menon, T., Sheldon, O. J., & Galinsky, A. D. (2014). Barriers to transforming hostile relations: Why friendly gestures can backfire. *Negotiation and Conflict Management Research, 7*(1), 17–37. doi:10.1111/ncmr.12023.

Mulkay, M., Clark, C., & Pinch, T. (1993). Laughter and the profit motive: The use of humor in a photographic shop. *Humor—International Journal of Humor Research, 6*(2), 163–193. doi:10.1515/humr.1993.6.2.163.

Nadler, J., & Shestowsky, D. (2006). Negotiation, information technology, and the problem of the faceless other. *Negotiation Theory and Research*, 145–172.

Naquin, C. E., & Paulson, G. D. (2003). Online bargaining and interpersonal trust. *Journal of Applied Psychology, 88*(1), 113–120.

Nilsen, D. L. (1970). Linguistic analysis of humor. *English Record, 20*(3), 41–56.

O'Quin, K., & Aronoff, J. (1981). Humor as a technique of social influence. *Social Psychology Quarterly*, *44*(4), 349–357.

Öberg, B.-M. (1995). *Negotiation processes as talk and interaction: Interaction analyses of informal negotiations*. Linköping: Linköping University.

Provine, R. (2000). *Laughter: A scientific investigation*. New York: Viking adult.

Quigley, B. M., & Tedeschi, J. T. (1996). Mediating effects of blame attributions on feelings of anger. *Personality and Social Psychology Bulletin, 22*(12), 1280–1288.

Raskin, V. (1985). *Semantic mechanisms of humor*. Dordrecht/Boston/Lancaster: D. Reidel Publishing Company.

Vuorela, T. (2005). Laughing matters: A case study of humor in multicultural business negotiations. *Negotiation Journal, 21*(1), 105–130. doi:10.1111/j.0748-4526.2005.00049.x.

Winterheld, H. A., Simpson, J. A., & Orina, M. M. (2013). It's in the way that you use it: Attachment and the dyadic nature of humor during conflict negotiation in romantic couples. *Personality and Social Psychology Bulletin, 39*(4), 496–508. doi:10.1177/0146167213479133.

Ziv, A. (1976). Facilitating effects of humor on creativity. *Journal of Educational Psychology, 68*, 318–322.

Chapter 6
Humor and Learning in the Workplace

Tabea Scheel

Abstract This chapter presents benefits and drawbacks of using humor in learning/for teaching and training. We introduce two theories about humor and learning, namely the Instructional Humor Processing Theory and the Perceived Humor Hypotheses. Among the consequences of humor in instruction are cognitive, social, as well as motivational and affective ones: Humor may enhance learning if tied to the course content, humor may increase teachers' immediacy and the presenters' likability, and humor may foster positive affect and thus motivation. However, it may reduce the perceived credibility of the presenter and does not necessarily improve effectiveness or performance. Also, the use of humor interacts with personality. We present findings about the mode of presentation, that is, about the use of humor in textbooks, tests, and online instruction. Research in school/university settings serves as the basis and nearly the only setting of previous research; we discuss the limited research on instruction in work contexts. Future research avenues as well as recommendations for practical use close this chapter. For instance, techniques recommended for teaching students (e.g., smile, relate humor to important information) can be applied to trainings or instruction in the work context.

Keywords Learning · Instructional Humor Processing Theory · Memory · Creativity · Immediacy · Credibility · Motivation · Affect · Textbooks · Online classrooms

6.1 Introduction

Research on the use of humor in workplace learning and training contexts is rare, even though formal or informal learning is an important activity in many workplaces. Thus, we provide a review of the use of humor in school or university teaching (adult settings). Several of these empirical findings may be applicable to

---

The original version of this chapter was revised: See the "Chapter Note" section at the end of this chapter for details. The erratum to this chapter is available at https://doi.org/10.1007/978-3-319-65691-5_9

T. Scheel and C. Gockel, *Humor at Work in Teams, Leadership, Negotiations, Learning and Health*, SpringerBriefs in Psychology,
DOI 10.1007/978-3-319-65691-5_6

the work context. Also, "teacher" and "college instructor" are professions and thus represent specific work contexts.

Several reviews on humor in school exist. Neuliep (1991) presented an extensive review of the findings through 1990. Also, in Martin's book (2007), a chapter on the use of humor in the classroom provides a comprehensive summary. Recently, Banas, Dunbar, Rodriguez, and Liu (2011) reviewed the knowledge of four decades of research on the use of humor in instruction. We will summarize these reviews with regard to findings useful for the work context, and discuss the limited research that has been conducted in applied work contexts. Knowledge about humor in classroom instruction might be appropriately transferred to professional (work) contexts, as suggested by the title of Berk's (1998) book about how to use humor in instruction: "Professors are from Mars, students are from Snickers: How to write and deliver humor in the classroom and in professional presentations."

6.2 Content and Frequency of Humor in Instruction

Content Teachers have been found to use humor in the classroom in a variety of ways, a considerable proportion being tendentious (Gorham & Christophel, 1992; Neuliep, 1991). Among the contents of teachers' humor in the classroom were personal/general anecdotes or stories, humor that was related or unrelated to the subject or topic, joke telling, brief humorous comments, self-disparaging humor, and unplanned humor (Neuliep, 1991; Wanzer, Frymier, Wojtaszczyk, & Smith, 2006) or offensive and other-disparaging types (Frymier, Wanzer, & Wojtaszczyk, 2008). Most often, funny stories, funny comments, jokes, and professional (positive) humor were used, as indicated by students as well as (three) professors (Torok, McMorris, & Lin, 2004). In a taxonomy of classroom humor, Neuliep (1991) came up with five categories, which are teacher-targeted humor (e.g., self-disclosure-related), student-targeted humor (e.g., error identification), untargeted humor (e.g., awkward comparison/incongruity), external source humor (e.g., historical incident), and nonverbal humor (e.g., affect display humor). These taxonomies differ in their level of abstraction, for instance, the content of humor or the person(s) it is directed at. Summing up, humor is as multifaceted in learning contexts as it is in other areas of life.

Frequency Banas et al. (2011) concluded that the frequency of humor was highly dependent on the measure (e.g., self-report vs. tape recordings). From analyzing responses of US high school teachers, Neuliep (1991) found an average frequency of two humorous attempts per session. In a study of US undergraduates, 60% reported that their professors always used humor and 70% indicated strong agreement that their professor was entertaining and witty (Torok et al., 2004). College instructors seem to use more humor than school teachers (Banas et al., 2011). However, most studies are outdated and conducted in single contexts. Given that most studies were conducted in the US, differences in humor frequency due to cultural norms are largely unknown.

6.3 Theories About Humor in Instruction

The three general theoretical approaches of humor, as introduced in Sect. 2.3, are also applicable to humor in learning and training contexts. Thus, humor in classrooms is based on incongruity and may lead to arousal in humor recipients. As far as learning takes place in a social context, superiority issues may be related to the use of humor. However, there are two approaches specifically referring to the learning and instruction context. Thus, in the following we introduce the Instructional Humor Processing Theory (IHPT) and the Perceived Humor Hypothesis. While the IHPT proposes a process model based on incongruity theory, the Perceived Humor Hypothesis states that the advantage of humorous material for memory is based on the perception of humor rather than incongruity.

Instructional Humor Processing Theory Introduced by Wanzer, Frymier, and Irwin (2010), the IHPT combines incongruity-resolution theory, disposition theory, and the elaboration likelihood model (ELM) of persuasion. Wanzer et al. (2010) explained why the humor of certain types of instructors may result in increased student learning, whereas the humor of others does not. First, students have to recognize incongruity in an instructor's message, and they must then resolve or interpret this incongruity. Otherwise, the message is non-humorous, confusing, or distracting. Given that the humor is perceived, its appropriateness is then judged. Appropriate humor (e.g., affiliative) results in positive affect, whereas inappropriate humor (e.g., disparaging) results in negative affect. ELM predicts that this positive affect *motivates* students to elaborate and process the humorous message, given that the humorous material enhances the *ability to process* (e.g., if it is related to course content), and thus learning and retention will be enhanced. Negative affect will more likely reduce motivation and the ability to process because it distracts students. In aiming to test the IHPT in a cross-sectional study including 292 US students, Goodboy, Booth-Butterfield, Bolkan, and Griffin (2015) reported that instructor humor was positively related to students' cognitive learning, extra effort, participation, and out-of-class communication—even when controlling for students' learning and grade orientations. However, Bolkan and Goodboy (2015) tested the IHPT against self-determination theory (SDT) with a sample of 300 US students. They found the indirect effect of humor on perceived cognitive learning through SDT higher than through IHPT. Thus, humor was effective through the fulfillment of the students' basic psychological needs according to SDT (i.e., autonomy, competence, relatedness) and not so much through the (motivating) increase in positive affect the IHPT states.

The Perceived Humor Hypothesis Carlson (2011) dissents with the IHPT in that he states that the positive effect of humor for memory is based on the very perception of humor rather than semantic elaboration or incongruity resolution. Carlson (2011) compared the assumptions about (1) semantic elaboration, (2) incongruity resolution, and (3) humor perception with related findings: (1) Differential semantic processing is central to the *context-dependent elaboration hypothesis*, meaning that more stored semantic knowledge—or a greater memory search—is needed for humorous than non-humorous material, resulting in greater recall. So recall is not about humor per se. However, Schmidt and Williams (2001) reported that the effects of humor were not due to increased rehearsal (though humor showed effects in intentional and incidental memory situations), thus challenging the importance of semantic elaboration. (2) Semantic incongruity creates a memory advantage for humorous materials due to the *(incongruity)-resolution* found by a semantic search. However, Schmidt (1994) reported that the effects of humor could not be explained by contextual surprise (even if expected humor effects emerged). Thus, the importance of incongruity resolution for the positive effect of humor on memory is objected. (3) The final assumption states that perceiving humor increases recall; that is, the successful resolution of incongruity must be *perceived as humorous* in order to be recalled better. In fact, retrieval processes seem to be influenced by humor: items that are recalled earlier in free recall situations had higher humor ratings (Schmidt, 2002). Thus, Carlson (2011) concluded that the positive effect of humor for memory is exclusively based on the perception of humor. In line with his reasoning, Carlson's (2011) own study involving Chilean students' ratings of humor suggested that only perceived humor explained the advantage in recall offered by humor (in contrast to inspiration), but neither semantic elaboration nor incongruity resolution did. Thus, whether or not the latter two mechanisms are significant for the recall advantage deserves further investigation. However, the perception of humor seems to be crucial for the positive memory effects of humor.

6.4 The Consequences of Humor in Instruction

Humor is said to have cognitive, social, and psychological (i.e., emotional) benefits on learning in college classrooms from the instructors' perspective (Lei, Cohen, & Russler, 2010). However, most propositions found mixed support in studies on university student samples, and very few studies were ever conducted in the work context. Moreover, some ways of using humor are associated with drawbacks. Thus, degrading remarks about students (especially if unrelated to the course), offensive humor (e.g., sexual, cynical), and excessive humor may be problematic in learning contexts (Lei et al., 2010).

In the following, we present empirical findings regarding cognitive, social, and psychological effects in learning. Most of the research was conducted in classrooms.

6.4.1 Cognitive Effects of Humor on Learning

Humor is used instrumentally to foster learning (Martin, 2007). The cognitive (i.e., educational) benefits consist of enhancing interest (including interest in boring subjects), increasing attention and motivation, elevating students' self-competence, as well as facilitating comprehension, creativity, problem-solving, and risk-taking (Lei et al., 2010; Neuliep, 1991). Accordingly, in their seminal study, Bryant, Comisky, Crane, and Zillmann (1980) found that (male) teachers' use of humor in tape-recorded class presentations was associated with students' perceived general effectiveness of teaching, especially when the humor was spontaneous as compared to prepared humor.

On the other hand, excessive humor may make students feel self-conscious or bored or lose focus on the content of the course (Lei et al., 2010). Even more important, humor may lead to misunderstandings, which cause distorted recall. This might be especially relevant when intelligence is low and thus understanding is impaired (e.g., for irony) or when cultural backgrounds differ and the frame of reference leads to different perceptions and appraisals of humor.

Memory, Attention, and Learning Attention (e.g., Zillmann, Williams, Bryant, Boynton, & Wolf, 1980), learning, and memory are said to be better with humor, especially when humor is related to the course.

Studies with experimental designs found evidence for beneficial memory effects of humor. Students' *retention* 6 weeks after viewing a lecture was superior for students in the topic-related humor condition than in the non- or unrelated humorous conditions (Kaplan & Pascoe, 1977). Also, Chilean students' ratings of humor in photographs, keywords, and phrases predicted *recall* performance (Carlson, 2011). However, only the *recognition* but not the recall performance of 165 US students was better when videos were humorous and relevant to the lecture material (Suzuki & Heath, 2014). Also, Schmidt (1994) largely supported the link between humor and *memory*: Humorous sentences were remembered better than non-humorous sentences in a variety of conditions (Schmidt, 1994) because humor increased attention and rehearsal relative to or at the expense of non-humorous material. The subjectively perceived humor of the sentences affected memory (Schmidt, 1994).

In contrast to studies with experimental designs, self-reported learning found mixed support for beneficial memory effects of humor. That is, three cross-sectional studies report contradictory results about students' self-assessed learning. Wanzer et al. (2010) found that course-related humor correlated with students' *learning*, especially teachers' self-disparaging humor. However, humor unrelated to the course and inappropriate forms of humor (i.e., offensive) were unrelated to learning, thus indicating the ambiguous (or context-dependent) role of this type of humor. Likewise, professors' use of humor helped students learn better (40% said often, 40% always)—however, students' perceptions of competence, effectiveness, and learning were unrelated to professors' use of humor (Torok et al., 2004). Furthermore, humor was not significantly related to students' affect toward the course and their cognitive learning in a study of 286 US students (Myers, Goodboy, & Members of COMM 600, 2014).

In conclusion, humor should be used for enhancing learning, but should be closely tied to the content of the course materials and rather be used infrequently in order to illustrate the most important content (Martin, 2007).

Performance and Creativity The supports for the effects of *dispositional humor* in instruction are sparse and inconsistent: Sense of humor was correlated with the intelligence, retention, and creativity of elementary school children (Hauck & Thomas, 1972). However, humor styles were not related to Belgian students' school performance (Saroglou & Scariot, 2002).

More studies about humor and performance as well as creativity were conducted with regard to *humor exposure*. In an experiment in higher education, Ziv (1988) found that, in a 14-week statistics course, an intervention group with course-relevant humor exhibited superior learning, that is, higher scores on the final exam, over the control group without humor. A second experiment replicated these findings (Ziv, 1988). Two experiments with 124 Australian students showed that exposure to humor increased persistence in two tasks (via amusement), and the humor–persistence link was stronger for persons higher in self-enhancing humor (Cheng & Wang, 2014). This underlines the self-regulative function of humor and provides further explanations for the persistence path of the Dual Pathway to Creativity Model (Nijstad, De Dreu, Rietzschel, & Baas, 2010). This model proposes that creativity is a function of cognitive flexibility and cognitive persistence. Thus, creativity may be influenced by personality or situation features through effects on either flexibility or persistence, or both (Nijstad et al., 2010). In an experiment with 80 US students, jokes and simple sentences of high or low imagery were presented prior to participants' attempts to solve tasks: Humor increased the speed of mental rotation (i.e., imaginal tasks) and slowed performance on analogies (i.e., verbal tasks) for men but not for women (Belanger, Kirkpatrick, & Derks, 1998). So, humor exposure may foster or hinder performance, but this might depend on gender.

Drawing on earlier research by Isen, Daubman, and Nowicki (1987) and Ziv (1976), Scheel, Bachmann, Gerdenitsch, and Korunka (2015) found that affect induction with four video conditions was more strongly related to mens' verbal creativity than to womens': In this experiment with 165 German/Austrian students, only the induction of positive affect with humor was associated with higher verbal creativity (fluency, appropriateness, flexibility, but not originality), but the inductions of neutral, negative, or positive non-humorous affect were not (Scheel et al., 2015). Filipowicz (2006) reported similar gender-dependent findings, with mens' creative performance being enhanced by positive affect induction but not womens'. He explained that different arousal levels might account for this finding (i.e., only men had higher arousal through positive affect) and concluded that pleasantness *and* activation may be necessary for positive affect to foster creativity. The role of humor was further highlighted when surprise—the inherent characteristic of humor—was found to fully mediate the relation between positive affect induction and creativity (Filipowicz, 2006). While these findings underscore the impact of positive affect on (creative) performance, direct evidence for the beneficial effects of humor in instruction on creativity is largely missing. Again, humor may be more enjoyable and may thus enhance motivation or activation.

6.4.2 Social Effects of Humor

According to Lei et al. (2010), the social benefits (i.e., relationships with students) of humor use include improvements in student morale, the establishing of professional relationships with students, the building of a sense of trust, fear and tension reduction, approachableness of the instructor, and creating a relaxed and positive learning climate. It also serves other interpersonal, social communication functions (e.g., status maintenance, norm enforcement; Martin, 2007). However, hostile forms of humor are caveats (Martin, 2007; Torok et al., 2004). For instance, ridiculing a student may serve the short-term goal of enforcing norms and correcting students' behavior (e.g., Bryant, Brown, Parks, & Zillmann, 1983) but has long-term detrimental effects on classroom climate (e.g., Janes & Olson, 2000).

Students appreciate a professors' use of humor (Bryant et al., 1980; Torok et al., 2004). However, humor might threaten *credibility* perceptions. While an older study did not find a significant relation between humor ratings and competence perceptions (Bryant et al., 1980), two more recent studies report contradictory results. That is, advisors' humor was positively related to advisee perceptions of advisor credibility (Wrench & Punyanunt-Carter, 2005). However, in an experiment with Canadian students, humorous individuals were seen as less intelligent and trustworthy (Bressler & Balshine, 2006). Also, excessive humor may jeopardize the credibility of the instructor (Lei et al., 2010; see also Bressler & Balshine, 2006; Bryant, Brown, Silberberg, & Elliott, 1981).

Among the most intensely discussed social consequences in the learning context are immediacy and empathy of the instructors; thus, we present findings regarding both constructs. Again, no studies in the work context exist.

Immediacy and Empathy Humor appears to belong to the broader set of teacher behaviors that contribute to a perception of immediacy in the classroom, which enhances students' evaluations of teachers and courses and perceived learning (Wanzer & Frymier, 1999). Immediacy behavior reduces psychological distance and enhances closeness between students and their teachers (Neuliep, 1991). Thus, immediacy is said to ensure that classes remain semiformal (Neuliep, 1991).

Both amount and type of humor are important for classroom climate (Stuart & Rosenfeld, 1994). Thus, low overall teacher humor was seen as less supportive by students. Offensive and hostile teacher humor is perceived as inappropriate (Frymier et al., 2008), defensive, and less supportive (Stuart & Rosenfeld, 1994).

On the other hand, students perceived professors as more caring when professors used humor, and the majority of the students thought that humor promotes a sense of community (Torok et al., 2004). Also, teachers' level of humor orientation, verbal aggressiveness, and nonverbal immediacy were related to students' ratings of teacher humor (Frymier et al., 2008). These studies focused on teachers as the producers of humor ("sender"). Additionally, the higher the students' own humor orientation and communication competence, the more appropriate they perceive the teacher humor (Frymier et al., 2008).

Though students' *empathy* was positively related to students' own positive, adaptive use of humor, and negatively to aggressive humor (but not to self-defeating humor, Hampes, 2010), there is no study about humor and empathy perceptions of teachers. Overall, the studies mentioned in this section relied on cross-sectional self-reports from US university students. Whereas benign humor (e.g., affiliative, self-enhancing) seems to be favorable for immediacy, other-disparaging humor (e.g., aggressive, offensive) tends to show the opposite effect.

6.4.3 Motivational and Affective Effects of Humor

Among the psychological benefits, Lei et al. (2010) and Neuliep (1991) saw enhancements of students' well-being (including mental and physical health), self-image, and self-esteem; an increased ability to cope with stress; anxiety/tension reduction; and the reversion of negatively conditioned feelings. Also, humor may reduce apprehension around potentially uncomfortable topics (e.g., sex education, Allen, 2014). In the following, we present empirical findings on motivation, affect, and appraisal.

Motivation Motivation may play an important role in why humor may be related to learning; the impact of teachers' (humorous) behavior seems relevant for motivation. Though they did not directly assess humor, two studies found a relation between teachers' immediacy and students' learning via *motivation*: Immediacy (e.g., verbal: uses humor in class; nonverbal: smiles at the class while talking) and students' state motivation had a combined impact on learning (Christophel, 1990). Also, state motivation mediated, but only the relation between verbal immediacy and affective learning (Frymier, 1994). In the above-mentioned study by Myers et al. (2014), humor was significantly related to students' affect toward the instructor, state motivation, and their communication satisfaction. That is, instructor humor seems to be relevant for learners' motivation. On the contrary, motivation was perceived as a student-owned state, and lack of motivation was rated as a teacher-owned problem: Negative teacher behavior (e.g., no sense of humor, loses temper) was perceived as central to college students' demotivation. And teachers' positive behavior (e.g., sense of humor) was perceived as central to motivation (Gorham & Christophel, 1992). Additionally, Saroglou and Scariot (2002) reported that students' negative humor styles (i.e., aggressive and self-defeating) were related to their low school motivation.

Affect and Appraisal Affect and cognitive appraisal are mechanisms that can potentially explain why humor is related to outcomes. Humor seems to attenuate affect. Advisors' humor was positively related to advisee affect in a graduate context, whereas verbal aggression was negatively related to affect (Wrench & Punyanunt-Carter, 2005). In an early experiment with tape recordings (hostile, non-hostile, non-humorous) by Dworkin and Efran (1967) using a sample of 50 male US students, humor significantly reduced reported feelings of anger and anxiety; and angry participants appreciated hostile humor more than non-angry participants. Experimental research (in advertising) found a beneficial effect of humor for reducing vulnerability to shame, especially for persons with higher fear of negative evaluation (Yoon, 2015).

There is one study showing that humor relates to appraisal. In a study of 81 Canadian students, Kuiper, McKenzie, and Belanger (1995) found that *cognitive appraisal* for a drawing task was related to sense of humor as measured by the Situational Humor Response Questionnaire (SHRQ), Coping Humor Scale (CHS), and the Sense of Humor Questionnaire (SHQ, metamessage sensitivity/MS, personal liking of humor/LH, but not emotional expressiveness/EE); that is, more humorous people *changed their perspective* more often for stressful (vs. pleasant) events. Higher humor levels were associated with *higher challenge/lower threat* appraisals, higher levels of *task motivation*, and more positive affect.

In sum, humor seems to be related to motivation, affect, and appraisal in learning contexts. However, the nature of the relationships has mostly been examined in correlational studies and the lab experiments are rather outdated. Moreover, studies about humor and learning in the work context with regard to psychological effects are lacking.

6.5 Mode of Presentation

Whether humor effects vary if used for verbal instruction, tests, textbooks, or online instruction is largely unknown. However, there is initial research about humor use in these different modes, though almost exclusively from school and not work contexts.

6.5.1 Humor in Textbooks and Tests

Humor in textbooks Humor in textbooks may be more enjoyable but did little for learning, memory, and interest and was even worse for the credibility of the author (Bryant et al., 1981; Klein, Bryant, & Zillmann, 1982). In 2014, Piaw published a study of effects of humor cartoons in a book about research methods and statistics (five volumes) in Malaysia. The majority of 379 readers (students) assessed the cartoons as making reading and learning fun, enhancing understanding and meaning, but around 5 percent responded negatively as humor reduced formality. In an experiment with 66 Malaysian school assistant principles, the book with cartoons was superior over the book with text-only in reading comprehension and reading motivation. Though humor in textbooks may be used to enhance their appeal, evidence for enhanced learning is still missing.

Humor in Tests Humor in tests is meant to enhance students' performance, their appreciation, and reduce anxiety.

Besides an experimental study by Berk and Nanda (2006), there is little evidence that students' actual *performance* benefits from humorous tests and exams. Berk and Nanda (2006) found that humor in test instructions (but not items) was significantly related to increased test performance of US students on constructed-response problem-solving items (but not on multiple-choice tests).

However, students seem to respond favorably to humorous items in tests (e.g., Deffenbacher, Deitz, & Hazaleus, 1981). McMorris, Boothroyd, and Pietrangelo (1997) recommended the use of appropriate and constructive humor on exams or tests in order to enhance enjoyment for students.

The attenuating effects of the use of humor on trait *anxiety* (e.g., as stated by Field, 2009) have not been unequivocally supported as some studies have provided support but others have presented contrary findings. That is, highly test-anxious students performed significantly better (Smith, Ascough, Ettinger, & Nelson, 1971) or worse (Deffenbacher et al., 1981) in the humor condition than those in the non-humorous condition. However, Berk and Nanda (2006) did not find humor to be a moderator of anxiety effects, but attributed this finding to the very low levels of pre-anxiety.

6.5.2 Online Instruction

Online humor seems to be beneficial for activation, engagement, and motivation of students, but little is known about learning success. However, students' perceptions of their skill development do not seem to differ between online and face-to-face courses (Fortune, Shifflett, & Sibley, 2006).

In a study of 43 students in an online class, those in the "humor-enhanced" condition were more *active* (e.g., posting) as compared with those in the non-humorous condition (Shatz & LoSchiavo, 2006). Likewise, in an experiment with 266 US students over an entire semester course, the students whose instructors' used humor via a course-based social network had higher *engagement* in this network (if students spend a high amount of time there) as compared to the control group with non-humorous instructors (Imlawi, Gregg, & Karimi, 2015). Also, students' network engagement was associated with higher students' motivation to learn and satisfaction with learning.

On the one hand, online students (Generations X and Y) are tech-savvy and may expect more entertainment in classes. On the other hand, online instructors found that it takes extra planning and effort to make humor happen in online classes (Taylor, Zeng, Bell, & Eskey, 2010). Special caution is indicated as written jokes cannot be revoked, and thus offensive topics (e.g., religion, race, gender, age, or bodily functions) should be avoided (Krovitz, 2007; cf. Taylor et al., 2010). However, the avoidance of offensive topics is an important rule to follow in offline settings, too.

6.6 Humor in Learning/Instruction in Work Contexts

Up to this point, all studies that have been cited were conducted in non-work contexts (irrespective of the fact that schools are teachers' workplaces). Though several aspects of humor in instruction may easily be transferred to work contexts (e.g., immediacy, attention, and creativity), empirical evidence is needed.

Two cross-sectional self-report studies in the work context of schools related humor to employees' psychological and cognitive outcomes. Principals' humor style was associated with teachers' work *motivation* (Recepoğlu, Kilinç, & Çepni, 2011), and using humor in the learning content of nursing courses promoted learners' critical thinking and emotional intelligence, according to qualitative interviews with teachers (Chabeli, 2008). However, both studies had methodological shortcomings and a very limited focus and thus deserve a more sophisticated replication.

A rather distal study related to the work context (though maybe to speeches by top management) was conducted by Greatbatch and Clark (2003): Gurus used verbal and nonverbal humor practices in their lectures to project clear message-completion points, to signal their humorous intent, to "invite" audience laughter, and to manipulate the relations between their use of humor and their core ideas and visions. That said, evidence for the effects of humor in learning and training or effects of humorous trainings in the work context is missing, thus being "unworked fields" in need of future research. Likewise, humor in work-related print products (e.g., brochures, guidelines) may enhance attention, but besides the higher appeal of (information/instructional) material, the beneficial function of humor for retention or even compliance needs to be tested.

6.7 Conclusions

The following statement has yet to find unequivocal support: "Humor appropriately used has the potential to humanize, illustrate, defuse, encourage, reduce anxiety, and keep people thinking" (Torok et al., 2004, p. 14). Also, with regard to Field's (2009) conclusion that humor can make students love statistics and that it can reduce anxiety but should be topic related, only the topic-related part has been empirically supported.

Though the use of humor for learning and instruction in the work context seems promising, its mechanisms or effects have yet to be measured. The benefits seem to stem from the positive side of humor styles, and the drawbacks from the negative side, including offensive humor. Rather than presenting ultimate knowledge, the findings presented in this chapter serve as the basis for future research in the work context.

6.7.1 Future Research

There is little research on the use of humor in learning/teaching or training, it is dated, and it has not fully explored the influences of different forms of humor, the placement of humor, and how well humor should be aligned with the concepts being taught. Also, the impact of student-initiated joking and related students' agency on classroom interactions (Davies, 2015) is an interesting field for future research in instruction and training contexts. The propositions on the beneficial functions of humor in instruction have found mixed support in studies that have primarily explored student samples as very few studies have been conducted in the work context. For instance, the role of humor in instructing employees with external or in-house trainers might be a worthwhile area of research. That said, virtually all aspects of the use of humor for training purposes are in urgent need of research applying sophisticated methods, including different sources and the work context. Additionally, methods from other disciplines may be transferred to psychological humor research (e.g., communications analyses, Reddington & Waring, 2015).

Accordingly, the following important research questions in this area are very broad and far from exhaustive:

1. Which previous findings are replicable in learning and training in work contexts?
2. What are the mechanisms for the effects of humor in learning and training in work contexts?
3. What are the boundary conditions for the consequences of humor; that is, under what circumstances are certain forms of humor effective?

6.7.2 Recommendations for Practice

Generally, humor that is judged as always *appropriate* (e.g., affiliative, self-enhancing) or *appropriate depending on the context* (e.g., self-disparaging, unplanned humor, jokes) should be preferred over inappropriate types (e.g., aggressive, offensive humor) in the classroom (Banas et al., 2011). Also, sexual themes should be avoided (e.g., Field, 2009). Likewise, ridiculing coworkers or subordinates may serve the short-term goal of enforcing norms or correcting behavior (e.g., Bryant et al., 1983), but has negative long-term effects on climate (see Janes & Olson, 2000, for classrooms).

Based on students' perception of appropriate humor in the classroom (Weaver & Cotrell, 2001), several techniques for developing appropriate humor for learning and instruction in the work context may be inferred but need to be tested (e.g., smile; use humorous stories; encourage a give-and-take climate). However, in order to avoid excessive humor, the techniques should be chosen adequately and sparsely. Similarly, Torok et al. (2004) adopted Provine's (2000) recommendations for increasing humor in the classroom, that is, increase interpersonal contact through face-to-face contact, create a casual and safe atmosphere, adopt a laugh-ready attitude, provide humorous materials, and remove social inhibitions. Aside from the removal of social inhibitions, these aspects are well-aligned with work contexts. For instance, humor may enhance the appeal of safety instructions by fostering positive affect and attention. Also, humor may be used to maintain a safe space to communicate across differences by challenging ill-informed or intolerant statements (Rocke, 2015).

Recommendations for further reading:

Banas, J. A., Dunbar, N., Rodriguez, D., & Liu, S.-J. (2011). A review of humor in educational settings: Four decades of research. *Communication Education, 60*(1), 115–144. doi:10.1080/03634523.2010.496867.

Lei, S. A., Cohen, J. L., & Russler, K. M. (2010). Humor on learning in the college classroom: Evaluating benefits and drawbacks from instructors' perspectives. *Journal of Instructional Psychology, 37*(4), 326–333.

Martin, R. A. (2007). *The psychology of humor: An integrative approach*. London: Elsevier Academic Press.

Neuliep, J. W. (1991). An examination of the content of high school teachers' humor in the classroom and the development of an inductively derived taxonomy of classroom humor. *Communication Education, 40,* 343–355.

References

Allen, L. (2014). Don't forget, thursday is test[icle] time! *Sex Education, 14*(4), 387–399. doi:10.1080/14681811.2014.918539.

Banas, J. A., Dunbar, N., Rodriguez, D., & Liu, S.-J. (2011). A review of humor in educational settings: Four decades of research. *Communication Education, 60*(1), 115–144. doi:10.1080/03634523.2010.496867.

Belanger, H. G., Kirkpatrick, L. A., & Derks, P. (1998). The effects of humor on verbal and imaginal problem solving. *Humor - International Journal of Humor Research, 11*(1), 21–31.

Berk, R. A. (1998). *Professors are from Mars, students are from Snickers: How to write and deliver humor in the classroom and in professional presentations*. Madison, WI: Magna Publications.

Berk, R. A., & Nanda, J. (2006). A randomized trial of humor effects on test anxiety and test performance. *Humor—International Journal of Humor Research, 19*(4), 425–454. doi:10.1515/HUMOR.2006.021.

Bolkan, S., & Goodboy, A. K. (2015). Exploratory theoretical tests of the instructor humor–student learning link. *Communication Education, 64*(1), 45–64. doi:10.1080/03634523.2014.978793.

Bressler, E. R., & Balshine, S. (2006). The influence of humor on desirability. *Evolution and Human Behavior, 27*(1), 29–39. doi:10.1016/j.evolhumbehav.2005.06.002.

Bryant, J., Brown, D., Parks, S. L., & Zillmann, D. (1983). Children's imitation of a ridiculed model. *Human Communication Research, 10*(2), 243–255. doi:10.1111/j.1468-2958.1983.tb00013.x.

Bryant, J., Brown, D., Silberberg, A. R., & Elliott, S. M. (1981). Effects of humorous illustrations in college textbooks. *Human Communication Research, 8*(1), 43–57.

Bryant, J., Comisky, P. W., Crane, J. S., & Zillmann, D. (1980). Relationship between college teachers' use of humor in the classroom and students' evaluations of their teachers. *Journal of Educational Psychology, 72*(4), 511.

Carlson, K. A. (2011). The impact of humor on memory: Is the humor effect about humor? *Humor - International Journal of Humor Research, 24*(1). doi:10.1515/humr.2011.002.

Chabeli, M. (2008). Humor: A pedagogical tool to promote learning. *Curationis, 31*(3), 51–59.

Cheng, D., & Wang, L. (2014). Examining the energizing effects of humor: The influence of humor on persistence behavior. *Journal of Business and Psychology*. doi:10.1007/s10869-014-9396-z.

Christophel, D. M. (1990). The relationships among teacher immediacy behaviors, student motivation, and learning. *Communication Education, 39,* 323–340.

Davies, C. E. (2015). Humor in intercultural interaction as both content and process in the classroom. *Humor - International Journal of Humor Research, 28*(3), 375–395. doi:10.1515/humor-2015-0065.

Deffenbacher, J. L., Deitz, S. R., & Hazaleus, S. L. (1981). Effects of humor and test anxiety on performance, worry, and emotionality in naturally occurring exams. *Cognitive Therapy and Research, 5*(2), 225–228.

Dworkin, E. S., & Efran, J. S. (1967). The angered: Their susceptibility to varieties of humor. *Journal of Personality and Social Psychology, 6*(2), 233–236.

Field, A. (2009). Can humour make students love statistics? *Humor and Statistics, 22*(3), 210–213.

Filipowicz, A. (2006). From positive affect to creativity: The surprising role of suprise. *Creativity Research Journal, 18*(2), 141–152.

Fortune, M. F., Shifflett, B., & Sibley, R. E. (2006). A comparison of online (high tech) and traditional (high touch) learning in business communication courses in Silicon Valley. *Journal of Education for Business, 81*(4), 210–214. doi:10.3200/JOEB.81.4.210-214.

Frymier, A. B. (1994). A model of immediacy in the classroom. *Communication Quarterly, 42*(2), 133–144.

Frymier, A. B., Wanzer, M. B., & Wojtaszczyk, A. M. (2008). Assessing students' perceptions of inappropriate and appropriate teacher humor. *Communication Education, 57*(2), 266–288. doi:10.1080/03634520701687183.

Goodboy, A. K., Booth-Butterfield, M., Bolkan, S., & Griffin, D. J. (2015). The role of instructor humor and students' educational orientations in student learning, extra effort, participation, and out-of-class communication. *Communication Quarterly, 63*(1), 44–61. doi:10.1080/01463373.2014.965840.

Gorham, J., & Christophel, D. M. (1992). Students' perceptions of teacher behaviors as motivating and demotivating factors in college classes. *Communication Quarterly, 40*(3), 239–252.

Greatbatch, D., & Clark, T. (2003). Displaying group cohesiveness: Humour and laughter in the public lectures of management gurus. *Human Relations, 56*(12), 1515–1544. doi:10.1177/00187267035612004.

Hampes, W. P. (2010). The relation between humor styles and empathy. *Europe's Journal of Psychology, 6*(3), 34–45.

Hauck, W. E., & Thomas, J. W. (1972). The relationship of humor to intelligence, creativity, and intentional and incidental learning. *The Journal of Experimental Education, 40*(4), 52–55.

Imlawi, J., Gregg, D., & Karimi, J. (2015). Student engagement in course-based social networks: The impact of instructor credibility and use of communication. *Computers & Education, 88,* 84–96. doi:10.1016/j.compedu.2015.04.015.

Isen, A. M., Daubman, K. A., & Nowicki, G. P. (1987). Positive affect facilitates creative problem solving. *Journal of Personality and Social Psychology, 52*(6), 1122.

Janes, L. M., & Olson, J. M. (2000). Jeer pressure: The behavioral effects of observing ridicule of others. *Personality and Social Psychology Bulletin, 26*(4), 474–485. doi:10.1177/0146167200266006.

Kaplan, R. M., & Pascoe, G. C. (1977). Humorous lectures and humorous examples: Some effects upon comprehension and retention. *Journal of Educational Psychology, 69*(1), 61.

Klein, D. M., Bryant, J., & Zillmann, D. (1982). Relationship between humor in introductory textbooks and student's evaluations of the texts' appeal and effectiveness. *Psychological Reports, 50*(1), 235–241. doi:10.2466/pr0.1982.50.1.235.

Krovitz, G. (2007, May 9). Using humor in online classes. *Educator's Voice*, *8*(2), 1–2.

Kuiper, N. A., McKenzie, S. D., & Belanger, K. A. (1995). Cognitive appraisals and individual differences in sense of humor: Motivational and affective implications. *Personality and Individual Differences, 19*(3), 359–372.

Lei, S. A., Cohen, J. L., & Russler, K. M. (2010). Humor on learning in the college classroom: Evaluating benefits and drawbacks from instructors' perspectives. *Journal of Instructional Psychology, 37*(4), 326–333.

Martin, R. A. (2007). *The psychology of humor: An integrative approach*. London: Elsevier Academic Press.

McMorris, R. F., Boothroyd, R. A., & Pietrangelo, D. J. (1997). Humor in educational testing: A review and discussion. *Applied Measurement in Education, 10*(3), 269–297. doi:10.1207/s15324818ame1003_5.

Myers, S. A., Goodboy, A. K., & Members of COMM 600. (2014). College student learning, motivation, and satisfaction as a function of effective instructor communication behaviors. *Southern Communication Journal, 79*(1), 14–26.

Neuliep, J. W. (1991). An examination of the content of high school teachers' humor in the classroom and the development of an inductively derived taxonomy of classroom humor. *Communication Education, 40,* 343–355.

Nijstad, B. A., De Dreu, C. K. W., Rietzschel, E. F., & Baas, M. (2010). The dual pathway to creativity model: Creative ideation as a function of flexibility and persistence. *European Review of Social Psychology, 21,* 34–77. doi:10.1080/10463281003765323.

Piaw, C. Y. (2014). The effects of humor cartoons in a series of bestselling academic books. *Humor - International Journal of Humor Research, 27*(3), 499–520. doi:10.1515/humor-2014-0069.

Provine, R. (2000). *Laughter: A scientific investigation*. New York: Viking Adult.

Recepoğlu, E., Kilinç, A. Ç., & Çepni, O. (2011). Examining teachers' motivation level according to school principals' humor styles. *Educational Research and Reviews, 6*(17), 928–934.

Reddington, E., & Waring, H. Z. (2015). Understanding the sequential resources for doing humor in the language classroom. *Humor - International Journal of Humor Research, 28*(1), 1–23. doi:10.1515/humor-2014-0144.

Rocke, C. (2015). The use of humor to help bridge cultural divides: An exploration of a workplace cultural awareness workshop. *Social Work with Groups, 38,* 152–169. doi:10.1080/01609513.2014.968944.

Saroglou, V., & Scariot, C. (2002). Humor Styles Questionnaire: Personality and educational correlates in Belgian high school and college students. *European Journal of Personality, 16*(1), 43–54. doi:10.1002/per.430.

Scheel, T., Bachmann, S., Gerdenitsch, C., & Korunka, C. (2015). *The humor-creativity pathway: Experimenting with affect.* Poster presentation at the 17th European Congress on Work and Organizational Psychology [EAWOP] (Oslo/Norway, 20.–23.05.2015).

Schmidt, S. R. (1994). Effect of humor on sentence memory. *Journal of Experimental Psychology, 20*(4), 953–967.

Schmidt, S. R. (2002). The humour effect: Differential processing and privileged retrieval. *Memory, 10*(2), 127–138.

Schmidt, S. R., & Williams, A. R. (2001). Memory for humorous cartoons. *Memory & Cognition, 29*(2), 305–311.

Shatz, M. A., & LoSchiavo, F. M. (2006). Bringing life to online instruction with humor. *Radical Pedagogy, 8*(2). Retrieved from http://www.radicalpedagogy.org/radicalpedagogy/Bringing_Life_to_Online_Instruction_with_Humor.html.

Smith, R. E., Ascough, J. C., Ettinger, R. F., & Nelson, D. A. (1971). Humor, anxiety, and task performance. *Journal of Personality and Social Psychology, 19*(2), 243–246.

Stuart, W. D., & Rosenfeld, L. B. (1994). Student perception of teacher humor and classroom climate. *Communication Research Reports, 11*(1), 87–97.

Suzuki, H., & Heath, L. (2014). Impacts of humor and relevance on the remembering of lecture details. *Humor—International Journal of Humor Research, 27*(1), 87–101. doi:10.1515/humor-2013-0051.

Taylor, C., Zeng, H., Bell, S., & Eskey, M. (2010). Examining the do's and don'ts of using humor in the online classroom. In *TCC Worldwide Online Conference* (Vol. 2010, pp. 31–46). Retrieved from http://www.editlib.org/p/43757/.

Torok, S. E., McMorris, R. F., & Lin, W.-C. (2004). Is humor an appreciated teaching tool? *College Teaching, 52*(1), 14–20.

Wanzer, M. B., & Frymier, A. B. (1999). The relationship between student perceptions of instructor humor and students' reports of learning. *Communication Education, 48,* 48–62.

Wanzer, M. B., Frymier, A. B., & Irwin, J. (2010). An explanation of the relationship between instructor humor and student learning: Instructional humor processing theory. *Communication Education, 59*(1), 1–18. doi:10.1080/03634520903367238.

Wanzer, M. B., Frymier, A. B., Wojtaszczyk, A. M., & Smith, T. (2006). Appropriate and inappropriate uses of humor by teachers. *Communication Education, 55*(2), 178–196. doi:10.1080/03634520600566132.

Weaver, R. L., & Cotrell, H. W. (2001). Ten specific techniques for developing humor in the classroom. *Education, 108*(2), 167–179.

Wrench, J. S., & Punyanunt-Carter, N. M. (2005). Advisor–advisee communication two: The influence of verbal aggression and humor assessment on advisee perceptions of advisor credibility and affective learning. *Communication Research Reports, 22*(4), 303–313. doi:10.1080/000368105000317599.

Yoon, H. (2015). Humor effects in shame-inducing health issue advertising: The moderating effects of fear of negative evaluation. *Journal of Advertising, 44*(2), 126–139.

Zillmann, D., Williams, B. R., Bryant, J., Boynton, K. R., & Wolf, M. A. (1980). Acquisition of information from educational television programs as a function of differently paced humorous inserts. *Journal of Educational Psychology, 72*(2), 170–180.

Ziv, A. (1976). Faciliating effects of humor on creativity. *Journal of Educational Psychology, 68*(3), 318–322.

Ziv, A. (1988). Teaching and learning with humor: Experiment and replication. *Journal of Experimental Education, 57*(1), 5–11.

Chapter 7
Humor in Health: How to Stay Healthy and Happy with Humor

Tabea Scheel

Abstract The saying "laughter is the best medicine" is explored in this chapter on humor and health. Though a large proportion of humor and health research is conducted in general contexts, empirical findings regarding the work context are increasing. Employees' and supervisors' affiliative and self-enhancing humor styles are found to be related to employees' mental health and work-related outcomes (e.g., performance, job satisfaction). Aggressive humor seems significant for outcomes in the work context, and self-defeating humor seems more relevant in general contexts of humor where it has been associated with (less) well-being, anxiety/stress, and depression. However, the role of cultural determination is largely unknown. Among the hypotheses about the mechanisms that link humor with health are the ideas that humor buffers the consequences of stressful events and facilitates social relationships by enhancing social support. Several physiological mechanisms can explain the link between humor and physical health. Given that humor and health are related, future research should analyze whether improved mental health can explain the link between humor and performance.

Keywords Mental health · Physiological health · Stress-buffering hypothesis · Social facilitation · Health at work · Well-being · Performance · Withdrawal

7.1 Introduction

The largest amount of humor research is conducted in the field of health—however, this may be less true in work contexts. Humor is said to be a resource or coping style that can protect against stress (e.g., Martin & Lefcourt, 1983), or it might be a demand itself (e.g., negative styles), and it affects mental as well as physical health.

A meta-analysis by Mesmer-Magnus, Glew, and Viswesvaran (2012) showed that employee humor is positively related to employee's mental health as well as

The original version of this chapter was revised: See the "Chapter Note" section at the end of this chapter for details. The erratum to this chapter is available at https://doi.org/10.1007/978-3-319-65691-5_9

T. Scheel and C. Gockel, *Humor at Work in Teams, Leadership, Negotiations, Learning and Health*, SpringerBriefs in Psychology,
DOI 10.1007/978-3-319-65691-5_7

work-related outcomes (i.e., performance). Although negative humor is often found to be detrimental to mental health, its specific role(s) are less clear. It seems that the "humor profile," that is, the individual composition of humor styles, is important. For instance, in one of our own cross-sectional studies in German, Swiss, and Belgian samples, positive humor showed the potential to reduce the detrimental relations between negative humor and several indicators of well-being (e.g., irritation, sleep, etc.; Gockel, Scheel, & Van de Ven, in prep.).

Whereas humors' general relationships with mental and physical health are described in detail by Martin (2001, 2004, 2007), our focus is on how humor is associated with mental health, well-being, and related attitudes (e.g., job satisfaction, commitment) in the work context. However, we will also refer to findings on humor in general, in order to encourage transfer to and replication in work contexts.

This chapter combines findings on mental health constructs and the related affective and cognitive outcomes that are relevant in the workplace, and it will highlight gaps in research. For instance, newer promising concepts such as job crafting (Tims, Bakker, & Derks, 2012) or passion for work (Forest, Mageau, Sarrazin, & Morin, 2011) can and should be integrated into humor research. General findings on humor and mental health will be mentioned before turning to the work context.

7.2 Humor and Mental Health

Humor is said to be favorable for mental health as it buffers the effects of stressful situations by changing perspectives and fostering distance from a problem. As mechanisms, we discuss how humor may buffer stress (e.g., via affect) as well as the social facilitation by humor. Social facilitation with regard to humor is meant in the literal sense, that is, humor may facilitate social relationships. (The term is also known in group research, with persons showing better performance in easy tasks in the presence of others. However, this phenomenon is not meant in this chapter.)

Findings with nonworking populations (mostly students) have mainly supported the humor-health link between (1) humor and well-being/perceived health, (2) humor and anxiety/stress, and (3) humor and depression. For the work context, Mesmer-Magnus et al. (2012) likewise concluded that a positive sense of humor (1) is associated with good physical and mental health, (2) buffers the negative effects of workplace stress on mental health, and (3) promotes effective functioning at work.

(Positive) humor attenuates stressful situations by fostering relaxation and reducing tension. Also, it allows a beneficial reinterpretation of stressful events and fosters a more optimistic attitude toward those situations (e.g., Martin, Puhlik-Doris, Larsen, Gray, & Weir, 2003). Also, humor facilitates social relationships by "lubricating" them (Martineau, 1972). The effects of humor on health have been explained by more effective biological responses (e.g., tension relief) due to enhanced quality of social support networks, including the availability of social support when needed in stressful times. These mechanisms (i.e., stress buffering and social facilitation) may hold for general as well as work contexts. Most findings from general contexts deserve replication in/adaptations for the work context. So far, most studies on humor and mental health at work involve self-reports and are correlational in nature. The most informative piece of work in this regard is the meta-analysis by Mesmer-Magnus et al. (2012) encompassing positive humor (styles). Based on 49 cross-sectional studies conducted in the work context (including studies up to and including the year 2008), Mesmer-Magnus et al. (2012) reported significantly positive relationships of employees' as well as supervisors' positive humor styles (i.e., affiliative, self-enhancing, coping collapsed) with employees' self-ratings of well-being and performance indicators. There is far less research including maladaptive humor like the negative humor styles. In the following section, general and work-related research about humor and mental health (including findings on negative humor) is presented.

7.2.1 Humor and Well-Being, Anxiety, and Depression

Well-being and perceived health Many cross-sectional, self-report studies in different cultures have found evidence for the relationship between humor and health: Scores in the SHQ (Sense of Humor Questionnaire) were found to be positively related to overall *health satisfaction* (Svebak, Martin, & Holmen, 2004), and self-enhancing humor (HSQ) correlated positively with *perceived health* (Kazarian & Martin, 2004; 2006) and *well-being* (Maiolino & Kuiper, 2014). Both positive humor styles (HSQ) were positively related to *well-being* (Dyck & Holtzman, 2013; Kazarian & Martin, 2004, 2006; Leist & Müller, 2012; Martin et al., 2003). Affiliative, self-enhancing, and coping humor are positively related to *mental health* (assessed by the Symptoms Checklist 90/SLC-90, reversed; Chen & Martin, 2007). Among the sense of humor facets, humor appreciation was most relevant (versus humor production/social uses, coping humor, and attitude toward humor) for *emotional well-being*, *personal development*, and the *effective functioning* of students (Herzog & Strevey, 2008).

Among the negative styles, self-defeating humor was negatively related to *well-being* and *mental health* (Dyck & Holtzman, 2013; Maiolino & Kuiper, 2014; Martin et al., 2003), whereas aggressive humor was not (Martin et al., 2003). However, Chen and Martin (2007) found that both negative styles were negatively related to *mental health.* The affiliative humor style was positively, and both negative humor styles were negatively related to *life satisfaction*, whereas the self-enhancing style was unrelated in the meta-analysis by Schneider (2015). Also, Cheung and Yue (2012) found only the affiliative of all styles positively related to life satisfaction.

However, challenging the association between humor and well-being on the basis of two cross-sectional self-report studies, Ruch and Heintz (2014) found that humor styles offered only little incremental validity in predicting psychological well-being once personality factors (the Big Five) were accounted for. Tests in the work context are owed.

Well-being and perceived health in work contexts: Positive employee humor was positively related to self-reported *health* (small effect; Mesmer-Magnus et al., 2012). In one of the few longitudinal studies over a time lag of three years with 34 Finnish police officers, sense of humor (self- and peer-rating) failed to predict *workplace well-being* (Kerkkänen, Kuiper, & Martin, 2004). However, the sample was very small.

Anxiety and stress The positive humor styles have been found to be related to lower trait *anxiety*, and the self-defeating style was related to higher trait *anxiety*, whereas the aggressive style was unrelated (Kuiper, Grimshaw, Leite, & Kirsh, 2004; Martin et al., 2003). Sense of humor (assessed by the Multidimensional Sense of Humor Scale/MSHS) was related to *worry*; more specifically, humor production was related to lower, and coping with humor was related to higher worry (Kelly, 2002). Sense of humor components were associated with *less fear* of death or serious disease, less negative bodily preoccupation, and less concern about pain, but the amount of humor was not correlated with different health habits (Kuiper & Nicholl, 2004).

In addition to these cross-sectional self-report studies, three experiments with students' state humor showed mixed results. Laughter (as a humor response) was not as effective as relaxation training in reducing physiological measures of *stress* but reduced *anxiety* to a comparable degree as relaxation (White & Winzelberg, 1992). However, watching a humorous video while jogging reduced psychological *distress* and enhanced positive *well-being* similarly to watching a non-humorous video (Szabo, 2003), though humor was also able to lower *anxiety* more than exercise (Szabo, 2003). But writing a narrative reduced *stress* responses regardless of humorous or non-humorous instructional videos; also, being more *successful* at writing decreased *mood disturbance* and *anxiety* (Lehmann, Burke, Martin, Sultan, & Czech, 2001).

Overall, (positive) humor may serve to reduce anxiety, though it may not always be superior to other means to this end (e.g., physical exercise).

Stress, coping, and anxiety in the work context: Positive employee humor was also negatively related to self-reported *stress*, and positively related to *coping effectiveness* (medium effects; Mesmer-Magnus et al., 2012). In a cross-sectional study of 349 US employees, the affiliative (but not the self-enhancing) humor style was related to lower *stress* (Romero & Arendt, 2011). In addition, the negative styles were included in this study: Whereas the self-defeating style was not related to stress, the aggressive style was related to higher stress. These findings indicate that it is essential to distinguish between types of humor in order to disentangle the relationships between humor and health. One of three *humorous coping* styles (i.e., antecedent-focused, but not generic or response-focused) was associated with lower negative *job-related affect* in a cross-sectional study of 2,094 employees (Doosje, De Goede, Van Doornen, & Van de Schoot, 2011). However, in a longitudinal study with 1,857 US army soldiers, humor (i.e., joking and making fun of the situation) showed only weak and inconsistent correlations with mental health symptoms (i.e., anxiety and depression; Britt, Crane, Hodson, & Adler, 2015).

As mentioned in Chap. 4, employees' perceived positive supervisor humor was related to lower perceived stress last month (Kim, Lee, & Wong, 2015), and aggressive humor was positively associated with stress and strain (Huo, Lam, & Chen, 2012; Kim et al., 2015).

In summary, positive humor is associated with lower stress, while aggressive humor seems to be related to higher stress in the work context. Self-defeating humor has—in contrast to general contexts—a weaker association with stress.

Depression In cross-sectional self-report studies, mostly involving students, adaptive (i.e., coping, affiliative, self-enhancing, skilled) humor was found to be related to lower *depression,* and maladaptive, self-focused (e.g., self-defeating, belabored) humor was associated with greater depression (Kuiper et al., 2004; also Kuiper & McHale, 2009), whereas other-focused humor (i.e., aggressive, rude) was unrelated to depression. The same relations with humor styles were found for *depression, depressive symptoms*, and *dysphoria* (Frewen, Brinker, Martin, & Dozois, 2008; Hugelshofer, Kwon, Reff, & Olson, 2006; Martin et al., 2003). However, in her meta-analysis with 37 cross-sectional studies (up to 2015; Schneider, 2015), with mixed samples (students amongst others), both positive humor styles were related to lower depressiveness, and both negative styles were related to higher depressiveness. Also, hinting at cross-cultural differences, humor styles were unrelated to depression in Armenian-Lebanese adults (Kazarian & Martin, 2006).

Other positive humor concepts support the picture: Sense of humor (assessed by the Situational Humor Response Questionnaire/SHRQ, Sense of Humor Questionnaire/SHQ) was linked to fewer *depressive symptoms* (Kuiper & Borowicz-Sibenik, 2005). Using humor to cope (CHS) with emotional difficulties was negatively related to *depression* (Freiheit, Overholser, & Lehnert, 1998). Humor (CHS, humor appreciation, humor creativity) was associated with lower *depression* in women (Overholser, 1992).

Several associations between humor and vulnerability factors for depression hint at a mediating role of humor. The self-defeating style (HSQ) was associated with *sociotropy* (e.g., dependency), and aggressive humor was associated with the *need for control* (an autonomy dimension), outcomes that both promote depression (Frewen et al., 2008). *Positive self-evaluative standards* were related to more use of affiliative humor, which in turn was related to lower depression (Kuiper & McHale, 2009); *negative self-evaluative standards* were associated with more self-defeating humor, which was related to higher depression. Self-enhancing and self-defeating humor styles mediated the relationship between *early maladaptive schemas* (self-schemas) and depressed mood (Dozois, Martin, & Bieling, 2009).

Thus, positive and adaptive humor is associated with lower depression in general contexts, while self-defeating humor is related to more depression, and aggressive humor seems less relevant.

Burnout and depression in the work context: In the work context, burnout as a construct is more relevant than depression. Positive employee humor was negatively related to *burnout*, its facets emotional exhaustion as well as depersonalization, and was positively related to personal accomplishment (all small effects;

Mesmer-Magnus et al., 2012). Other self-report studies published after 2008 (i.e., not included in the meta-analyses) support the humor-burnout link: Both positive styles were related to lower *burnout* in a cross-sectional study of 1,192 Belgian employees (mostly white collar, full-time, permanent employees; Van den Broeck, Vander Elst, Dikkers, De Lange, & De Witte, 2012). As one of the very few diary studies, a two-week study of 57 Dutch employees in the automotive sector showed that employees were more *emotionally exhausted* on days when they expressed maladaptive humor (Guenter, Schreurs, Van Emmerik, Gijsbers, & Van Iterson, 2013). Though this was a novel, multilevel approach in the field of humor, unfortunately, the two positive styles (affiliative, self-enhanced) and the two negative styles (aggressive, self-defeating) of the Humor Styles Questionnaire (HSQ) were combined in an adaptation (with eight items each). Thus, the role of single styles cannot be further analyzed. In a cross-sectional study of 133 US psychotherapists, Malinowski (2013) found that self-defeating humor related to emotional exhaustion and depersonalization, whereas self-enhancing humor related to personal accomplishment. In another cross-sectional study of 951 Australian occupational therapists, Poulsen et al. (2014) showed that a low frequency of having a "belly laugh" was associated with burnout. However, no causal inferences can be drawn. Thus, positive humor is related to lower—and the negative styles to more—burnout, especially with regard to the emotional exhaustion facet. However, in the longitudinal study by Britt et al. (2015), humor showed only weak and inconsistent correlations with mental health symptoms, which included depression.

In sum, positive and adaptive humor seems to be generally related to better mental health, less anxiety, stress, depression, and burnout, though effects are only small to medium. Self-defeating humor shows the opposite relation with well-being, and thus, is maladaptive especially in general contexts. Aggressive humor, in turn, seems less relevant for well-being in general contexts but in work contexts, where it is related with lower well-being.

As most studies are of North-American origin, the nonsignificant association of any humor styles with depression in the Lebanese context is of special interest. Certainly, cultural conditions have to be considered in future research. Also, the rare longitudinal research only produces weak or nonsignificant associations in contrast to correlational designs. Thus, whether humor is only a short-term phenomenon for well-being needs to be clarified.

7.2.2 Humor and Work-Related Outcomes

Though unusual at first glance in a chapter about health, the relationship between humor and broader work-relevant variables will be discussed. Employee well-being and productivity are closely interwoven. Thus, we present empirical findings regarding humor and two main aspects in work and organizational psychology, that is, performance (performance, work engagement) and retention (withdrawal, job satisfaction), which may indirectly relate to the mental well-being of employees.

Performance Positive employee (and perceived positive supervisor) humor were related to higher *employee work performance* (small to medium effects; Mesmer-Magnus et al., 2012). For example, peer-rated humor was positively related to the performance under stress (final course grades) of 159 army soldiers, especially active (self-produced) humor (Bizi, Keinan, & Beit-Hallahmi, 1988). Additionally, in the study of supervisor-subordinate dyads by Kim et al. (2015) mentioned above, employees' perceived self-enhancing humor of supervisors (but not affiliative, aggressive and self-defeating) was positively related to supervisors' rating of this employees' job performance.

Work engagement Two studies supported the link between positive humor and higher work engagement (Van den Broeck et al., 2012; Guenter et al., 2013). Both positive styles were related to higher work engagement in a study with Belgian employees (Van den Broeck et al., 2012). An interaction between humor and job characteristics was found: Low role conflict and social support (but not workload) interacted with positive humor in predicting higher work engagement (Van den Broeck et al., 2012). In the Dutch diary study by Guenter et al. (2013), employees were more engaged on days when they expressed adaptive humor, but they were not less engaged on days when they expressed maladaptive humor (Guenter et al., 2013). The above-mentioned study of 951 Australian therapists by Poulsen et al. (2014) about laughter and burnout also revealed that high levels of work engagement were reported by the rapists with a higher frequency of having a "belly laugh".

Overall, positive and adaptive humor seem to be positively linked to performance and work engagement, while negative humor seems rather unrelated and is less frequently investigated.

Withdrawal Positive employee and perceived positive supervisor humor were likewise related to lower *work withdrawal* (small, respectively, medium effect; Mesmer-Magnus et al., 2012). Published after the meta-analysis and only in Korean, a cross-sectional self-report study of 275 Korean nurses from six hospitals found that humor (Sense of Humor Questionnaire/SHQ-6) was indirectly (via job satisfaction) related to *intentions to quit* (Kim, 2013). Three other cross-sectional self-report studies showed that humor/fun at work was related to withdrawal or intention to stay: When the women (but not men) of 317 Australian employees perceived high levels of tolerance for workplace incivility (aggressive humor), they decreased their work withdrawal behavior (Loi, Loh, & Hine, 2013). Coworker socializing and manager support for fun were negatively related to turnover among 296 US servers, mediated by attachment (Tews, Michel, & Allen, 2014), whereas fun at work was indirectly related to less turnover via attachment. In a study of 184 Brazilian interns by Sobral and Islam (2015), supervisors' use of appropriate (i.e., positive) humor was—through satisfaction—related with higher intention to stay (i.e., willingness to accept permanent employment). As a counterpart to withdrawal, Romero and Arendt (2011) reported that both positive humor styles were associated with higher *organizational commitment* and that aggressive (but not self-defeating) humor was negatively associated with organizational commitment in a sample of 349 US employees. Overall, there seems to be a tendency for favorable relationships between positive humor and (lower) withdrawal. Attachment and job satisfaction seem to mediate this relationship.

Job Satisfaction Positive employee humor was related to higher *job satisfaction*, but the 90% Confidence Interval included zero. Positive supervisor humor was found to be positively related to employee *job satisfaction* (medium effect; Mesmer-Magnus et al., 2012). The meta-analysis included two cross-sectional employee self-report studies on humor orientation (HO) and *job satisfaction*: The humor orientation of 142 US nurses (Wanzer, Booth-Butterfield, & Booth-Butterfield, 2005) and the humor orientation of 186 students (Booth-Butterfield, Booth-Butterfield, & Wanzer, 2007) were associated with higher *self-perceived coping efficacy*, which in turn mediated the link between humor orientation and *job satisfaction*. Coping may be one of the mechanisms that can account for effects of humor in the work context, an idea that is in line with the stress-buffering hypothesis (see Sect. 7.3 for a discussion). Humor (Sense of Humor Questionnaire/SHQ-6) was significantly positively related to *job satisfaction*. In the above-mentioned study of Brazilian interns, supervisor's use of positive humor was associated with a higher level of intern satisfaction, whereas the use of negative humor was negatively related to satisfaction (Sobral & Islam, 2015). However, these cross-sectional studies treat humor as a predictor of satisfaction but do not explain causality—authors of a qualitative study of 75 US internship students concluded that humor was used as a *response* to workplace dissatisfaction (Garner, Chandler, & Wallace, 2015).

Especially positive and coping humor (including sense of humor) seems favorable for (less) withdrawal and higher job satisfaction. Self-defeating humor was seldomly assessed and of little relevance. Aggressive humor was maladaptive when expressed by supervisors.

Overall, experiences of humor can take many forms in the work context. For example, Van Wormer and Boes (1997) found five aspects of humor to be prevalent in emergency rooms, and these might also be relevant in other workplaces: tension-relieving nonsense, plays on words, sense of the preposterous and incongruous, gallows humor, and foolish jesting. The general impression of the studies presented here is that adaptive humor in employees (as well as in supervisors) is beneficial for employees' mental health and work-related outcomes, but maladaptive forms of humor seem to be detrimental. Self-defeating humor does not appear to have an impact, but aggressive humor seems to be related to outcomes in the work context, whereas, in general contexts of humor and well-being, anxiety/stress, and depression, it seems to be the opposite. However, the findings are not consistent, and the quality of most studies does not allow far-reaching conclusions to be drawn about causal relationships, generalizability, or the explicit differentiation between distinctive humor styles. Also, health needs to be tested as a mediator between humor and relevant work-related outcomes.

Both cross-sectional and self-report studies have indicated that relationships might not be straightforward; two potential explanations for the association between humor and well-being will be discussed in the next sections: the stress-buffering role of humor (Sect. 7.3) and humor as social facilitator (Sect. 7.4).

7.3 Humor and the Stress-Buffering Hypothesis

Among the most often discussed ideas about why humor should be related to better health is the hypothesis that humor buffers the detrimental consequences of stressful situations on mental health. The *positive emotional states* that accompany laughter and humor offer a possible explanation, as well as the *ability to cope more effectively* with stress due to more favorable cognitive appraisal and attributions (Martin, 2001). (For a comprehensive review of the psychological, behavioral, and biological mechanisms of the stress-health link, see Schneiderman, Ironson, & Siegel, 2005.) In this regard, two mechanisms have been discussed: (1) humor as a moderator between stressors and mental health through affect and coping, and (2) humor as an antecedent of several mediators of mental health.

7.3.1 Stress-Buffering Through Affect and Coping

Humor might buffer the detrimental effects of stress on mental health via affect and coping. In three studies of Canadian students, Martin and Lefcourt (1983) reported evidence for the stress-buffering role of humor for five out of six humor measures: The association between *life events* and *mood states* was moderated by scores in the Situational Humor Response Questionnaire (SHRQ), the Sense of Humor Questionnaire (SHQ—personal liking, but not meta-message sensitivity), and the CHS, the ability to produce humor (comedy routine, experiment), and the ability to create witty monologs while watching a stressful movie. One mechanism that they discussed is the ability to reduce negative affect or increase positive affect through humor. Experiments with states of humor supported this mechanism: Cann, Holt, and Calhoun (1999) found that an external humorous event could alter negative emotional responses to stressors, but sense of humor was also important: After observing a stress-arousing movie, brief exposure to a humorous videotape was the most effective strategy for both reducing *anxiety* and increasing *positive affect* relative to a waiting condition, while a non-humorous video only reduced anxiety. The meta-message sensitivity scale (ability to recognize humor in a situation) from the SHQ (Sense of Humor Questionnaire) was the most consistent predictor of anxiety and affect as compared with the CHS, SHQ, and MSHS (Multidimensional Sense of Humor Scale), but this meta-message sensitivity scale was the only nonsignificant scale in the study by Martin and Lefcourt (1983). Following *experimentally* induced *stress*, humor production led to lower negative affect, tension, and psychophysiological reactivity compared with the production of a serious narrative—regardless of a persons' level of trait-humor (Situational Humor Response Questionnaire/SHRQ; Newman & Stone, 1996). Thus, humor production may be an effective coping strategy even for persons who do not typically use humor to cope with stress. However, Lehmann et al. (2001; see Sect. 7.2.1) reported that writing a narrative is beneficial regardless of humor.

Martin, Kuiper, Olinger, and Dance (1993) summarized three studies that demonstrated the moderating effect of humor, that is, people who exhibit a lot of humor have less negative affect in response to adverse life circumstances: Greater humor levels were associated with a more positive self-concept (i.e., actual-ideal discrepancies, *self-esteem*, standards of self-evaluation; Kuiper & Martin, 1993); greater (coping) humor levels (CHS) in women were related to less *stress* and more positive and self-protective *cognitive appraisals* at event times (Kuiper, Martin, & Olinger, 1993); and—in a daily diary study—greater sense of humor facilitated greater positive affect in response to negative/positive life events and thus a more positive *orientation toward life* (Kuiper, Martin, & Dance, 1992). Thus, in addition to buffering the effects of stress by reducing negative affect, humor is also said to play an important role in enhancing the enjoyment of positive life experiences.

Also, *laughter*—as a reaction to humor—is seen as a buffer. Kuiper and Martin (1998) recorded the actual frequency of laughter of 80 participants for a 3-day period as well as *stressful life events* every evening and *positive* and *negative affect* in the mornings and evenings: A higher number of stressful life events was associated with greater negative affect for people who did not laugh frequently but unrelated for people who laughed more. (The same moderation regarding positive affect held only for males; thus, men who laughed frequently had higher positive affect after stressful life events.) Cognitive appraisals and emotion-focused coping strategies were discussed as the mechanism behind this effect.

Two self-report studies support the association between humor and affect: In a longitudinal study of 120 US students, self-enhancing humor was positively related to stable positive affect, negatively so to stable negative affect, and stable affect served as a mediator between humor and resilience, well-being, and distress (Cann & Colette, 2014). Also, Edwards and Martin (2014) conducted a cross-sectional study with 176 Canadian students; the positive styles (HSQ) were positively related to positive affect, and the negative styles were related to higher negative affect.

As positive emotional states do not necessarily depend on humor, humor and laughter provide a means to this end.

In addition to altering affect, the stress-buffering function of humor has been linked to *coping* attitudes. While the appreciation of neutral humor in jokes was found to be positively related to active coping and *positivity in reframing*, the appreciation of sick humor (e.g., disgusting jokes) was positively related to *coping styles* reflecting emotional expression and the use of humor as coping, and negatively related to measures of *religion* (Saroglou & Anciaux, 2004) [Capps (2006), in a review, even stated that humor counters religious melancholy and argued for a religion of humor]. Two studies showed that sense of humor was related to perceptions of stressors: People with a high sense of humor (Multidimensional Sense of Humor Scale/MSHS) were more likely to use the *positive reappraisal of stress* and *problem-solving coping strategies* and to report less current *anxiety* than persons with a low sense of humor (Abel, 2002)—despite experiencing a similar number of everyday problems.

Humor is not only related to coping but may be a coping device itself (e.g., see Kuiper et al., 1993 above). In an intervention study, humor was one of the *emotion-*

focused coping strategies that was negatively related to *distress* one day before, three days after, and three months after surgery for women with cancer (Roussi, Krikeli, Hatzidimitriou, & Koutri, 2007).

Interestingly, humor was related to coping with physical complaints, but not to negative affect, in a study by Kuiper and Harris (2009): the positive styles were associated with facilitative *coping* strategies (e.g., changing ones' perspective), and aggressive humor was linked to dysfunctional coping patterns (e.g., greater denial).

In summary, positive humor seems to be beneficially related to affect and coping strategies, an association which accounts for the stress-buffering role of humor for mental health. Thus, sense of humor (CHS, Situational Humor Response Questionnaire/SHRQ) moderated the relationship between *stressful events* and *depressive symptoms* two months later; however, it did not moderate the relationship between *stressful events* and *anxiety* (Nezu, Nezu, & Blissett, 1988). Also, Porterfield (1987) found no evidence that sense of humor moderates the impact of negative life events on *depression* or physical illness: Independent of life stress, sense of humor was found to be directly related to lower depression. Much like the evidence for the stress-buffering role of humor in work contexts (see next Sect. 7.3.2), the findings are inconclusive and demand more sophisticated research.

7.3.2 The Stress-Buffering Hypothesis at Work

This section mainly refers to empirical findings in the work setting. A few studies tested the moderating role of humor directly; however, most studies report the direct link between humor and mental health.

Several studies in the work context found empirical support for the stress-buffering hypothesis. In the meta-analysis by Mesmer-Magnus et al. (2012), employees' use of positive humor (coping and affiliative) partially buffered the negative effects of perceived workplace stress on burnout such that the extent of humor explained one to nine percent of the variance in burnout. A subsequent longitudinal study supported the stress-moderator hypothesis: Coping humor (Coping Humor Scale/CHS) buffered the relationships of traumatic events with *burnout* and *post-traumatic stress disorder* (six months later), but not *absenteeism,* in a study of 179 US firefighters (Sliter, Kale, & Yuan, 2014).

Without directly testing the moderating role, several studies support a humor-health link. In a cross-sectional study of 508 US task force personnel (Internet Crime Against Children), more frequent use of lighthearted humor was related to lower STS (secondary traumatic stress), whereas more frequent use of gallows humor was related to higher STS—or the other way around (Craun & Bourke, 2014). In line with this, semi-structured interviews with 14 crime scene investigators indicated that they use humor for stress-reduction so that job tasks could be completed (Vivona, 2014). Taking a rather different perspective, in an interview study by Tanay, Wiseman, Roberts, and Ream (2014) in a UK adult cancer ward, patients reported to use humor consciously during their interactions with the nurses in an attempt to help nurses cope with the stress in clinical practice.

However, two additional cross-sectional self-report studies challenge the humor-health moderation hypothesis (Healy & McKay, 2000): In contrast to studies on students (Nezu et al., 1988; Szabo, 2003), Healy and McKay (2000) found no evidence for the moderating effect of coping humor (CHS) on the relationship between *stress* and *mood* in a study of 129 primarily female Australian nurses. While avoidance coping and work overload perceptions were related to mood disturbance, *job satisfaction* but not coping humor moderated the stress-mood link (Healy & McKay, 2000). Also, no interaction between job characteristics (role conflict, social support, and workload) and humor were found in the prediction of burnout (Van den Broeck et al., 2012). Failing to show a direct humor-health link, Kim (2013) did not find humor (Sense of Humor Questionnaire/SHQ-6) to be significantly related to job *stress* in the Korean nurse study (Kim, 2013). These results do not line up with the mitigating effects of humor on stress (e.g., Mesmer-Magnus et al., 2012). Also, other than in general contexts (i.e., Edwards & Martin, 2014), in a cross-sectional study of 235 employees in India, aggressive humor was not related to negative affect at work (Goswami, Nair, & Grossenbacher, 2015). Overall, humor seems to buffer stress at work, though contrary findings exist.

In line with Kuiper and Martin's (1998) previous finding that greater negative affect was associated with a larger number of stressful life events for individuals with a lower frequency of actual *laughter* but unrelated for individuals with more laughter, Scheel, Putz, and Kurzawa (2017) found evidence that laughter during work breaks may buffer workplace demands. In a cross-sectional self-report study involving 170 employees from four German retail stores, time pressure was positively related to affective irritation (i.e., nervousness). However, laughing with colleagues during breaks moderated the link between time pressure and irritation such that this link became nonsignificant as the frequency of laughter increased. Thus, laughter as a pleasurable social break activity may buffer between job demands and mental health.

A promising framework for the investigation of the buffering role of humor in the work context is the *Job demands-resources model* (JD-R Model; e.g., Demerouti, Bakker, Nachreiner, & Schaufeli, 2001), that is, humor is a resource that seems to act as a buffer between job demands and well-being (affective path) as well as between job demands and performance (energy or motivational path). The findings of the association between humor and burnout (see Sect. 7.2.1) as well as humor and work engagement (see Sect. 7.2.2; e.g., Guenter et al., 2013; Poulsen et al., 2014) support the affective as well as the motivational path of the JD-R Model.

In summary, humor seems to have the potential to buffer between stressors and mental health in the work context, though research is not fully consistent and deserves replication with more sophisticated methods than cross-sectional designs. Evidence for the roles of affect and coping with regard to humor in the work context is largely missing (Sect. 7.3.1), also the role of potential mediators relevant for the work context needs to be clarified (Sect. 7.3.2). While positive humor (i.e., affiliative, coping) seems to be the most promising, it may be worthwhile to investigate the composition of humor rather than isolated styles. Future studies should investigate the mitigating role of positive humor styles buffering the effects of negative humor styles. The JD-R Model may be used as the basis for future research on the buffering role of humor in the work context.

7.3.3 Stress-Buffering of Humor by Promoting Mediators of Mental Health

Several direct relationships between humor and beneficial affective and attitudinal qualities may add to the explanation of the stress-buffering role of humor. Optimism, hope, self-esteem, resilience, and happiness may be seen as proxies for mental health, and humor may enhance these mediators.

One of the few studies which analyzed the mediation directly was conducted by Cann and colleagues. The association between sense of humor and *perceived stressors* was mediated by positive personality qualities (*optimism, hope, happiness*; Cann & Etzel, 2008). Eight weeks later (time 2), these qualities mediated the association of self-enhancing and self-defeating humor styles at time 1 with *perceived stress* at time 2 (Cann, Stilwell, & Taku, 2010).

Several cross-sectional studies support the direct relationship between humor styles and optimism as well as happiness: Whereas in the meta-analysis by Schneider (2015) both positive humor styles were positively, and the negative styles negatively related to *optimism*, in another study only the self-enhancing humor style (but not the other styles) was found to be positively related to optimism by Martin et al. (2003). Ford, McCreight, and Richardson (2014) report a positive correlation between both positive humor styles and *happiness*, and a negative correlation between both negative humor styles and happiness, in a study of 109 US online workers (Amazons' Mechanical Turk).

An experiment by Vilaythong, Arnau, Rosen, and Mascaro (2003) even showed that *hopefulness* may be manipulated in the short-term: state *hopefulness* increased after a humorous video relative to a neutral video, while the severity (but not the quantity) of recently experienced stressors was found to be related to lower state hopefulness (Vilaythong et al., 2003).

Cross-sectional evidence for a significant relationship between humor and several favorable dispositions were reported: Positive humor styles, coping humor (CHS, humor appreciation, humor creativity) and sense of humor (Situational Humor Response Questionnaire/SHRQ, Sense of Humor Questionnaire/SHQ) have been found to be related to higher *self-esteem* (Kuiper & Borowicz-Sibenik, 2005; Kuiper et al., 2004; Leist & Müller, 2012; Martin et al., 2003; Overholser, 1992; Zhao, Wang & Kong, 2014), whereas the aggressive style was unrelated and the self-defeating style was negatively related to self-esteem (except in Leist & Müller,

2012). However, in the meta-analysis by Schneider (2015), the affiliative humor style was positively, and the aggressive humor style negatively related to self-esteem, while both self-directed styles were unrelated. Both positive styles were positively, and self-defeating negatively, related to *social* self-esteem as well as *self-competency judgments*, and the aggressive humor style was unrelated (Kuiper et al., 2004). A combination of high positive and low negative humor styles has been found to be beneficial for *self-regulatory strategies* (Galloway, 2010; Leist & Müller, 2012). Edwards and Martin (2014) found both positive styles to be related to *resilience*. However, Cann and Colette (2014) reported mediation by stable affect only between self-enhancing humor and resilience in a longitudinal study (see above).

These mostly cross-sectional self-report studies on students suggest that the link between humor and health might be mediated by affective or attitudinal characteristics that might be relevant in the work context too, for instance, occupational self-efficacy.

7.4 Humor and Social Facilitation

Another prominent explanation for the link between humor and health is the facilitation of social contacts and thus social support. Social facilitation is characterized by the higher availability of social support for humorous persons (e.g., Dyck & Holtzmann, 2013). Also, social competence might be one of the factors aligned with social facilitation through humor. On the contrary, the negative humor styles seem detrimental for social facilitation.

7.4.1 Social Facilitation by Social Support Through Humor

Social support is discussed as a mediator of the relationship between humor and outcomes. This argument implies a significant relationship between humor and social support, and the mediation of the humor and mental health link by social support.

There is general, but cross-sectional, evidence for the significant association of humor and social support. The self-enhancing style was found to be positively and the self-defeating style negatively related to *satisfaction with social support* (Martin et al., 2003), whereas the other-directed styles (i.e., affiliative, aggressive) were found to be unrelated. However, aggressive humor seemed to be related to higher levels of the availability of social support among men and the lower availability of social support among women, a finding that might be explained by different role expectations. Also, humor (CHS, humor appreciation, humor creativity) was found to be associated with lower *loneliness* in men only (Overholser, 1992). As one possible precondition for social support, Hampes (1999) found that humor (CHS,

Multidimensional Sense of Humor Scale/MSHS, and Situational Humor Response Questionnaire/SHRQ, but the SHRQ only for women) was positively related to general *trust* (in people or in the world) in a cross-sectional self-report study of students.

There is initial support for the mediation of social support between the positive styles and mental well-being. Kuiper and McHale (2009) suggested that the use of affiliative humor might foster the development and maintenance of social support networks, which in turn might enhance well-being (social self-esteem, lower depression) such that a greater use of self-defeating humor might lead to maladaptive support networks and thus impede psychological well-being. In fact, the perceived availability of support was found to mediate the positive relationship between positive humor styles and well-being (i.e., depressive symptoms, life satisfaction) and the negative association between self-defeating humor and well-being (Dyck & Holtzman, 2013). Likewise, social support and self-esteem fully mediated the relationship between affiliative as well as self-enhancing humor and life satisfaction (Zhao et al., 2014). However, both studies were cross-sectional self-report studies with students. Thus, sound evidence is still missing.

But why should humor be related to higher social support? As one of the mechanisms between humor and social support, social competence will be discussed in the next section.

7.4.2 Humor, Social Competence, and Social Support

Social competence is discussed as a mediator of the relationship between humor and social support, that is, humor should be related to social competence, which in turn is related to social support. In fact, several studies support the association between humor and social competence as well as related constructs. For instance, the positive humor styles and trait cheerfulness were found to be positively correlated with various domains of *social competence*; self-enhancing humor and trait cheerfulness were found to be positively (and trait bad mood negatively) related to *emotional intelligence* (Yip & Martin, 2006). Aggressive and self-defeating humor was negatively associated with the *ability to accurately perceive emotions,* and negative humor styles and bad mood were negatively related to social competence in this cross-sectional self-report study (Yip & Martin, 2006). Likewise, aggressive humor was related to lower *interpersonal skills* (emotional support, conflict management; Kuiper et al., 2004). These cross-sectional self-report studies are complemented by Nezlek and Derks' (2001) two-week study, which found that CHS scores were positively related to how pleasurable people found their *interactions*, how confident they felt in their interactions, and how much time they spent with others. However, these relationships were moderated by *depression* (lower depression—higher strength) but not by social skills, loneliness, or social anxiety.

Humor is related to social competence; however, the support for this (beneficial) link between positive or coping humor and social competence is largely cross-sectional, as is the similar unfavorable link between negative humor styles and social competence. Also, the mediating role of social competence for the association between humor and social support remains to be tested.

7.4.3 *Empirical Evidence for Humor and Social Facilitation in the Work Context*

A few studies investigated the association between humor and concepts related to social facilitation in the work context, but none included a mediation of the humor-mental health link by social support. Thus, Romero and Arendt (2011) reported that the positive styles were associated with higher *team cooperation*, and affiliative (but not self-enhancing) humor was related to higher *satisfaction with coworkers* for US employees. Also, aggressive (but not self-defeating) humor was negatively related to both outcomes. [Emotional contagion may be one of the mechanisms behind the humor-cohesion link (see Sect. 2.3.4).] Challenging the links between humor and *social support* found in non-work contexts, Bowling et al. (2004; in Mesmer-Magnus et al., 2012) reported that measures of reciprocity (OCB, social competence) were related to social support availability, but measures of attraction (including sense of humor) were not. In this cross-sectional self-report study of 123 US high-school teachers and staff members, social support appeared to be a moderator of the relationship between stressor and strain regardless of humor.

In summary, evidence for the social facilitation hypotheses of the humor-health link for the work context is largely missing.

7.5 Humor and Physical Health

Several reviews were published on the physiology of humor (Fry, 1994), how humor and laughter are related to physical health (Martin, 2001), and how the sense of humor is related to physical health (Martin, 2004). Fry and Savin (1988) concluded that an enhancement of circulatory efficiency due to laughter is beneficial for physiological survival. Fry (1994) described biological processes and physiological changes that were due to laughter, which can benefit health even without humor. Martin (2001) summarized mechanisms that are said to link humor to health, and Martin (2004), in the introduction to a Special Issue of the International Journal of Humor Studies, reviewed findings on how the sense of humor is related to health, immunity, pain, and well-being.

Overall, there is more evidence for an association between humor and mental than physiological health. Svebak et al. (2004) found an interesting significant "psychological" interaction: When daily activities were rated as important, *bodily complaints* decreased with higher SHQ (Sense of Humor Questionnaire), but when they were rated as unimportant, complaints increased with higher SHQ. Also, increased numbers of *physical symptoms* were found to be associated with higher levels of *negative affect* but were unrelated to humor styles (Kuiper & Harris, 2009).

Evidence of physiological health effects of humor in the work context is rare. Kerkkänen et al. (2004) did not find significant associations, but despite the longitudinal design, the small sample ($N = 34$ Finnish police officers) prevents any conclusions from being drawn. With a bigger sample of 2,094 employees, but only cross-sectional assessment, Doosje et al. (2011) reported that one of three *humorous coping* styles (i.e., antecedent-focused, but not generic or response-focused) was associated with fewer instances of upper *respiratory tract infections*. However, the correlation was extremely low.

In the following, the physiological mechanisms between humor and health are discussed.

Physiological Evidence for Laughter, Humor and Health According to Fry (1994), humor has an impact by stimulating the central nervous system; that is, during periods of *laughter*, activities in various bodily systems increase (e.g., heart rate, pulmonary ventilation, muscle activity, brain activity, skin temperature, hormone production, circulation of immune substances), and pain perception decreases. In a subsequent refractory/relaxation phase, heart rate, blood pressure, respiratory rate, and muscle activity drop. Finally, greater social and psychological animation persists. While the stimulation phase is aligned with Berlyne's (1969) arousal theory of humor, the latter phase reflects Freud's catharsis theory of humor (see Sect. 2.3.3). That is, humor has a cathartic, pressure-releasing effect.

Laboratory experiments investigated humor in relation to blood pressure, pain tolerance, discomfort threshold, physiological stress measures and neuro-immune parameters (see Martin, 2001, 2004). However, studies on laughter and blood pressure have produced controversial findings. The arterial blood pressure of older men was found to increase during mirthful *laughter*, followed by a decrease below the level of resting pressure (Fry & Savin, 1988). Female students with higher levels of *coping humor* (CHS, Situational Humor Response Questionnaire/SHRQ) had lower systolic blood pressure in stressful situations, but the opposite results were found for male students (Lefcourt, Davidson, Prkachin, & Mills, 1997).

The stress-moderating effect of humor was found for *pain tolerance* in the cold pressor task (i.e., the time an arm was held in a cold water container) (Lefcourt et al., 1997; Weisenberg, Tepper, & Schwarzwald, 1995; Zweyer, Velker, & Ruch, 2004) and the tolerance of physical discomfort (blood-pressure cuff tolerance; Cogan, Cogan, Waltz, & McCue, 1987; Zillmann, Rockwell, Schweitzer, & Sundar, 1993), though relaxation (Cogan et al., 1987) or tragedy (Zillmann et al., 1993) were likewise beneficial in comparison with other non-humorous conditions. With respect to cognitive stress (induced by mental arithmetic), laughter was not as effective as relaxation training in reducing physiological measures of stress (White & Winzelberg, 1992). An exposure to comedy was found to be related to *immunity and analgesic* effects (Martin, 2001). Several neuro-immune parameters were heightened (i.e., natural killer cell activity) as a response to mirthful *laughter*

(Berk, Felten, Tan, Bittman, & Westengard, 2001); humor presentation/*appreciation* was found to enhance secretory immunoglobulin A (IgA) concentration (Lefcourt, Davidson-Katz, & Kueneman, 1990; McClelland & Cheriff, 1997), especially for students with a higher *sense of humor* (Situational Humor Response Questionnaire/SHRQ; Lefcourt et al., 1990).

Overall, empirical evidence for the physiological mechanisms of laughter and humor are not entirely consistent and deserve replication in a work context with work-relevant criteria. For instance, pain tolerance might be less important in most work contexts, while cortisol levels are an accepted indicator of stress. To our knowledge, only one study reported about cortisol in this regard: in an intervention study with 66 long-term care residents in Taiwan, Laughing Qigong affected cognitive impairment, mood states, and depression in a positive way—but not cortisol levels (Hsieh, Chang, Tsai, & Wu, 2015).

Self-report evidence for laughter, humor, and health In contrast to laboratory studies, self-report measures of humor have demonstrated only a few significant correlations with immunity, pain tolerance, self-reported illness symptoms, or stress-moderating effects on physical health, and none with *longevity* (Martin, 2001). Thus, humor (Multidimensional Sense of Humor Scale/MSHS) was not related to most of the eight *health* indicators but to (less) physical role limitations, more energy/less fatigue, higher emotional wellness (Boyle & Joss-Reid, 2002). Humor (Sense of Humor Questionnaire/SHQ) had no relation to blood pressure in neither a large-scale study of Norwegian adults (Svebak et al., 2004) nor a small longitudinal study (Kerkkänen et al., 2004), and was not related to the prevalence of common bodily complaints (Svebak et al., 2004) or physical health levels (Kerkkänen et al., 2004).

The ambiguous nature of the association between trait humor and health is demonstrated by the following studies. McClelland and Cheriff (1997) found that people with an appreciation of a *good sense of humor* had a higher resistance to respiratory infections (see also Doosje et al., 2011, for similar findings in the work context), whereas a greater production of humor was related to more colds—possibly due to more exposure. Moreover, sense of humor was (cross-sectionally) associated with higher *body mass* and a greater risk for *cardiovascular disease* (Kerkkänen et al., 2004). Cheerfulness was related to engaging in risky activities and to early death in a life-cycle study (Martin et al., 2002, reviewed in Martin, 2004). Finally, the ability to generate humor was negatively related to *longevity* in comedians (Rotton, 1992). Also, humor is associated with higher *substance abuse* (Edwards & Martin, 2012; Kerkkänen et al., 2004; Martin et al., 2002, reviewed in Martin, 2004).

In sum, the humor-health hypothesis is quite popular—even dental health appears to be related to humor (Dumitrescu, Toma, & Lascu, 2010). But evidence is far from conclusive. Studies have mostly been experimental, thus examining the induction of a state of humor. Also, typical samples are comprised of students. Field studies often challenge experimental findings and the humor-health hypotheses. More so, studies in work contexts are largely missing.

7.6 Conclusion: Humor and (Mental) Health at Work

Humor seems to buffer the consequences of stress by influencing affect and coping, and by fostering social support. However, research for the work context is preliminary, at best.

Overall, laughter and humor might benefit well-being and thus health at the workplace, though they might not be the only devices. Whereas for example, relaxation (as compared with laughter) may be even more effective for reducing physiological stress, the incremental benefits of humor might lie on the psychological side (White & Winzelberg, 1992). However, certain aspects of humor (as a trait) are related to risk-taking behavior and therefore to worse health outcomes. This might be due to a third underlying variable (e.g., sensation-seeking). Fortunately, most workplaces offer limited opportunities to engage in life-endangering risk-taking behaviors; thus, workplace mortality is hopefully unrelated to humor. However, when it comes to bullying by means of aggressive humor, victims might experience serious health consequences. Findings in general contexts do not hint at a detrimental effect of aggressive humor on mental health (except for dysfunctional coping patterns; Kuiper & Harris, 2009), but self-defeating humor has been shown to affect mental health. In work contexts, the findings go in the opposite direction: Aggressive humor usually has unfavorable relationships with mental health, whereas self-defeating humor seems less important. But cultural differences might also play a role in the associations between humor and health; however, there is no systematic research on this.

7.6.1 Future Research

All of the studies cited above require replication in work contexts, in different cultures, and with better methods. Also, studies in atypical workforce samples (volunteers, the unemployed) are scarce. In particular, causal relationships have been understudied, for instance, with regard to the stress-buffering hypothesis and social facilitation. Differences between work and non-work contexts with regard to the humor-social facilitation link should be investigated further: Is the study by Bowling et al. (2004) replicable? In other words, is social support a stressor-strain moderator regardless of humor? If so, is the higher availability of social support for humorous persons (e.g., Dyck & Holtzman, 2013) not transferable to the work context, and what are the reasons? For example, while friends are chosen with regard to their personality characteristics (e.g., sense of humor), coworkers are usually not—thus, is the interpersonal matching of humor styles one reason for the differences between contexts?

It seems worthwhile to study the associations of—among others—two promising concepts with humor and mental health. *Job crafting* (Tims et al., 2012) revises employees' work identities and the extent to which their work is meaningful by "the physical and cognitive changes individuals make in the task or relational boundaries of their work" (Wrzesniewski & Dutton, 2001, p. 179). Job crafting might benefit from the use of positive humor, especially the dimension of increasing social job resources, as humor may facilitate social support (e.g., by supervisors). Likewise, using aggressive humor might be detrimental for job crafting. Job crafting was found to be positively related to work engagement (Tims et al., 2012), and future research could investigate job crafting as a mediator between the use of humor and mental health.

Passion is a strong inclination toward an activity that people like and find important, invest time and energy in, and include as part of their identity (Vallerand et al., 2003). While harmonious passion for work is a motivational force that leads a person to volitionally choose to engage in work activities, obsessive passion for work is characterized by an internal pressure and a lack of control over the urge to work (Forest et al., 2011). Harmonious passion was found to be positively and obsessive passion negatively related to mental health (e.g., Forest et al., 2011). Future studies could investigate the potential mediating role of humor styles, that is, whether harmonious passion is related to positive humor styles and obsessive passion to negative humor styles.

7.6.2 Practical Implications

Using affiliative humor at work will be beneficial for mental health if the frequency of humor remains within acceptable limits. Supervisors, in particular, should use positive types of humor with their subordinates. The differentiation between positive and negative humor styles, with respect to either oneself or organizational agents, can be useful when thinking about an individuals' use of humor; that is, the ability to distinguish between humor styles with their specific functions in everyday life may help to foster the positive styles (e.g., trying to see the funny aspects of awkward situations) and to avoid the negative styles. Self-defeating humor is potentially unfavorable for mental health, and aggressive humor challenges relationship quality.

Given that laughter has physiological benefits (e.g., relaxation) it may be sensible to enable—or at least permit—laughter at the workplace. Laughing may be one of the fruitful ways to counter stressful situations.

Laughing may not be the *best* medicine, but one of several medicines.

Recommendations for Further Reading:

On mental health and humor at work:

Guenter, H., Schreurs, B., Van Emmerik, I. H., Gijsbers, W., & Van Iterson, A. (2013). How adaptive and maladaptive humor influence well-being at work: A diary study. *Humor, 26*(4), 573–594.

Mesmer-Magnus, J., Glew, D. J., & Viswesvaran, C. (2012). A meta-analysis of positive humor in the workplace. *Journal of Managerial Psychology, 27*(2), 155–190.

On mental health and humor:

Martin, R. A. (2007). *The psychology of humor: An integrative approach.* London: Elsevier Academic Press.

Martin, R. A., Puhlik-Doris, P., Larsen, G., Gray, J., & Weir, K. (2003). Individual differences in uses of humor and their relation to psychological well-being: Development of the Humor Styles Questionnaire. *Journal of Research in Personality, 37*(1), 48–75.

On biological/physical health and humor:

Fry, W. F. (1994). The biology of humor. *Humor-International Journal of Humor Research, 7*(2), 111–126.

Martin, R. A. (2001). Humor, laughter, and physical health: Methodological issues and research findings. *Psychological Bulletin, 127*(4), 504–519.

Martin, R. A. (2004). Sense of humor and physical health: Theoretical issues, recent findings, and future directions. *Humor, 17*(1/2), 1–20.

References

Abel, M. H. (2002). Humor, stress, and coping strategies. *Humor—International Journal of Humor Research, 15*(4), 365–381.

Berk, L. S., Felten, D. L., Tan, S. A., Bittman, B. B., & Westengard, J. (2001). Modulation of neuroimmune parameters during the eustress of humor-associated mirthful laughter. *Alternative Therapies in Health and Medicine, 7*(2), 62–76.

Berlyne, D. E. (1969). Arousal, reward and learning. *Annals of the New York Academy of Sciences, 159*(3), 1059–1070.

Bizi, S., Keinan, G., & Beit-Hallahmi, B. (1988). Humor and coping with stress: A test under real-life conditions. *Personality and Individual Differences, 9*(6), 951–956.

Booth-Butterfield, M., Booth-Butterfield, S., & Wanzer, M. (2007). Funny students cope better: Patterns of humor enactment and coping effectiveness. *Communication Quarterly, 55*(3), 299–315.

Bowling, N. A., Beehr, T. A., Johnson, A. L., Semmer, N. K., Hendricks, E. A., & Webster, H. A. (2004). Explaining potential antecedents of workplace social support: Reciprocity or attractiveness? *Journal of Occupational Health Psychology, 9*(4), 339–350.

Boyle, G. J., & Joss-Reid, J. M. (2002). Relationship of humour to health: A psychometric investigation. *British Journal of Health Psychology, 9*(1), 51–66.

Britt, T. W., Crane, M., Hodson, S. E., & Adler, A. B. (2015). Effective and ineffective coping strategies in a low-autonomy work environment. *Journal of Occupational Health Psychology, 21*(2), 154–168. doi:10.1037/a0039898.

Cann, A., & Collette, C. (2014). Sense of humor, stable affect, and psychological well-being. *Europe's Journal of Psychology, 10*(3), 464–479. doi:10.5964/ejop.v10i3.746.

Cann, A., & Etzel, K. C. (2008). Remembering and anticipating stressors: Positive personality mediates the relationship with sense of humor. *Humor—International Journal of Humor Research, 21*(2), 157–178.

Cann, A., Holt, K., & Calhoun, L. G. (1999). The roles of humor and sense of humor in responses to stressors. *Humor—International Journal of Humor Research, 12*(2), 177–193.

Cann, A., Stilwell, K., & Taku, K. (2010). Humor styles, positive personality and health. *Europe's Journal of Psychology, 6*(3), 213–235.

Capps, D. (2006). The psychological benefits of humor. *Pastoral Psychology, 54*(5), 393–411.

Chen, G.-H., & Martin, R. A. (2007). A comparison of humor styles, coping humor, and mentalhealth between Chinese and Canadian university students. *Humor—International Journal of Humor Research, 20*(3), 215–234.

Cheung, C., & Yue, X. D. (2012). Sojourn students' humor styles as buffers to achieve resilience. *International Journal of Intercultural Relations, 36*(3), 353–364.

Cogan, R., Cogan, D., Waltz, W., & McCue, M. (1987). Effects of laughter and relaxation on discomfort thresholds. *Journal of Behavioral Medicine, 10*(2), 139–144.

Craun, S. W., & Bourke, M. L. (2014). The use of humor to cope with secondary traumatic stress. *Journal of Child Sexual Abuse, 23*(7), 840–852. doi:10.1080/10538712.2014.949395.

Demerouti, E., Bakker, A. B., Nachreiner, F., & Schaufeli, W. (2001). The job demands-resources model of burnout. *Journal of Applied Psychology, 86,* 499–512.

Doosje, S., De Goede, M. P. M., Van Doornen, L. J. P., & Van de Schoot, R. (2011). The associations of humorous coping styles, affective states, job demands and job control with the frequency of upper respiratory tract infection. *SA Journal of Industrial Psychology, 37*(2), 9. doi:10.4102/sajip.v37i2.863

Dozois, D. J. A., Martin, R. A., & Bieling, P. J. (2009). Early maladaptive schemas and adaptive/maladaptive styles of humor. *Cognitive Therapy and Research, 33*(6), 585–596.

Dumitrescu, A. L., Toma, C., & Lascu, V. (2010). Relationship of humour and oral health status. *Romanian Journal of Internal Medicine, 48*(4), 333–339.

Dyck, K. T. H., & Holtzman, S. (2013). Understanding humor styles and well-being: The importance of social relationships and gender. *Personality and Individual Differences, 55*(1), 53–58.

Edwards, K. R., & Martin, R. A. (2012). Do humorous people take poorer care of their health? Associations between humor styles and substance use. *Europe's Journal of Psychology, 8*(4), 524–534.

Edwards, K. R., & Martin, R. A. (2014). The conceptualization, measurement, and role of humor as a character strength in positive psychology. *Europe's Journal of Psychology, 10*(3), 505–519. doi:10.5964/ejop.v10i3.759.

Ford, T. E., McCreight, K. A., & Richardson, K. (2014). Affective style, humor styles and happiness. *Europe's Journal of Psychology, 10*(3), 451–463. doi:10.5964/ejop.v10i3.766.

Forest, J., Mageau, G. A., Sarrazin, C., & Morin, E. M. (2011). "Work is my passion": The different affective, behavioural, and cognitive consequences of harmonious and obsessive passion toward work. *Canadian Journal of Administrative Sciences/Revue canadienne des sciences de l'administration, 28*(1), 27–40.

Freiheit, S. R., Overholser, J. C., & Lehnert, K. L. (1998). The association between humor and depression in adolescent psychiatric inpatients and high school students. *Journal of Adolescent Research, 13*(1), 32–48.

Frewen, P. A., Brinker, J., Martin, R. A., & Dozois, D. J. A. (2008). Humor styles and personality-vulnerability to depression. *Humor—International Journal of Humor Research, 21* (2), 179–195. doi: 10.1515/HUMOR.2008.009

Fry, W. F., & Savin, W. M. (1988). Mirthful laughter and blood pressure. *Humor—International Journal of Humor Research, 1*(1), 49–62.

Fry, W. F. (1994). The biology of humor. *Humor—International Journal of Humor Research, 7*(2), 111–126.

Galloway, G. (2010). Individual differences in personal humor styles: Identification of prominent patterns and their associates. *Personality and Individual Differences, 48*(5), 563–567.

Garner, J. T., Chandler, R. C., & Wallace, J. D. (2015). Nothing to laugh about: Student interns' use of humor in response to workplace dissatisfaction. *Southern Communication Journal, 80*(2), 102–118. doi:10.1080/1041794X.2014.986586.

Gockel, C., Scheel, T., & Van de Ven, B. (in prep.). *Positive humor style as a buffer for the detrimental effects of negative humor styles on well-being: Studies in three countries.*

Goswami, A., Nair, P. K., & Grossenbacher, M. A. (2015). Impact of aggressive humor on dysfunctional resistance. *Personality and Individual Differences, 74,* 265–269.

Guenter, H., Schreurs, B., Van Emmerik, I. H., Gijsbers, W., & Van Iterson, A. (2013). How adaptive and maladaptive humor influence wellbeing at work: A diary study. *Humor—International Journal of Humor Research, 26*(4), 573–594.

Hampes, W. P. (1999). The relationship between humor and trust. *Humor—International Journal of Humor Research, 12,* 253–260.

Healy, C. M., & McKay, M. F. (2000). Nursing stress: The effects of coping strategies and job satisfaction in a sample of Australian nurses. *Journal of Advanced Nursing, 31*(3), 681–688.

Herzog, T. R., & Strevey, S. J. (2008). Contact with nature, sense of humor, and psychological well-being. *Environment and Behavior, 40*(6), 747–776.

Hsieh, C.-J., Chang, C., Tsai, G., & Wu, H.-F. (2015). Empirical study of the influence of a Laughing Qigong Program on long-term care residents: LQP on long-term care residents. *Geriatrics & Gerontology International, 15*(2), 165–173. doi:10.1111/ggi.12244.

Hugelshofer, D. S., Kwon, P., Reff, R. C., & Olson, M. L. (2006). Humour's role in the relation between attributional style and dysphoria. *European Journal of Personality, 20*(4), 325–336.

Huo, Y., Lam, W., & Chen, Z. (2012). Am I the only one this supervisor is laughing at? Effects of aggressive humor on employee strain and addictive behaviors. *Personnel Psychology, 65*(4), 859–885.

Kazarian, S. S., & Martin, R. A. (2004). Humour styles, personality, and well-being among Lebanese university students. *European Journal of Personality, 18*(3), 209–219.

Kazarian, S. S., & Martin, R. A. (2006). Humor styles, culture-related personality, well-being, and family adjustment among Armenians in Lebanon. *Humor—International Journal of Humor Research, 19*(4), 405–423.

Kelly, W. E. (2002). An investigation of worry and sense of humor. *The Journal of Psychology, 136*(6), 657–666.

Kerkkänen, P., Kuiper, N. A., & Martin, R. A. (2004). Sense of humor, physical health, and well-being at work: A three-year longitudinal study of Finnish police officers. *Humor—International Journal of Humor Research, 17*(1/2), 21–36.

Kim, J. (2013). Structural equation modeling for humor, job satisfaction, job stress and intention to turnover. *Journal of Korean Academy of Nursing Administration, 19*(2), 265.

Kim, T.-Y., Lee, D.-R., & Wong, N. Y. S. (2015). Supervisor humor and employee outcomes: The role of social distance and affective trust in supervisor. *Journal of Business and Psychology*. doi:10.1007/s10869-015-9406-9.

Kuiper, N. A., & Borowicz-Sibenik, M. (2005). A good sense of humor doesn't always help: Agency and communion as moderators of psychological well-being. *Personality and Individual Differences, 38*(2), 365–377.

Kuiper, N. A., Grimshaw, M., Leite, C., & Kirsh, G. (2004). Humor is not always the best medicine: Specific components of sense of humor and psychological well-being. *Humor—International Journal of Humor Research, 17*(1/2), 135–168.

Kuiper, N. A., & Harris, A. L. (2009). Humor styles and negative affect as predictors of different components of physical health. *Europe's Journal of Psychology, 5*(1), 1–18.

Kuiper, N. A., & Martin, R. A. (1993). Humor and self-concept. *Humor—International Journal of Humor Research, 6*(3), 251–270. doi:10.1515/humr.1993.6.3.251.

Kuiper, N. A., & Martin, R. A. (1998). Laughter and stress in daily life: Relation to positive and negative affect. *Motivation and Emotion, 22*(2), 133–153.

Kuiper, N. A., Martin, R. A., & Dance, K. A. (1992). Sense of humour and enhanced quality of life. *Personality and Individual Differences, 13*(12), 1273–1283.

Kuiper, N. A., Martin, R. A., & Olinger, L. J. (1993). Coping humour, stress, and cognitive apraisals. *Canadian Journal of Behavioural Science/Revue canadienne des sciences du comportement, 25*(1), 81–96.

Kuiper, N. A., & McHale, N. (2009). Humor styles as mediators between self-evaluative standards and psychological well-being. *The Journal of Psychology, 143*(4), 359–376.

Kuiper, N. A., & Nicholl, S. (2004). Thoughts of feeling better? Sense of humor and physical health. *Humor—International Journal of Humor Research, 17*(1/2), 37–66.

Lefcourt, H. M., Davidson-Katz, K., & Kueneman, K. (1990). Humor and immune-system func-tioning. *Humor—International Journal of Humor Research, 3*(3), 305–322. doi:10.1515/humr.1990.3.3.305.

Lefcourt, H. M., Davidson, K., Prkachin, K. M., & Mills, D. E. (1997). Humor as a stress moderator in the prediction of blood pressure obtained during five stressful tasks. *Journal of Research in Personality, 31,* 523–642.

Lehmann, K. M., Burke, K. L., Martin, R., Sultan, J., & Czech, D. R. (2001). A reformulation of the moderating effects of productive humor. *Humor—International Journal of Humor Research, 14*(2), 131–161.

Leist, A. K., & Müller, D. (2012). Humor types show different patterns of self-regulation, self-esteem, and well-being. *Journal of Happiness Studies, 14*(2), 551–569.

Loi, N. M., Loh, J. M. I., & Hine, D. W. (2013). Don't rock the boat—The moderating role of gender in the relationship between workplace incivility and work withdrawal. *Journal of Management Development, 34*(2), 169–186. doi:10.1108/JMD-12-2012-0152.

Maiolino, N. B., & Kuiper, N. A. (2014). Integrating humor and positive psychology approaches to psychological well-being. *Europe's Journal of Psychology, 10*(3), 557–570. doi:10.5964/ejop.v10i3.753.

Malinowski, A. J. (2013). Characteristics of job burnout and humor among psychotherapists. *Humor—International Journal of Humor Research, 26*(1), 117–133. doi:10.1515/humor-2013-0007.

Martin, L. R., Friedman, H. S., Tucker, J. S., Tomlinson-Keasey, C., Criqui, M. H., & Schwartz, J. E. (2002). A life course perspective on childhood cheerfulness and its relation to mortality risk. *Personality and Social Psychology Bulletin, 28*(9), 1155–1165.

Martin, R. A. (2001). Humor, laughter, and physical health: Methodological issues and research findings. *Psychological Bulletin, 127*(4), 504–519.

Martin, R. A. (2004). Sense of humor and physical health: Theoretical issues, recent findings, and future directions. *Humor—International Journal of Humor Research, 17*(1/2), 1–20.

Martin, R. A. (2007). *The psychology of humor: An integrative approach.* London: Elsevier Academic Press.

Martin, R. A., Kuiper, N. A., Olinger, L., & Dance, K. A. (1993). Humor, coping with stress, self-concept, and psychological well-being. *Humor—International Journal of Humor Research, 6*(1), 89–104.

Martin, R. A., & Lefcourt, H. M. (1983). Sense of humor as a moderator of the relation between stressors and moods. *Journal of Personality and Social Psychology, 45*(6), 1313–1324.

Martin, R. A., Puhlik-Doris, P., Larsen, G., Gray, J., & Weir, K. (2003). Individual differences in uses of humor and their relation to psychological well-being: Development of the Humor Styles Questionnaire. *Journal of Research in Personality, 37*(1), 48–75.

Martineau, W. H. (1972). A model of social functions of humor. In J. H. Goldstein & P. E. McGhee (Eds.), *The psychology of humor* (pp. 101–125). New York: Academic.

McClelland, D. C., & Cheriff, A. D. (1997). The immunoenhancing effects of humor on secretary IgA and resistance to respiratory infections. *Psychology and Health, 12*(3), 329–344.

Mesmer-Magnus, J., Glew, D. J., & Viswesvaran, C. (2012). A meta-analysis of positive humor in the workplace. *Journal of Managerial Psychology, 27*(2), 155–190.

Newman, M. G., & Stone, A. A. (1996). Does humor moderate the effects of experimentally-induced stress? *Annals of Behavioral Medicine, 18*(2), 101–109.

Nezlek, J. B., & Derks, P. (2001). Use of humor as a coping mechanism, psychological adjusment, and social interaction. *Humor—International Journal of Humor Research, 14*(4), 395–414.

Nezu, A. M., Nezu, C. M., & Blissett, S. E. (1988). Sense of humor as a moderator of the relation between stressful events and psychological distress: A prospective analysis. *Journal of Personality and Social Psychology, 54*(3), 520–525.

Overholser, J. C. (1992). Sense of humor when coping with life stress. *Personality and Indivi-dual Differences, 13*(7), 799–804.

Porterfield, A. L. (1987). Does sense of humor moderate the impact of life stress on psychological and physical well-being? *Journal of Research in Personality, 21*(3), 306–317.

Poulsen, A. A., Meredith, P., Khan, A., Henderson, J., Castrisos, V., & Khan, S. R. (2014). Burnout and work engagement in occupational therapists. *British Journal of Occupational Therapy, 77*(3), 156–164. doi:10.4276/030802214X13941036266621.

Romero, E. J., & Arendt, L. A. (2011). Variable effects of humor styles on organizational outcomes. *Psychological Reports, 108*(2), 649–659. doi:10.2466/07.17.20.21.PR0.108.2.649.659.

Rotton, J. (1992). Trait humor and longevity: Do comics have the last laugh? *Health Psychology, 11*(4), 262–266.

Roussi, P., Krikeli, V., Hatzidimitriou, C., & Koutri, I. (2007). Patterns of coping, flexibility in coping and psychological distress in women diagnosed with breast cancer. *Cognitive Therapy and Research, 31*(1), 97–109.

Ruch, W. F., & Heintz, S. (2014). Humour styles, personality, and psychological well-being: What's humour got to do with it? *The European Journal of Humour Research, 1*(4), 1–24.

Saroglou, V., & Anciaux, L. (2004). Liking sick humor: Coping styles and religion as predictors. *Humor—International Journal of Humor Research, 17*(3), 257–278.

Scheel, T., Putz, D., & Kurzawa, C. (2017). Give me a break: Laughing with colleagues guards against ego depletion. *European Journal of Humour Research, 5*(1), 36–51. doi: 10.7592/EJHR2017.5.1.scheel

Schneider, M. (2015). *Humor ist, wenn's wirkt! Metaanalyse zum Zusammenhang von Humor und psychischer Gesundheit (Diploma Thesis).* Austria: University of Vienna.

Schneiderman, N., Ironson, G., & Siegel, S. D. (2005). Stress and health: Psychological, behavioral, and biological determinants. *Annual Review of Clinical Psychology, 1*(1), 607–628.

Sliter, M., Kale, A., & Yuan, Z. (2014). Is humor the best medicine? The buffering effect of co-ping humor on traumatic stressors in firefighters. *Journal of Organizational Behavior, 35* (2), 257–272.

Sobral, F., & Islam, G. (2015). He who laughs best, leaves last: The influence of humor on the attitudes and behavior of interns. *Academy of Management Learning & Education, 14*(4), 500–518. doi:10.5465/amle.2013.0368.

Svebak, S., Martin, R. A., & Holmen, J. (2004). The prevalence of sense of humor in a large, unselected county population in Norway: Relations with age, sex, and some health indicators. *Humor—International Journal of Humor Research, 17*(1/2), 121–134.

Szabo, A. (2003). The acure effects of humor and exercise on mood and anxiety. *Journal of Leisure Research, 35*(2), 152–162.

Tanay, M. A., Wiseman, T., Roberts, J., & Ream, E. (2014). A time to weep and a time to laugh: humour in the nurse—patient relationship in an adult cancer setting. *Supportive Care in Cancer, 22*(5), 1295–1301. doi:10.1007/s00520-013-2084-0.

Tews, M. J., Michel, J. W., & Allen, D. G. (2014). Fun and friends: The impact of workplace fun and constituent attachment on turnover in a hospitality context. *Human Relations, 67*(8), 923–946.

Tims, M., Bakker, A. B., & Derks, D. (2012). Development and validation of the job crafting scale. *Journal of Vocational Behavior, 80*(1), 173–186.

Vallerand, R. J., Blanchard, C., Mageau, G. A., Koestner, R., Ratelle, C., Léonard, M., et al. (2003). Les passions de l'âme: On obsessive and harmonious passion. *Journal of Personality and Social Psychology, 85,* 756–767.

Van den Broeck, A., Vander Elst, T., Dikkers, J., De Lange, A., & De Witte, H. (2012). This is funny: On the beneficial role of self-enhancing and affiliative humour in job design. *Psicothema, 24*(1), 87–93.

Van Wormer, K., & Boes, M. (1997). Humor in the emergency room: A social work perspective. *Health and Social Work, 22*(2), 87–92.

Vilaythong, A. P., Arnau, R. C., Rosen, D. H., & Mascaro, N. (2003). Humor and hope: Can humor increase hope? *Humor—International Journal of Humor Research, 16*(1), 79–89.

Vivona, B. D. (2014). Humor functions within crime scene investigations: Group dynamics, stress, and the negotiation of emotions. *Police Quarterly, 17*(2), 127–149. doi:10.1177/1098611114531418.

Wanzer, M., Booth-Butterfield, M., & Booth-Butterfield, S. (2005). "If we didn't use humor, we'd cry": Humorous coping communication in health care settings. *Journal of Health Communication, 10*(2), 105–125.

Weisenberg, M., Tepper, I., & Schwarzwald, J. (1995). Humor as a cognitive technique for increasing pain tolerance. *Pain, 63*(2), 207–212.

White, S., & Winzelberg, A. (1992). Laughter and stress. *Humor—International Journal of Humor Research, 5*(4), 343–355.

Wrzesniewski, A., & Dutton, J. E. (2001). Crafting a job: Revisioning employees as active crafters of their work. *Academy of Management Review, 26,* 179–201.

Yip, J. A., & Martin, R. A. (2006). Sense of humor, emotional intelligence, and social competence. *Journal of Research in Personality, 40*(6), 1202–1208.

Zhao, J., Wang, Y., & Kong, F. (2014). Exploring the mediation effect of social support and self-esteem on the relationship between humor style and life satisfaction in Chinese college students. *Personality and Individual Differences, 64,* 126–130.

Zillmann, D., Rockwell, S., Schweitzer, K., & Sundar, S. S. (1993). Does humor facilitate coping with physical discomfort? *Motivation and Emotion, 17*(1), 1–21.

Zweyer, K., Velker, B., & Ruch, W. (2004). Do cheerfulness, exhilaration, and humor production moderate pain tolerance? A FACS study. *Humor—International Journal of Humor Research, 17*(1/2), 85–120.

Chapter 8
Two Emerging Topics for Humor Research and Practice: Diversity and Virtuality

Tabea Scheel and Christine Gockel

Abstract In this concluding chapter, we discuss two important new avenues for humor research. First, globalization, as well as demographic changes in organizations, increase diversity with regard to age, gender, nationality, and so on. Thus, there will also be more diversity in communication, the expression of emotions, and the use of humor within work units. As one consequence, humorous comments may be accompanied by misunderstandings. In worse cases, the workflow might suffer. Second, due to increasing workplace flexibility in organizations, more communication will take place virtually, for instance, via email, chat, or skype. All of these media transmit less information than traditional face-to-face communication. Therefore, it becomes more difficult for receivers to decipher those social and emotional cues that signal that a comment is not meant seriously. More misunderstandings in humorous communications should result. We discuss to what extent these misunderstandings might be mitigated by the use of emoticons and other virtual signals of emotions. Taken together, leaders and employees alike are advised to establish some common ground for their humorous communications in their work units.

Keywords Diversity · Age · Gender · Culture · Virtuality · Computer-mediated communication (CMC) · Face-to-face (FTF) communication · Virtual teams · Emoticons · Media richness theory

8.1 Diverse Humor

High hopes are connected to the use of humor, as "Humor is the universal language that can speak across generations and cultures" (Lurie & Monahan, 2015, p. 82).

Humor is part of every social system (Martineau, 1972) and its consequences depend on cultural values (Gruber, Mauss, & Tamir, 2011). In a more and more globalized workforce, this issue becomes central for the performance in

---

The original version of this chapter was revised: See the "Chapter Note" section at the end of this chapter for details. The erratum to this chapter is available at https://doi.org/10.1007/978-3-319-65691-5_9

T. Scheel and C. Gockel, *Humor at Work in Teams, Leadership, Negotiations, Learning and Health*, SpringerBriefs in Psychology,
DOI 10.1007/978-3-319-65691-5_8

cross-national cooperations. But also, sex or gender roles in "developed countries" are undergoing fundamental changes, with calls for women's quota, and more women in high-status positions. Thus, the question whether women use humor as much and with the same purpose as men becomes ever more salient. Finally, due to demographic changes in the industrialized world, the issues of aging workforces and thus individual performance, as well as cross-generational issues, arise.

8.1.1 Cultural Diversity

Aligning cultural values with humor research is relevant for conclusions about "culture-specific humor." As cultural values determine perceptions, attitudes and social interactions of people, they also affect perceptions, attitudes and social interactions with regard to humor. Literally far-ranging studies about basic human values (Schwartz, 1992), cultural values (Hofstede, 1980) and culture-based leadership types (GLOBE study, House et al., 1999, 2004) find culture-dependent differences in work values. Building on findings from Hofstede (1980), the cross-sectional GLOBE study confirms nine cultural dimensions across work contexts in 62 countries. Those are: power distance, uncertainty avoidance, humane orientation, collectivism (institutional), collectivism (in-group), assertiveness, gender egalitarianism, future orientation, and performance orientation (House et al., 2004). Later, another dimension concerning long- versus short-term orientation was introduced (Minkov & Hofstede, 2012).

For example, cultures high in power distance (i.e., hierarchy) may not tolerate aggressive humor against supervisors, high in-group collectivism may foster affiliative humor with in-group members but aggressive humor towards out-group members, and low gender egalitarianism may inhibit certain humor types for women (e.g., aggressive). Humane orientation may be aligned with self-enhancing humor. For instance, Lundquist (2014) analyzed Danish humor characteristics (ironic, self-ironic, sarcastic, direct, no taboos) in professional settings, using a linguistic and a historico-sociological approach. She ascribed what she called "campfire mentality" to the horizontal, flat structure and low power distance in Danish work relationships.

Based on Hofstedes' (1980) cultural dimensions, Kalliny, Cruthirds, and Minor (2006) predicted how culture relates to humor use in a comparison between (mostly students) Americans (mostly Hispanics) and Arabs (Egyptian, Lebanese). Likewise, Kazarian and Martin (2006) compared Armenian-Lebanese and American students, Chen and Martin (2007) compared Chinese and Canadian students, and Kazarian and Martin (2004) Lebanese, Canadian and Belgian students. The HSQ was cross-culturally stable (e.g., Kazarian & Martin, 2004). Of the positive styles, *affiliative* humor was not more prevalent in collectivistic cultures (Arabs) than in the USA (Kalliny et al., 2006), and Lebanese scored even lower than Canadians or Belgians on affiliative humor (Kazarian & Martin, 2004). However, affiliative humor correlated positively with self-assessed horizontal collectivism in the latter study.

Self-enhancing humor was higher in individualistic cultures (USA) than in Arab samples (Kalliny et al., 2006). Accordingly, Canadians (but not Belgians) scored higher than Lebanese on self-enhancing humor (Kazarian & Martin, 2004). However, self-enhancing humor correlated positively with self-assessed horizontal collectivism in the latter study.

Of the negative humor styles, *self-defeating* humor was higher in cultures with low power distance (USA; Kalliny et al., 2006), but Lebanese, Canadian and Belgian students did not differ in their self-defeating humor (Kazarian & Martin, 2004). However, self-defeating humor was positively related to self-assessed vertical collectivism in the latter study.

Contrary to assumptions, *aggressive* humor was not different between masculine cultures (i.e., low gender equality; Arab countries) and a low masculine culture (USA). Accordingly, aggressive humor was not lower in cultures high in uncertainty avoidance (entailing avoiding the risk of offending someone). However, Lebanese students scored lower than Belgians (but not Canadians) on aggressive humor (Kazarian & Martin, 2004). Aggressive humor was negatively associated with (self-assessed) horizontal collectivism and positively with individualism in the latter study.

Summarized, Arabs were lower in self-enhancing and self-defeating humor than Americans, while affective and aggressive humor did not differ (Kalliny et al., 2006). However, Armenian-Lebanese (Kazarian & Martin, 2006) and Chinese (compared to Canadian students, Chen & Martin, 2007) scored lower than Americans in all four styles, Chinese especially regarding aggressive humor. Thus, the inconsistent findings, as well as the differences when comparing national samples versus self-assessed cultural values, deserve more thorough analyses. For instance, whether nations (rather than regions) are the adequate unit of analysis for values is controversial as nations may be culturally heterogeneous (Minkov & Hofstede, 2014). Homogenous and distinct national clusters of value measures (Schwartz's 21 Value Items) were found for (a total of 316) regions of most European countries and randomly formed groups. While groups from some countries were 100% homogenous (e.g., Netherlands, Denmark, Norway, Estonia), other countries seem more heterogeneous with regard to the cultures of their regions (e.g., Greece 54% homogeneous, Switzerland 57%; 60% Russia, 81% France and Germany, 83% Spain).

On the one hand, there may be more similarities than differences, on the other hand, even between cultures perceived as similar as the German and the Austrian, differences may be detectable: Austrian knowledge workers rated their positive humor styles at work higher than their German counterparts, while no differences were found for the negative styles (Scheel, Gerdenitsch, & Korunka, 2016). Thus, when conducting future research, the heterogeneity has to be taken into account.

Cultural diversity implies that a common reference frame may be missing, while shared culture promotes affiliation and humor plays a special role in interpersonal relations (Curry & Dunbar, 2013). Results of an experiment showed that the degree of shared appreciation for both sets of stimuli (non-humorous: first lines of novels; humorous: jokes) had a positive effect on affiliation, and only humorous stimuli had an effect on altruism (Curry & Dunbar, 2013). This is especially important as cooperation requires that persons are able to identify and associate with others who have compatible preferences and shared background knowledge. These findings imply potential problems for virtual work (see next section).

Cultural diversity and work The findings so far are of a general kind—studies in the work context are rare. Though the following examples refer to the work context, they are rather anecdotal. Within cultures, the respective *Communities of Practice* (a linguistic approach) is of importance for understanding the ways humor is and humor must be used. Murata (2014) examined Japanese and New Zealand *business meetings*: though humor serves as a relational practice, its manifestations are distinctive in each community of practice/workplace culture—the relational practice is enacted through humor in ways that meet the underlying expectations of each country. For instance, the use of humor contributes to the construction of the status relationships.

Maemura (2014) found humor and laughter in Japanese groups to be determined by *kuuki* of *negotiations*; Japanese conversations are governed by implicitly defined conversational rules—*kuuki*—of a social interaction. Understanding group dynamics in a high-context culture like Japan is essential—likely to imagine what a challenge that means for foreigners!

In a review of ethnic diversity to be regarded in using humor in *counseling,* Maples et al. (2001) report general differences: Native Americans seem to use humor with the purpose of reaffirming and enhancing the sense of connectedness, in being part of a family/clan/tribe. Asian Americans use humor for strengthening family ties, bound to insiders, and very conditional humor (based on trust), implying no direct teasing and no self-defeating humor, as those kinds violate the boundaries of respect. Latinos (i.e., Mexican Americans, Puerto Ricans, Cuban Americans living in the US) are reported to have a gender-based world in which jokes have sexual meanings and gender roles and gender-settings are important. African Americans rather play with stereotypes they hold about themselves, but favor integrity, that is, humor must be genuine and congruent with beliefs. Needless to say, whether these assumptions about humor use in diverse ethnicities hold in general needs further empirical research. Maples et al. (2001) derive recommendations for using humor in counseling: (1) both must be comfortable with humor, (2) efficacy must be the purpose for humor in counseling, (3) mutual trust and respect are precondition, (4) the timing and pacing is important, that is, the right to use humor must be earned, and (5) humor has to be tailored or customized to the cultural orientation. On the one hand, it seems plausible to generalize these recommendations to coaching and training contexts, on the other hand, there is a huge research gap.

8.1.2 Gender Diversity

Empirical evidence for gender differences in the use of humor is inconsistent. Neither Thorson and Powell (1993) nor Vilaythong, Arnau, Rosen, and Mascaro

(2003) found significant differences between genders as measured by the Multidimensional Sense of Humor Scale (MSHS).

However, with regard to *humor production,* Thorson and Powell (1993) report higher scores for men than women, majority US students. In the same line, in one of the rare studies from work context with 123 teachers and staff members of a small-town US high school (Bowling et al., 2004), men indicated higher generation of humor (assessed with several sense of humor scales) than women. Also, in a study were the US undergrad business students responded to a hypothetical, socially awkward situation at work (Cox, Read, & Van Auken, 1990), men had higher humor responses than women, while women had higher helping responses. The authors concluded that humor seems to be less a part of communicative patterns of women. However, women showed higher coping humor (Thorson & Powell, 1993).

Besides humor production, most gender differences are reported with regard to the higher *aggressive humor* of men (e.g., Dyck & Holtzman, 2013; Greengross & Miller, 2008; Liu, 2012). Likewise, (French and US) male students seem to *appreciate* aggressive or dark humor more than their female counterparts (Aillaud & Piolat, 2012; Prerost, 1995). In line, US male students (but not female students) found cartoons funnier the more sexual the themes were, while for women (but not men) the funniness of the cartoons decreased with increasing sexism (Love & Deckers, 1989). Admittedly, the majority of these studies are based on (mostly US) students' self-reports or hypothetical situations. Additionally, given that gender stereotypes changed in the last decades, especially the last two studies are outdated. However, Kuipers (2015) argues for differences in the appreciation of jokes between genders from a sociological perspective, supporting the assumption that women find offensive jokes less funny than men. This applies to aggressive, ethnic or sick humor rather than sexual humor. Among the reasons suggested, the sensitivity of women is said to be higher and the aim of communication and joke telling is said to be different. While men aim to create a sense of community with other men by sharing offensive jokes, women use other strategies for this (e.g., gossip). An important notion by Kuipers (2015) says that "in terms of content the standard joke repertoire also seemingly has little to offer women" (p. 185).

In a meta-analysis on gender and humor including 141 cross-sectional studies, men scored higher than women in a general humor factor (Coner, 2016; Scheel & Nestler, in preparation). However, moderator analyses revealed that, for positive humor, no differences between men's and women's humor were found. The significantly higher ratings for men were mainly found for aggressive and sexual humor. Most interestingly, differences were larger for other- as compared for self-rating, and also for newer as compared to older studies. The latter finding was especially unexpected, however, methods and procedures changed over the decades and became more sophisticated. Interesting for this volume were also the contexts: while for relationships and schools, gender differences were significant, for work context they were not.

Culture and gender Like general findings of gender and humor, gender and culture may interact regarding humor. However, empirical evidence supports gender differences regardless of culture: Canadian, Belgian and Lebanese men rated higher on negative humor styles (i.e., aggressive, self-defeating) as compared to women (Chen & Martin, 2007; Kazarian & Martin, 2004). Also, American/US, Arab and Hong Kong men scored higher on aggressive humor as compared with their female counterparts (Greengross & Miller, 2008; Kalliny et al., 2006; Liu, 2012). Armenian-Lebanese men scored higher than women on all four humor styles, especially the negative forms (Kazarian & Martin, 2006).

Summarized, even in cultures low in masculinity (USA) aggressive humor use differed between genders with men having higher ratings (e.g., Kalliny et al., 2006). Thus, the preliminary evidence speaks for higher aggressive humor use of males than females across these cultures. However, this was not found for negative humor styles of Chinese men as compared to women's (Chen & Martin, 2007). Also, Chinese men scored higher on the Coping Humor Scale (CHS) than women.

8.1.3 Age Diversity

Humor is age-related, that is, what we find funny, how we use humor and the extent of laughter seems to depend on our age. As to humor *preferences*: while in childhood clownish behavior, visual surprise and slapstick are preferred, in adolescence subtleties and irreverent behavior are appreciated, and in adulthood diversity and individuality (Buijzen & Valkenburg, 2004).

The *use* of humor seems slightly to depend on age, too. Though Proyer, Ruch, and Müller (2010) report that sense of humor was generally stable across life span, in a large-scale study with 65,333 Norwegian adults, Svebak, Martin, and Holmen (2004) found a negative relationship between age and scores in the Sense of Humor Questionnaire (SHQ); in younger cohorts, the scores were slightly higher for males. Also, aggressive (or other-deprecating) humor declined with age in a sample of male students between 18 and 30 years (Greengross & Miller, 2008).

Accordingly, our expression of *laughter* seems to decline with age (though positive mood increased) (Proyer et al., 2010). However, Martin and Kuiper (1999) reported this decline in self-assessed laughing frequency with age only for women, but not for men.

As age-related changes in the face—like smile wrinkles—impede decoding of displayed emotions (Hess, Adams, Simard, Stevenson, & Kleck, 2012), social interactions in which emotions are communicated reciprocally (e.g., Duchenne-smile versus non-Duchenne; Hess & Bourgeois, 2010) might be affected by age.

Summarized, humor preferences and the expression of laughter seem to change with age. Also, sense of humor and aggressive humor seem to decline with age, though the evidence is inconsistent and hints at gender effects. On the one hand, when workforces grow older, they may seem more serious, thus causing cross-generational differences and sometimes misunderstandings. On the other hand, older workforces may show higher positive mood.

Culture and age Age seems to be associated with the decline of specific humor styles across cultures, thus, age, as well as gender, may be the more important conditions as compared with culture. For instance, younger Chinese, Canadian and Armenian-Lebanese respondents had higher affiliative and aggressive humor (Chen & Martin, 2007; Kazarian & Martin, 2006). In the Armenian-Lebanese sample, self-defeating (but not self-enhancing) humor correlated negatively with age (Kazarian & Martin, 2006).

8.1.4 Future Research

Cultural differences in humor use need to be comprehensively assessed. Subsequently, the consequences of these potential differences and similarities in work contexts need to be investigated. Likewise, gender differences in humor need to be investigated regarding their impact in work contexts. Given that there seem to be differences between the humor used by men and women, and that humor serves several functions in the work context, the implications for, for instance, gender equality or justice issues have to be investigated. There is little research about intergenerational effects of humor use, let alone about the different kinds of humor in this regard. As age is usually also connected with senior positions, the interplay between position and age may be especially interesting for effects of humor and humor climate, but also challenging to disentangle. Finally, the interaction of gender, age and ethnic diversity in the use of humor and its effect in the work context need to be taken into account in future studies. For instance, teams may include diverse members regarding age and ethnic background, creating "fault lines" with regard to humor.

One issue that is widely neglected in research about diversity is to account for persons with diverse mental or physiological handicaps. First, are there differences in humor use related to handicaps? Second, what implications do these differences have for the work context, for instance, for workplace integration or socialization? Who is allowed to make jokes, what stereotypes may be manifested with jokes, or how is humor to be used between handicapped and non-handicapped employees?

8.1.5 Recommendations

Generally, intercultural differences should not mask the huge intracultural differences between persons. As shown, cultural differences may become negligible once gender and age differences are factored in. Also, humor use may differ considerably despite having the same gender, age or handicap. That said, the recommendations given here are of a very general nature. (1) It is advisable to step back and observe the humor of the counterpart or coworker until you have a clue about the meaning of the different styles of the respective culture (as well as gender and age group) and the respective person. (2) Start with simple actions like smiling, laughing, and benign spontaneous funny remarks. (3) In the beginning, avoid jokes, as they are usually context and culture dependent. At best, no one will laugh because your counterpart does not understand it. At worst, it will cause misunderstandings, offense, and irritation. (4) Avoid negative forms of humor, especially the aggressive style, at least until the relationships are developed and trustful, and you understand the meaning of negative forms in the culture of your counterpart. (5) Employ self-defeating humor only if you are sure you will not undermine your status and the other will not interpret it as a weakness.

In summary, as much or less diverse people might be, trust and mutual respect are fundamental preconditions for a truly functional way of using humor.

8.2 Humor in Computer-Mediated Communication

Most people regularly use computer-mediated communication. For example, in 2016 in Germany, 76% of the population used smartphones (Bitkom, 2016) and in 2015, around 667 million WhatsApp messages were sent per day (VATM, 2015). Currently, 30% of organizations offer some kind of work in virtual teams or telework to employees with a college degree (Staufenbiel Institut, 2016).

Because humor occurs in almost all interactions, it should also occur in most computer-mediated interactions. Thus, a closer look at the differences between face-to-face (FTF) and computer-mediated communication (CMC) is warranted. We focus especially on CMC as it occurs in virtual teams because these teams represent a frequent form of team work in today's organizations and their cooperation is built on CMC. We first explain differences between FTF and CMC, present relevant research findings, and highlight implications for humor usage in CMC.

8.2.1 Important Definitions

CMC differs from FTF communication in two dimensions of social presence (Manstead, Lea, & Goh, 2011). On a physical dimension, nonverbal cues and visibility can be diminished in CMC. Depending on the medium, it might be more difficult to decode others' humorous messages because important pieces of information are not transmitted. On the second dimension, the social dimension, the extent to which other people are salient is reduced. This might lead to less perspective-taking when drafting humorous messages and explain a tendency to more aggressive humor.

In a work context, most CMC occurs in the context of virtual teams. In those teams, members are geographically and temporally dispersed, and cooperation depends on technology (Martins, Gilson, & Maynard, 2004). Virtual teams often have members from different organizations, cultures, or with different native languages, which might lead to very different norms regarding the expression of humor. Also, because virtual teams are generally diverse, all findings and conclusions about diversity from the previous section apply to virtual teams as well.

8.2.2 *Virtual Teamwork*

Virtual teamwork can also be described with different dimensions that help us understand humor usage. Four dimensions are particularly relevant in the context of humor.

First, virtual teamwork can be described in regards to synchronicity (Kirkman & Mathieu, 2005). It explains to what extent communication is synchronous, i.e., taking place in real time versus delayed. In FTF communication there is usually an immediate response after humorous comments, whereas in CMC the response is delayed. Speakers cannot get immediate feedback after their humor attempts, which might lead to more misunderstandings in the long run.

Second, the informational value is important (Kirkman & Mathieu, 2005). Some technological tools possess more informational value than others because they also transmit nonverbal or paraverbal signals. For example, in a video conference team members can see each others' gestures and hear each others' tone of voice, which makes it easier to decode humorous messages.

The third dimension refers to organizational membership (Chudoba, Wynn, Lu, & Watson-Manheim, 2005). Members can come from different areas in the same organization or from different organizations, and all units might have their own norms regarding humor usage.

Finally, the fourth dimension refers to cultural differences (Hoch & Kozlowski, 2014), which entail differences in humor usage norms. It might be perfectly acceptable to make fun of one's boss in one culture, but be a taboo in another. Thus, the more differences there are between members of a team, the more information has to be exchanged in order to prevent misunderstandings (Kauffeld, Handke, & Straube, 2016).

8.2.3 *Relevant Research Findings*

Although there is not much research about humor usage in CMC and in virtual teams, three general trends in findings of virtual teamwork can be transferred well to humor usage.

In general, there is less communication overall in virtual than in FTF teams (Andres, 2012). Communication in virtual teams is often text-based and therefore requires more effort than FTF communication. Also, there is less socio-emotional communication (Mesmer-Magnus, DeChurch, Jimenez-Rodriguez, Wildman, & Shuffler, 2011). Thus, a stronger focus on the task in communications in virtual teams can be found (Kauffeld et al., 2016) and conflicts are generally detected later than in FTF teams (Hertel, Geister, & Konradt, 2005). These findings imply that humor is used less often in virtual teams and that misunderstandings about humor may be increased due to communication delays and/or language difficulties.

The second relevant research finding is that there is no or reduced visibility of emotional cues, which greatly increases the possibility of misunderstandings (Axtell, Fleck, & Turner, 2004). Nonverbal communication helps to reduce the ambiguity of emotion expressions and can either intensify or downplay a spoken message (Derks, Fischer, & Bos, 2008). For example, the expression "My boss gave me great feedback this morning" can be meant literally or ironically with completely different implications. One can only detect potential irony based on a "play frame" that usually accompanies humorous messages (Eisenberg, 1986). Thus, depending on the medium, in CMC important information might not be transmitted. In text-based CMC, senders of humorous messages need to express their humorous intent in the text (hahaha!) or in symbols like emoticons. Also, senders usually do not get immediate feedback about their message. They often cannot hear laughter, but need to wait patiently for some kind of text-based or symbol-based response.

Emoticons (or gifs) present one possibility to add humorous intent to a written message. They should thus have the same function as nonverbal communication. Research has shown that women tend to use emoticons more often to communicate humor of solidarity, whereas men tend to use them more often to communicate sarcasm (Wolf, 2000). However, the use of emoticons certainly depends on the context and the relevant team norms. Although emoticons function like an emblem for a person's feelings, there is one crucial difference between using emoticons and nonverbal behavior for a humorous message: Emoticons are always placed in a text deliberately and voluntarily (Derks et al., 2008). Therefore, spontaneity is greatly reduced. Another area of life, where people deliberately use emblems to amuse others, is the social network Facebook. Research has shown that Facebook users employ a variety of profile cues to demonstrate high humor orientation (e.g., self-related anecdotes or pop-culture references, Pennington & Hall, 2014). These cues are then used by observers to infer humor orientation.

The third relevant research finding is that people show more uninhibited behavior in CMC and insult each other more easily (Martins et al., 2004). It is not entirely clear if the rise in uninhibited behavior is due to lack of visibility or to changes in norms. There are first hints that a lack of visible cues predicts this kind of behavior (Castellá, Abad, Alonso, & Silla, 2000). Thus, aggressive humor should occur more often in CMC. And because of the reduced visibility of emotional cues, it should also be misunderstood often. It is therefore advisable to avoid aggressive humor in CMC.

8.2.4 Future Research

Because of the paucity of research in this area, humor researchers have many possibilities to advance knowledge. First, they could compare the use of humor in different media to have more information about what kind of humor is used by whom. Second, they could interview senders and receivers about their intentions and perceptions of humor. Because humor is mostly used intentionally and often text-based in CMC, senders should be able to explain why they used humor; and because humor attempts also require an intentional and text-based response, receivers should be able to describe how funny they found the humor and what they believed the effects were. In contrast, in FTF groups humor is used much more spontaneously, and interviews about sender intentions and receiver perceptions would therefore not be possible. Third, one could easily study intentions and perceptions in a lab setting to examine cause-and-effect relationships. In this kind of setting, it is generally much easier to manipulate humor because receivers do not see who sends the humor. Humor in CMC fits the experimental method, and a variety of interesting research questions can be answered in the laboratory.

8.2.5 Recommendations

People using CMC seem to have found ways of coping with the restrictions of this kind of communication—for example, by using emoticons, gifs, or by verbalizing their emotions and intentions (Derks et al., 2008).

Media Richness Theory (Daft & Lengel, 1986) provides some suggestions about how to use communication media in order to get certain information across from sender to receiver. The assumption is that different media are suited differently for transferring certain kinds of information. More specifically, rich and ambiguous information (like negative feedback) should be transmitted FTF for better understanding. And simple and clear information can be transmitted with less rich media like email.

To conclude, working in a virtual team and using humor requires intercultural competencies, clear rules about behavior, regular checks on members' moods, as well as open and immediate feedback about problems. Additionally, one needs to keep in mind that it takes more time to use humor effectively in CMC because it is usually constructed and risky. Nevertheless, we believe it is worth the effort.

References

Aillaud, M., & Piolat, A. (2012). Influence of gender on judgment of dark and nondark humor. *Individual Differences Research, 10*(4), 211–222.

Andres, H. P. (2012). Technology-mediated collaboration, shared mental model and task performance. *Journal of Organizational and End User Computing (JOEUC), 24*(1), 64–81.

Axtell, C. M., Fleck, S. J., & Turner, N. (2004). Virtual teams: Collaborating across distance. *International Review of Industrial and Organizational Psychology, 19,* 205–248.

Bitkom. (2016). Anteil der Smartphone-Nutzer in Deutschland in den Jahren 2012 bis 2016. In Statista - Das Statistik-Portal. Retrieved from https://de.statista.com/statistik/daten/studie/585883/umfrage/anteil-der-smartphone-nutzer-in-deutschland/.

Bowling, N. A., Beehr, T. A., Johnson, A. L., Semmer, N. K., Hendricks, E. A., & Webster, H. A. (2004). Explaining potential antecedents of workplace social support: Reciprocity or attractiveness? *Journal of Occupational Health Psychology, 9*(4), 339–350. doi:10.1037/1076-8998.9.4.339.

Buijzen, M., & Valkenburg, P. M. (2004). Development a typology of humor in audivisual media. *Media Psychology, 6,* 147–167. doi:10.1207/s1532785xmep0602_2.

Castellá, V. O., Abad, A. Z., Alonso, F. P., & Silla, J. P. (2000). The influence of familiarity among group members, group atmosphere and assertiveness on uninhibited behavior through three different communication media. *Computers in Human Behavior, 16*(2), 141–159.

Chen, G.-H., & Martin, R. A. (2007). A comparison of humor styles, coping humor, and mental health between Chinese and Canadian university students. *Humor, 20*(3), 215–234. doi:10.1515/HUMOR.2007.011.

Chudoba, K. M., Wynn, E., Lu, M., & Watson-Manheim, M. B. (2005). How virtual are we? Measuring virtuality and understanding its impact in a global organization. *Information Systems Journal, 15*(4), 279–306.

Coner, W. (2016). *Geschlechterdifferenzen im Bereich Humor - eine Metaanalyse* [*Gender differences in the domain of humor—A metaanalysis*] (Unpublished Master's Thesis). University of Vienna, Austria.

Cox, J. A., Read, R. L., & Van Auken, P. M. (1990). Male-female differences in communicating job-related humor: An exploratory study. *Humor, 3*(3), 287–295.

Curry, O. S., & Dunbar, R. I. M. (2013). Sharing a joke: The effects of a similar sense of humor on affiliation and altruism. *Evolution and Human Behavior, 34*(2), 125–129. doi:10.1016/j.evolhumbehav.2012.11.003.

Daft, R. L., & Lengel, R. H. (1986). Organizational information requirements, media richness and structural design. *Management Science, 32*(5), 554–571.

Derks, D., Fischer, A. H., & Bos, A. E. R. (2008). The role of emotion in computer-mediated communication: A review. *Computers in Human Behavior, 24*(3), 766–785. doi:10.1016/j.chb.2007.04.004.

Dyck, K. T. H., & Holtzman, S. (2013). Understanding humor styles and well-being: The importance of social relationships and gender. *Personality and Individual Differences, 55*(1), 53–58. doi:10.1016/j.paid.2013.01.023.

Eisenberg, A. R. (1986). Teasing: Verbal play in two mexicano homes. In B. B. Schieffelin & E. Ochs (Eds.), *Language socialization across cultures* (pp. 183–198). Cambridge: Cambridge University Press.

Greengross, G., & Miller, G. F. (2008). Dissing oneself versus dissing rivals: Effects of status, personality, and sex on the short-term and long-term attractiveness of self-deprecating and other-deprecating humor. *Evolutionary Psychology, 6*(3), 393–408.

Gruber, J., Mauss, I. B., & Tamir, M. (2011). A dark side of happiness? How, when, and why happiness is not always good. *Perspectives on Psychological Science, 6*(3), 222–233. doi:10.1177/1745691611406927.

Hertel, G., Geister, S., & Konradt, U. (2005). Managing virtual teams: A review of current empirical research. *Human Resource Management Review, 15*(1), 69–95.

Hess, U., Adams, R. B., Simard, A., Stevenson, M. T., & Kleck, R. E. (2012). Smiling and sad wrinkles: Age-related changes in the face and the perception of emotions and intentions. *Journal of Experimental Social Psychology, 48*(6), 1377–1380. doi:10.1016/j.jesp.2012.05.018.

Hess, U., & Bourgeois, P. (2010). You smile–I smile: Emotion expression in social interaction. *Biological Psychology, 84*(3), 514–520. doi:10.1016/j.biopsycho.2009.11.001.

Hoch, J. E., & Kozlowski, S. W. (2014). Leading virtual teams: Hierarchical leadership, structural supports, and shared team leadership. *Journal of Applied Psychology, 99*(3), 390–403.

Hofstede, G. H. (1980). *Culture's consequences: International differences in work-related values*. Thousand Oaks, CA: Sage.

House, R. J., et al. (Eds.). (2004). *Culture, leadership, and organizations: The GLOBE study of 62 societies*. Thousand Oaks, CA: Sage.

House, R. J., Hanges, P. J., Ruiz-Quintanilla, S. A., Dorfman, P. W., Javidan, M., Dickson, M., et al. (1999). Cultural influences on leadership and organizations: Project GLOBE. *Advances in Global Leadership, 1*, 171–233.

Kalliny, M., Cruthirds, K. W., & Minor, M. S. (2006). Differences between American, Egyptian and Lebanese humor styles: Implications for international management. *International Journal of Cross Cultural Management, 6*(1), 121–134. doi:10.1177/1470595806062354.

Kauffeld, S., Handke, M. S. L., & Straube, M. S. J. (2016). Verteilt und doch verbunden: Virtuelle Teamarbeit. *Gruppe. Interaktion. Organisation. Zeitschrift Für Angewandte Organisation spsychologie (GIO), 47*(1), 43–51.

Kazarian, S. S., & Martin, R. A. (2004). Humour styles, personality, and well-being among Lebanese university students. *European Journal of Personality, 18*(3), 209–219. doi:10.1002/per.505.

Kazarian, S. S., & Martin, R. A. (2006). Humor styles, culture-related personality, well-being, and family adjustment among Armenians in Lebanon. *Humor—International Journal of Humor Research, 19*(4), 405–423. doi: 10.1515/HUMOR.2006.020.

Kuipers, G. (2015). *Good humor, bad taste: A sociology of the joke*. Berlin: De Gruyter.

Kirkman, B. L., & Mathieu, J. E. (2005). The dimensions and antecedents of team virtuality. *Journal of Management, 31*(5), 700–718.

Liu, K. W. Y. (2012). Humor styles, self-esteem and subjective happiness. *Humor, 1*, 21–41.

Love, A. M., & Deckers, L. H. (1989). Humor appreciation as a function of sexual, aggressive, and sexist content. *Sex Roles, 20*(11–12), 649–654.

Lundquist, L. (2014). Danish humor in cross-cultural professional settings: Linguistic and social aspects. *Humor—International Journal of Humor Research, 27*(1), 141–163. doi: 10.1515/humor-2013-0044.

Lurie, A., & Monahan, K. (2015). Humor, aging, and life review: Survival through the use of humor. *Social Work in Mental Health, 13*(1), 82–91.

Maemura, Y. (2014). Humor and laughter in Japanese groups: The kuuki of negotiations. *Humor—International Journal of Humor Research, 27*(1), 103–119. doi:10.1515/humor-2013-0049.

Manstead, A. S. R., Lea, M., & Goh, J. (2011). Facing the future: Emotion communication and the presence of others in the age of video-mediated communication. In A. Kappas & N. Krämer (Eds.), *Face-to-face communication over the Internet: Issues, research, challenges* (pp. 144–175). Cambridge: Cambridge University Press.

Maples, M. F., Dupey, P., Torres-Rivera, E., Phan, L. T., Vereen, L., & Garrett, M. T. (2001). Ethnic diversity and the use of humor in counseling: Appropriate or inappropriate? *Journal of Counseling & Development, 79*(1), 53–60.

Martin, R. A., & Kuiper, N. A. (1999). Daily occurrence of laughter: Relationships with age, gender, and Type A personality. *Humor, 12*(4), 355–384.

Martineau, W. H. (1972). A model of the social functions of humor. In J. Goldstein &, P. McGhee (Eds.), *The psychology of humor* (pp. 101–125). New York: Academic Press.

Martins, L. L., Gilson, L. L., & Maynard, M. T. (2004). Virtual teams: What do we know and where do we go from here? *Journal of Management, 30*(6), 805–835.

Mesmer-Magnus, J. R., DeChurch, L. A., Jimenez-Rodriguez, M., Wildman, J., & Shuffler, M. (2011). A meta-analytic investigation of virtuality and information sharing in teams. *Organizational Behavior and Human Decision Processes, 115*(2), 214–225.

Minkov, M., & Hofstede, G. (2012). Hofstede's fifth dimension: New evidence from the World Values Survey. *Journal of Cross-Cultural Psychology, 43*(1), 3–14. doi:10.1177/0022022110388567.

Minkov, M., & Hofstede, G. (2014). Clustering of 316 European regions on measures of values: Do Europe's countries have national cultures? *Cross-Cultural Research, 48*(2), 144–176. doi:10.1177/1069397113510866.

Murata, K. (2014). An empirical cross-cultural study of humour in business meetings in New Zealand and Japan. *Journal of Pragmatics, 60,* 251–265. doi:10.1016/j.pragma.2013.09.002.

Pennington, N., & Hall, J. A. (2014). An analysis of humor orientation on Facebook: A lens model approach. *Humor—International Journal of Humor Research, 27*(1), 1–21. doi:10.1515/humor-2013-0053.

Prerost, F. J. (1995). Sexual desire and the dissipation of anger arousal through humor appreciation; gender and content issues. *Social Behavior and Personality, 23*(1), 45–52.

Proyer, R. T., Ruch, W., & Müller, L. (2010). Sense of humor among the elderly: Findings using the German version of the SHS. *Zeitschrift Für Gerontologie Und Geriatrie, 43*(1), 19–24. doi:10.1007/s00391-009-0082-0.

Scheel, T., Gerdenitsch, C., & Korunka, C. (2016). Humor at work: Validation of the short work-related Humor Styles Questionnaire (swHSQ). *HUMOR, 29*(3), 439–465. doi:10.1515/humor-2015-0118.

Scheel, T., & Nestler, S. (in preparation). Gender differences in humor use—a meta-analysis.

Schwartz, S. H. (1992). Universals in the content and structure of values: Theory and empirical tests in 20 countries. In M. Zanna (Ed.), *Advances in experimental social psychology* (vol. 25, pp. 1–65). New York: Academic Press.

Staufenbiel Institut. (2016.). Welche Arbeitszeitmodelle über feste Wochenarbeitszeiten hinaus bietet Ihr Unternehmen den Hochschulabsolventen?. In Statista - Das Statistik-Portal. Retrieved from https://de.statista.com/statistik/daten/studie/408854/umfrage/arbeitszeitmodelle-fuer-hochschulabsolventen-in-deutschen-unternehmen/.

Svebak, S., Martin, R. A., & Holmen, J. (2004). The prevalence of sense of humor in a large, unselected county population in Norway: Relations with age, sex, and some health indicators. *Humor, 17*(1/2), 121–134.

Thorson, J. A., & Powell, F. C. (1993). Development and validation of a multidimensional sense of humor scale. *Journal of Clinical Psychology, 49*(1), 13–23. doi:10.1002/1097-4679(199301)49:13.0.CO;2-S.

VATM. (2015). Anzahl der verschickten SMS- und WhatsApp-Nachrichten in Deutschland von 1999 bis 2014 und Prognose für 2015 (in Millionen pro Tag). In Statista - Das Statistik-Portal. Retrieved from https://de.statista.com/statistik/daten/studie/3624/umfrage/entwicklung-der-anzahl-gesendeter-sms–mms-nachrichten-seit-1999/.

Vilaythong, A. P., Arnau, R. C., Rosen, D. H., & Mascaro, N. (2003). Humor and hope: Can humor increase hope? *Humor, 16*(1), 79–89.

Wolf, A. (2000). Emotional expression online: Gender differences in emoticon use. *CyberPsychology & Behavior, 3*(5), 827–833.

Erratum to: Humor at Work in Teams, Leadership, Negotiations, Learning and Health

Tabea Scheel and Christine Gockel

Erratum to: T. Scheel and C. Gockel, *Humor at Work in Teams, Leadership, Negotiations, Learning and Health*, SpringerBriefs in Psychology, http://doi.org/10.1007/978-3-319-65691-5

In the original version of the book, chapter author names have to be included in respective chapter opening page and Laura Vetter as contributing author for Chapter 4. The erratum book has been updated with the changes.

The updated online version of this book can be found at http://doi.org/10.1007/978-3-319-65691-5

T. Scheel and C. Gockel, *Humor at Work in Teams, Leadership, Negotiations, Learning and Health*, SpringerBriefs in Psychology,
DOI 10.1007/978-3-319-65691-5_9

Appendix

A.1 Humor Measures

In this appendix, we provide a selection of useful scales for assessing humor at work. Contiguous to describing the content, example items, and the scale's format, we indicate internal consistencies. Only approximately half of the original sources give factor analytical reports, especially not in the last century's publications. Thus, we add a note (and the respective page number of the source) if these analyses are available.

A.1.1 Coping Humor Scales

Doosje, Landsheer, Goede, and Doornen (2012) provide an extensive overview over humorous coping scales. We will briefly describe the humorous coping measures they classify as generic (Coping Humor Scale, CHS; Multidimensional Sense of Humor Scale, MSHS-C; Brief COPE, humorous coping scale/BCOPE-H). Of the specific humorous coping measures (e.g., Relational Humor Inventory, RHI, De Koning & Weiss, 2002), only the self-enhancing subscale of the Humor Styles Questionnaire (HSQ-SE; Martin, Puhlik-Doris, Larsen, Gray, & Weir, 2003) will be introduced in a subsequent section. The Questionnaire of Occupational Humorous Coping (QOHC) is one of the few scales specific for the workplace.

Coping Humor Scale, CHS (Martin & Lefcourt, 1983). The CHS measures the degree to which respondents make use of humor as a means of coping with stressful experiences. It consists of seven self-report statements (e.g., "I usually look for something comical to say when I am in tense situations" or "It has been my experience that humor is often a very effective way of coping with problems.") that are each rated on a 4-point Likert scale, ranging from *strongly disagree* (1) to *strongly agree* (4). The reported internal consistency was Cronbach's α of 0.61.

Brief COPE Inventory—subscale humor (Carver, 1997). This 2-item subscale is taken from the short version of the COPE by Carver, Scheier, and Weintraub (1989). Respondents are asked whether, when faced with stressful situations, they

T. Scheel and C. Gockel, *Humor at Work in Teams, Leadership, Negotiations, Learning and Health*, SpringerBriefs in Psychology,
DOI 10.1007/978-3-319-65691-5

usually act in ways reflecting the specific coping styles (i.e., "I've been making jokes about it." and "I've been making fun of the situation.") on a 4-point Likert scale from *never* (1) to *very much* (4). A Cronbach's α of 0.73 was reported for this subscale.

Multidimensional Sense of Humor Scale, MSHS (Thorson & Powell, 1993). Measuring several elements of the personal construct of sense of humor (creativity, coping, and appreciation) with four subscales across 24 items: (1) humor production/elements of humor creativity and social uses of humor (12 items, e.g., "I can often crack people up with the things I say."), (2) coping and uses of coping humor (5 items, e.g., "Uses of wit or humor help me master difficult situations."), (3) attitude toward humorous people (5 reversed items, e.g., "People who tell jokes are a pain in the neck."), (4) attitudes toward humor itself (2 items, e.g., "I appreciate those who generate humor."). Statements have to be rated by a 5-point Likert scale from *strongly disagree* (1) to *strongly agree* (5). The reported internal consistency for the total scale was $\alpha = 0.92$. Factor analyses are reported (i.e., Thorson & Powell, 1993, p. 21).

At work:
Questionnaire of Occupational Humorous Coping, QOHC (Doosje, De Goede, Van Doornen, & Goldstein, 2010). This 23-item scale focuses on coping humor at the workplace. Being partly based on the model of emotion regulation by Gross (2001), it contains four subscales of humorous coping methods, that is, antecedent-focused/reappraisal (9 items, e.g., "When I have to work more to finish something I am able to see the humor in the situation."), response-focused (4 items, e.g., "When my work makes me feel tense, I make jokes to avoid that feeling."), instrumental affiliative (3 items, e.g., "When a colleague's behavior bothers me, I let him or her know by making an appropriate joke.") and instrumental aggressive-manipulative (7, e.g., "When a colleague gets on my nerves, I use humor to get back at him or her."). The items have to be rated on a 5-point Likert scale from *never* (1) to *very often* (5). Cronbach's α was 0.82 for the antecedent-focused/reappraisal subscale, $\alpha = 0.80$ for the response-focused subscale, $\alpha = 0.73$ for the instrumental affiliative subscale and $\alpha = 0.80$ for the instrumental aggressive-manipulative subscale. Results of factor analyses are provided (i.e., Doosje et al., 2010, p. 294).

A.1.2 Personality/Sense of Humor Scales

The State-Trait-Cheerfulness-Inventory (STCI) covers exhilaratability as a trait and a state, while the SHS is based on playfulness as underlying concept of sense of humor. Cann, Holt, and Calhoun (1999) report that the CHS correlates (cross-sectionally) most with other humor scales (SHQ, SHRQ, MSHS), which suggests that dealing with potentially stressful experiences is a dominant dimension of sense of humor. In contrast, the Situational Humor Response Questionnaire

(SHRQ) and the Sense of Humor Questionnaire (SHQ)-Personal Liking assess an overall humor factor regardless of whether humor is used in coping with stress.

State-Trait-Cheerfulness-Inventory, STCI (Ruch, Köhler, & Van Thriel, 1996; Ruch, Köhler, & Van Thriel, 1997). This inventory is based on a state-trait model of exhilaratability. Three concepts are captured as both, states and traits (cheerfulness, seriousness, bad mood). The trait form (Ruch et al., 1996) contains 60 items (international form with 106 items). The 30-item state form of cheerfulness (Ruch et al., 1997) represents the segment of positive affectivity related to exhilaratability, with three 10-item subscales: cheerfulness (e.g., "I am ready to have some fun."), seriousness (e.g., "I'm prepared to do a task in earnest."), and bad mood (e.g., "I am sad.") . A 4-point Likert scale format from *strongly disagree* (1) to *strongly agree* (4) was chosen. For the trait form, internal consistency ranged from $\alpha = 0.81$ for seriousness to $\alpha = 0.92$ for cheerfulness and $\alpha = 0.93$ for bad mood (Ruch et al., 1996). Factor analyses are reported (i.e., Ruch et al., 1996, p. 332). For the state form, Cronbach's α was 0.93 and 0.94 for cheerfulness and bad mood, respectively, but only $\alpha = 0.55$ for seriousness (Ruch et al., 1997). Factor analysis was only mentioned without giving details.

Sense of Humor Scale, SHS (McGhee, 1994, 1996). This scale covers *playfulness* as the basis for *sense of humor*, which is measured with six less basic, hierarchically organized factors or humor skills: enjoyment of humor, seriousness and negative mood, playfulness and positive mood, laughter, verbal humor, finding humor in everyday life, laughing at yourself, and finding humor under stress. Proyer, Ruch, and Müller (2010) report reliabilities for the total scale from $\alpha = 0.90$ to 0.93 for five samples. However, subscale reliabilities varied between $\alpha = 0.44$ and 0.90, with lowest scores for enjoyment and laughing.

Multidimensional Sense of Humor Scale, MSHS (Thorson & Powell, 1993). This scale is described above (in the coping humor section). Herzog and Strevey (2008) combined 45 items of various sense of humor scales to a sense of humor "composite" and found all of them falling into the four categories suggested by Thorson and Powell (1993): humor production and social uses, coping humor, humor appreciation, and attitude toward humor (i.e., humor appreciation).

Situational Humor Response Questionnaire, SHRQ (Martin & Lefcourt, 1984). The SHRQ covers the degree to which subjects respond with mirth (i.e., laugh and smile) in a variety of different situations with 21 items. Eighteen descriptions of typical real-life pleasant and unpleasant situations that a person might encounter are provided (e.g., "You are eating in a restaurant with some friends and a waiter accidentally spilled a drink on you."). Respondents indicate the degree to which they would have responded with laughter on a range from *I would not have found anything particularly amusing* (1) to *I would have laughed heartily much of the time* (5). Three items were nonsituational/ general self-report items (e.g., "How important is it for you to have friends who are easily amused?"). Cronbach's α ranged from $\alpha = 0.70$ to $\alpha = 0.83$.

Sense of Humor Questionnaire, SHQ-6 (Svebak, 1996). The original SHQ (Svebak, 1974) assessed sense of humor with the subscales metamessage sensitivity, personal liking of humor, and emotional expressiveness, but the latter scale showed poor psychometric properties (Kuiper & Martin, 1998). The originally 7-item subscales metamessage sensitivity and personal liking are reduced to a total of six items in the short version, the SHQ-6. While metamessage sensitivity covers an individuals' ability to recognize or notice humor in various life situations (e.g., "I can usually find something comical, witty, or humorous in most situations."), the liking of humor includes attitudes towards humor, particularly the degree to which an individual likes humor and values the humorous role (reversed, e.g., "A humorist is typically perceived by others as a person who lacks the courage of his convictions."). Respondents indicate their agreement using a 4-point Likert scale ranging from *strongly disagree* (1) to *strongly agree* (4). The inter-item correlations for the three item pairs of the SHQ-6 ranged from 0.38 to 0.62. Results of factor analyses are provided (i.e., Svebak, 1996, p. 357).

A.1.3 Humor Types

The Humorous Behavior Deck-Revised (HBD-R) and the Humor Styles Questionnaire (HSQ) distinguish specific types of how humor is used. The short work-related HSQ (swHSQ) covers humor styles specific for the workplace.

Humorous Behavior Deck-Revised, HBD-R (Kirsh & Kuiper, 2003). The HBD-R is the revision of the Humorous Behavior Q-Sort Deck, HBQD (Craik, Lampert, & Nelson, 1996), which covered five bipolar humor types (e.g., socially warm vs. cold, competent vs. inept, reflective vs. boorish, earthy vs. repressed, benign vs. mean-spirited) and consisted of 100 statements describing specific forms of everyday humorous conduct as self- or peer descriptions. The 100 statements with individual items of humor-related characteristics and behaviors, that is, positive and negative forms of everyday humorous conduct (e.g., "maintains group morale through humor" versus "smiles inappropriately"), had to be sorted into nine categories ranging from *very uncharacteristic* (1) to *neutral* (5) to *very characteristic* (9). The HBD-R consists of 32 self-report items that assess the degree to which participants engage in one positive and two negative components of sense of humor. The factors skilled and adept use of humor (positive other-focused, e.g., "I use good-natured jests to put others at ease."), rude humor (negative other-focused, e.g., "I am sarcastic.") and belabored humor (negative self-focused, e.g., "I react in an exaggerated way to mildly humorous comments.") had to be rated on a 7-point Likert scale ranging from *extremely uncharacteristic of me* (1) to *extremely characteristic of me* (7). Factor analyses are provided (i.e., Kirsh & Kuiper, 2003, p. 42).

Humor Styles Survey, HSS (Philbrick, 1989; see Recepoğlu, Kilinç, & Çepni, 2011). The HSS was developed on basis of the four styles from Babad (1974), who reported that 46% of 81 female undergraduates were producers, 24.9% were appreciators, 5.9% were reproducers, and the remaining were classified as non-humorous.

Humor Styles Questionnaire, HSQ (Martin et al., 2003). The 32-item HSQ (Martin et al., 2003) distinguishes two positive (i.e., affiliative, self-enhancing) from two negative styles (i.e., self-enhancing, aggressive) of the use of humor, which denote specific ways in which people use humor in their lives (Martin et al., 2003) in a general way. The four subscales consist of eight items each, with sample items like "I enjoy making people laugh." (affiliative), "If I am feeling depressed, I can usually cheer myself up with humor." (self-enhancing), "If someone makes a mistake, I will often tease them about it." (aggressive) and "I will often get carried away in putting myself down if it makes my family or friends laugh." (self-defeating). The 7-point Likert scale ranges from 1 = *totally disagree* to 7 = *totally agree*. Cronbach's α ranged from 0.77 for aggressive humor to α = 0.80 for self-defeating as well as affiliative humor and α = 0.81 for the self-enhancing humor style. Factor analyses and loadings are described (i.e., Martin et al., 2003, pp. 58/59).

At work:
Short, work-related Humor Styles Questionnaire, swHSQ (Scheel, Gerdenitsch & Korunka, 2016). This 12-item version of the HSQ assesses specific ways in which people use humor at their workplace and includes items appropriate for and adapted to the work context, while avoiding negatively coded items.The expression *at work* was added where appropriate, and the terms family, friends, and so forth were replaced by *my colleagues*. The four subscales have three items each: affiliative (e.g., "I enjoy making my colleagues laugh."), self-enhancing (e.g., "If I am feeling depressed at work, I can usually cheer myself up with humor."), aggressive (e.g., "If someone makes a mistake at work, I will often tease them about it."), and self-defeating (e.g., "I will often get carried away in putting myself down if it makes my colleagues laugh."). Participants are asked to indicate the degree to which the statements applied to them on a 5-point Likert scale ranging from 1 = *not at all* to 5 = *completely*. Cronbach's alphas in two samples were α = 0.62/0.71 for aggressive humor, α = 0.72/0.83 for self-defeating humor, α = 0.71/0.80 for self-enhancing humor, and α = 0.82/0.86 for affiliative humor. Factor analyses are displayed (i.e., Scheel et al., 2016, p. 451).

A.1.4 Use of Humor in Communication

Humor Orientation Scale, HO (Booth-Butterfield & Booth-Butterfield, 1991; Wanzer, Booth-Butterfield & Booth-Butterfield, 2005). This 17-item scale measures an individual's tendency to use humor (content) regularly in social interaction (i.e., communication). Self-reports as well as partner ratings (e.g., "I regularly tell jokes and funny stories when I am in a group.") are assessed in a 5-point Likert-type format ranging from 1 = *strongly disagree* to 5 = *strongly agree* (Wanzer et al., 2005). The latter source reports a Cronbach's α of 0.93.

Humor Assessment, HA (Wrench & Richmond, 2000; cf. Wrench & Richmond, 2004). This instrument covers 16 self-report items which "measure an individual's use of humor in interpersonal communication contexts" (Wrench & Richmond, 2004, p. 307). The scale is used with a 5-point Likert format ranging from 1 = *strongly disagree* to 5 = *strongly agree*. Internal consistency was $\alpha = 0.95$.

A.1.5 Humor at Work

Several scales aim at assessing humor at work with a broader focus, including general fun at work, hierarchical humor, and organizational issues. Two scales for the focus on workplace humor were already introduced above: the QOHC for assessing coping humor, and the swHSQ for assessing humor styles at work.

Fun at Work Scale—subscale global fun at work (McDowell, 2005; in Fluegge, 2008). This scale includes 24 items in four subscales (six items each). The first three factors (socializing with coworkers, celebrating at work, personal freedoms) were measured by the degree they occur at the workplace by a 5-point Likert scale from *never* (1) to *almost always* (5). The fourth factor, global fun at work (e.g., "this is a fun place to work") was assessed with a 5-point Likert agreement scale from *strongly disagree* (1) to *strongly agree* (5). The items are displayed in the appendix of Fluegge's (2008) dissertation (p. 82). Cronbach's α ranged from 0.74 to 0.85 for personal freedoms and socializing with coworkers, respectively, to $\alpha = 0.88$ for celebrating at work and $\alpha = 0.95$ for global fun at work.

Leader humor (Avolio, Howell, & Sosik, 1999). This scale covers leader's use of humor in terms of frequency of occurrence with five items on a 5-point Likert scale from *not at all* (0) to *frequently, if not always* (4). Sample items include "uses humor to take the edge off during stressful periods" and "makes us laugh at ourselves when we are too serious." An earlier version with six items was used by Dubinsky, Yammarino, Jolson, and Spangler (1995). Reliability was reported with $\alpha = 0.90$.

Supervisor humor (Decker & Rotondo, 2001). This questionnaire assesses respondent's perception of his/her manager's use of positive humor and negative humor on a five-point Likert scale of agreement from *strongly disagree* (1) to *strongly agree* (5). The seven items on perceived enjoyment or use of humor resemble positive humor with five items (e.g., "has good sense of humor," "tells jokes") and negative humor with two items (e.g., "uses insult humor"). The reliability reported was $\alpha = 0.86$ and $\alpha = 0.82$ for positive and negative humor, respectively. Factor analyses are reported (i.e., Decker & Rotondo, 2001, p. 463).

Short scale for evaluating affiliative and aggressive humor in groups (Curseu & Fodor, 2016). Purpose of this scale is to assess affiliative and aggressive humor with four items respectively, with the group being the referent. Items capture the perceptions of group members as initiators, targets and as receivers of humor. Scale format is not described; sample items include "…my team mates regularly told jokes and funny stories." and "… some group members disturbed the group by making ironic and inappropriate anecdotes and remarks." for the affiliative and the aggressive humor, respectively. Reliabilities for the affiliative humor subscale were $\alpha = 0.89$ at the individual and 0.92 at the group level of analysis, and for the aggressive humor $\alpha = 0.88$ and 0.93, at the individual and group level, respectively. Results of factor analysis are reported (i.e., Curseu & Fodor, 2016, p. 12).

Humor Climate Questionnaire, HCQ (Cann, Watson & Bridgewater, 2014). The HCQ assesses positive and negative styles of humor in the workplace climate with 16 items on a 7-point Likert scale from *totally disagree* (1) to *totally agree* (7). The four factors, consisting of four items each, cover positive humor (e.g., "humor is often used to encourage or support coworkers"), negative humor (e.g., "the humor used by my coworkers can often make someone in the group feel bad"), outgroup humor (e.g., "my coworkers often make jokes about 'management'"), and supervisor support with reversed items (e.g., "my supervisor believes that humor distracts from getting work done"). Cronbach's α ranged from 0.81 for supervisor support and $\alpha = 0.83$ for negative humor to $\alpha = 0.87$ and 0.89 for positive and outgroup humor, respectively. Factor analyses are reported (i.e., Cann et al., 2014, p. 315).

Humor At Work, HAW (Rawlings & Findlay, 2016). The HAW assesses the humor climate within workplace settings with 13 items on a 7-point Likert scale from *strongly disagree* (1) to *strongly agree* (7). Two subscales cover pleasant climate (8 items; e.g., "I like to share funny things that happen to me with the men I work with.") and unpleasant climate (5 items; e.g., "People use humour in this workplace for nasty reasons."). Reliability was Cronbach's α of 0.78 for both subscales. Factor loadings are displayed in a path model (i.e., Rawlings & Findlay, 2016, p. 64).

References

Avolio, B. J., Howell, J. M., & Sosik, J. J. (1999). A funny thing happened on the way to the bottom line: Humor as a moderator of leadership style effects. *Academy of Management Journal, 42*(2), 219–227. doi: 10.2307/257094.

Babad, E. (1974). A multi-method approach to the assessment of humor: A critical look at humor tests. *Journal of Personality, 42*(4), 618–631. doi: 10.1111/j.1467-6494.1974.tb00697.x.

Booth-Butterfield, S., & Booth-Butterfield, M. (1991). Individual differences in the communication of humorous messages. *Southern Journal of Communication, 56*(3), 205–218. doi: 10.1080/10417949109372831.

Cann, A., Holt, K., & Calhoun, L. G. (1999). The roles of humor and sense of humor in responses to stressors. *Humor—International Journal of Humor Research, 12*(2), 177–194. doi: 10.1515/humr.1999.12.2.177.

Cann, A., Watson, A. J., & Bridgewater, E. A. (2014). Assessing humor at work: The humor climate questionnaire. *Humor—International Journal of Humor Research, 27*(2), 307–323. doi: 10.1515/humor-2014-0019.

Carver, C. S. (1997). You want to measure coping but your protocol' too long: Consider the brief cope. *International Journal of Behavioral Medicine, 4*(1), 92–100. doi: 10.1207/s15327558ijbm0401_6.

Carver, C. S., Scheier, M. F., & Weintraub, J. K. (1989). Assessing coping strategies: A theoretically based approach. *Journal of Personality and Social Psychology, 56*(2), 267–283. doi: 10.1037/0022-3514.56.2.267.

Craik, K. H., Lampert, M. D., & Nelson, A. J. (1996). Sense of humor and styles of everyday humorous conduct. *Humor—International Journal of Humor Research, 9*(3–4), 273–302. doi: 10.1515/humr.1996.9.3-4.273.

Curseu, P. L., & Fodor, O. C. (2016). Humor and group atmosphere: Development of a short scale for evaluating affiliative and aggressive humor in groups. *Team Performance Management: An International Journal, 22*(7/8). Retrieved from http://www.emeraldinsight.com/doi/abs/10.1108/TPM-04-2015-0022.

Decker, W. H., & Rotondo, D. M. (2001). Relationships among gender, type of humor, and perceived leader effectiveness. *Journal of Managerial Issues, 13*(4), 450–465.

De Koning, E., & Weiss, R. L. (2002). The relational humor inventory: Functions of humor in close relationships. *American Journal of Family Therapy, 30*(1), 1–18. doi: 10.1080/019261802753455615.

Doosje, S., De Goede, M., Van Doornen, L., & Goldstein, J. (2010). Measurement of occupational humorous coping. *Humor—International Journal of Humor Research, 23*(3), 275–305. doi: 10.1515/humr.2010.013.

Doosje, S., Landsheer, J. A., Goede, M. P. M., & Doornen, L. J. P. (2012). Humorous coping scales and their fit to a stress and coping framework. *Quality & Quantity, 46*(1), 267–279. doi: 10.1007/s11135-010-9348-2.

Dubinsky, A. J., Yammarino, F. J., Jolson, M. A., & Spangler, W. D. (1995). Transformational leadership: An initial investigation in sales management. *The Journal of Personal Selling and Sales Management, 15*(2), 17–31. doi: 10.1080/08853134.1995.10754018.

Fluegge, E. R. (2008). *Who put the fun in functional? Fun at work and its effects on job performance* (Doctoral dissertation). Retrieved from ProQuest Dissertations and Theses database. (UMI No. 3322919).

Gross, J. J. (2001). Emotion regulation in adulthood: Timing is everything. *Current Directions in Psychological Science, 10*(6), 214–219. doi: 10.1111/1467-8721.00152.

Herzog, T. R., & Strevey, S. J. (2008). Contact with nature, sense of humor, and psychological well-being. *Environment and Behavior, 40*(6), 747–776. doi: 10.1177/0013916507308524.

Kirsh, G. A., & Kuiper, N. A. (2003). Positive and negative aspects of sense of humor: Associations with the constructs of individualism and relatedness. *Humor—International Journal of Humor Research, 16*(1), 33–62. doi: 10.1515/humr.2003.004.

Kuiper, N. A., & Martin, R. A. (1998). Laughter and stress in daily life: Relation to positive and negative affect. *Motivation and Emotion, 22*(2), 133–153. doi: 10.1023/A:1021392305352.

Martin, R. A., & Lefcourt, H. M. (1983). Sense of humor as a moderator of the relation between stressors and moods. *Journal of Personality and Social Psychology, 45*(6), 1313–1324. doi: 10.1037/0022-3514.45.6.1313.

Martin, R. A., & Lefcourt, H. M. (1984). Situational humor response questionnaire: Quantitative measure of sense of humor. *Journal of Personality and Social Psychology, 47*(1), 145–155. doi: 10.1037/0022-3514.47.1.145.

Martin, R. A., Puhlik-Doris, P., Larsen, G., Gray, J., & Weir, K. (2003). Individual differences in uses of humor and their relation to psychological well-being: Development of the Humor Styles Questionnaire. *Journal of Research in Personality, 37*(1), 48–75. doi: 10.1016/S0092-6566(02)00534-2.

McDowell, T. (2005). Fun at work: Scale development, confirmatory factor analysis, and links to organizational outcomes. *Dissertation Abstracts International: Section B. Science and Engineering, 65*(12), 6697.

McGhee, P. (1994). *How to develop your sense of humor: An 8 step training program for learning to use humor to cope with stress*. Dubuque, IA.: Kendall/Hunt Publishing Company.

McGhee, P. (1996). *Health, healing and the amuse system: humor as survival training*. Dubuque, IA.: Kendall/Hunt Publishing Company.

Philbrick, K. T. (1989). *The use of humor and effective leadership styles* (Doctoral dissertation). Retrieved from ProQuest Dissertations and Theses database. (UMI No. 9021898).

Proyer, R. T., Ruch, W., & Müller, L. (2010). Sense of humor among the elderly: Findings using the German version of the SHS. *Zeitschrift Für Gerontologie Und Geriatrie, 43*(1), 19–24. doi: 10.1007/s00391-009-0082-0.

Rawling, M., & Findlay, B. (2016). The development and validation of the Humor at Work (HAW) scale. *Humor—International Journal of Humor Research,* 249–75. doi: 10.1515/humor-2015-0097.

Recepoğlu, E., Kilinç, A. Ç., & Çepni, O. (2011). Examining teachers' motivation level according to school principals' humor styles. *Educational Research and Reviews, 6*(17), 928–934. doi: 10.5897/ERR11.178.

Ruch, W., Köhler, G., & Van Thriel, C. (1996). Assessing the "humorous temperament": Construction of the facet and standard trait forms of the State-Trait-Cheerfulness-Inventory—STCI. *Humor—International Journal of Humor Research, 9*(3–4), 303–339. doi: 10.1515/humr.1996.9.3-4.303.

Ruch, W., Köhler, G., & Van Thriel, C. (1997). To be in good or bad humor: Construction of the state form of the State-Trait-Cheerfulness-Inventory—STCI. *Personality and Individual Differences, 22*(4), 477–491. doi: 10.1016/S0191-8869(96)00231-0.

Scheel, T. E., Gerdenitsch, C., & Korunka, C. (2016). Humor at work: Validation of the short and work-related Humor Styles Questionnaire (swHSQ). *Humor—International Journal of Humor Research, 29*(3), 439–465. doi: 10.1515/humor-2015-0118.

Svebak, S. (1974). Revised questionnaire on the sense of humor. *Scandinavian Journal of Psychology, 15*(1), 328–331. doi: 10.1111/j.1467-9450.1974.tb00597.x.

Svebak, S. (1996). The development of the sense of humor questionnaire: From SHQ to SHQ-6. *Humor—International Journal of Humor Research, 9*(3–4), 341–362. doi: 10.1515/humr.1996.9.3-4.341.

Thorson, J. A., & Powell, F. C. (1993). Development and validation of a multidimensional sense of humor scale. *Journal of Clinical Psychology, 49*(1), 13–23. doi: 10.1002/1097-4679(199301)49:13.0.CO;2-S.

Wanzer, M., Booth-Butterfield, M., & Booth-Butterfield, S. (2005). "If we didn't use humor, we'd cry": Humorous coping communication in health care settings. *Journal of Health Communication, 10*(2), 105–125. doi: 10.1080/10810730590915092.

Wrench, J. S., & Richmond, V. P. (2000, November). *The relationships between teacher humor assessment and motivation, credibility, verbal aggression, affective learning, perceived learning, and learning loss.* Paper presented at the National Communication Association's Convention, Seattle, WA.

Wrench, J. S., & Richmond, V. P. (2004). Understanding the psychometric properties of the humor assessment instrument through an analysis of the relationships between teacher humor assessment and instructional communication variables in the college classroom. *Communication Research Reports, 21*(1), 92–103. doi: 10.1080/08824090409359971.

Printed by Printforce, the Netherlands